PAPER CRAFTS

PHOTOGRAPHY BY PETER WILLIAMS

Select Editions

This edition published in 2001 in Canada by
Select Editions
8036 Enterprise Street
Burnaby, BC Canada V5A 1V7
Ph: (604) 415-2444 Fax: (604) 415-3444

© Anness Publishing Limited 2001

Produced by
Anness Publishing Limited
Hermes House
88–89 Blackfriars Road
London SE1 8HA

Publisher: Joanna Lorenz
Project Editors: Catherine Barry,
Charlotte Berman, Emma Clegg, Rebecca Clunes,
Clare Nicholson
Designers: Graham Harmer, Lilian Lindblom,
Roger Walker
Photographer: Peter Williams
Stylist: Georgina Rhodes
Step Photographers: Rodney Forte, Mark Wood
Illustrators: Madeleine David, Lucinda Ganderton,
Vana Haggerty, Robert Highton
Production Controller: Yolande Denny

Previously published in five separate volumes as
part of the New Crafts series: Papermaking, Paper
Cutting, Papier Mache, Cardboard and Bookworks

10 9 8 7 6 5 4 3 2 1

NOTE
Bracketed terms are intended for American readers.

DISCLAIMER
Learning a new craft can be tremendous fun, filling many rewarding hours, but certain materials and equipment
may need to be handled with great care. The author and publishers have made every effort to ensure that all the instructions
in this book are accurate and safe, and therefore cannot accept liability for any resultant injury, damage or loss
to persons or property, however it may arise.

CONTENTS

CRAFTS USING PAPER

PAPER WAS INVENTED IN CHINA IN ABOUT AD105. IT WAS THE IDEAL WRITING MEDIUM TO RECORD THE IMPORTANT INFORMATION OF THE EMPEROR'S COURT, BUT IT WAS ALSO SOON RECOGNIZED AS A CRAFT FORM IN ITS OWN RIGHT.

THIS BOOK IS DIVIDED INTO FIVE SECTIONS, EACH CONCENTRATING ON A TRADITIONAL PAPER TECHNIQUE. EACH SECTION BEGINS WITH A BRIEF HISTORY OF HOW THE PARTICULAR CRAFT DEVELOPED AND CHANGED THROUGHOUT THE YEARS, AND HOW IT IS USED TODAY. THIS IS FOLLOWED BY A GALLERY OF EXCITING PROJECTS BY CONTEMPORARY ARTISTS, PRESENTING SOME OF THEIR BEST, MOST INNOVATIVE WORK. THE BOOK THEN TURNS TO WHAT YOU CAN ACHIEVE YOURSELF: THE TOOLS AND TECHNIQUES YOU WILL NEED TO GET STARTED, FOLLOWED BY A WHOLE RANGE OF PRACTICAL PROJECTS FOR YOU TO TRY.

Right: This sturdy shopping basket is made from brightly painted cardboard, woven using traditional techniques.

Below: A simple papercut can make an eye-catching doily that will transform a plate of fruit into a tempting treat.

The rough texture and slight imperfections of hand-made paper make it perfect to use in many craft projects. But hand-made paper is also wonderful to write on, and a Greetings Card or a note on Embossed Writing Paper is sure to be appreciated. One of the delightful things about making your own paper is the different effects that can be achieved: try textured paper, moulded paper or laminated paper, either for practical use or for display.

Hand-made paper is often used in paper cutting, as the Jam Pot Covers or the Picture Frame projects show. But a papercut can be equally as effective on thin card or tissue paper, as used in the Paper Flowers and Cake Tin projects. Once you are confident with the techniques you can create some truly spectacular results, such as the beautiful White Lace Scherenschnitte or the simple but strong dove design cut into a lampshade.

The versatility of papier mâché projects is endless, both in the objects you can make and in the finish. The striking African Pot is painted to resemble clay, and the Petal Picture Frame gleams silver, perfect for displaying cameo pictures.

lightly scented paper and lace, or make the perfect gift for a keen gardener: a Garden Notebook, with miniature garden tools scattered on the moss paper cover.

These ideas show a small range of the many ways in which paper can be used. Whatever your level of skill, time frame or purpose, there is a project somewhere in the book that is perfect for you.

Far left: This wastepaper basket uses cardboard made from recycled newspaper, giving it an attractive speckled finish.

Left: Several sorts of hand-made paper are used in this greetings card, which is suitable for any occasion.

Although it is an unusual craft medium, cardboard can produce some surprisingly delicate effects, such as the Chandelier or the Oak Leaf Frame. Cardboard's strength lends itself easily to larger projects, too, such as a Child's Chair, sturdy enough to take the inevitable knocks and bumps.

Bookworks is the art of binding a book in such a way that it reflects its intended purpose. Cover a Christening Book with

Right: Brightly coloured Chinese lanterns make wonderful decorations for both summer and winter parties.

Below: A profusion of ribbons draws attention to these pretty paper bowls, which can be filled with small gifts or chocolates.

INTRODUCTION

Although paper is mass-produced industrially, papermaking is an ancient hand-made craft now increasingly adopted by contemporary artists.

Producing your own sheet of paper is incredibly satisfying. During the making process, paper pulp can be dyed, shaped into bowls and embossed or cast over interesting shapes. Delicate tissue paper can be laminated to produce a strong, translucent surface, and petals, leaves and grasses can be embedded in the pulp while it is still wet. Finished hand-made paper can be decorated with embroidery or paints and inks.

The 24 projects in this section, each explained with step-by-step instructions, show how you can combine these techniques to make highly individual and achievable designs. This, combined with inspiring examples of contemporary work in the gallery section, will give you a rich array of ideas and techniques with which to make your own personal paper creations.

HISTORY OF PAPERMAKING

PAPERMAKING HAS A LONG HISTORY, BUT FOR CENTURIES THE TECHNIQUE, DEVISED IN CHINA, WAS A WELL-HIDDEN SECRET. ONCE INTRODUCED TO THE WEST, PAPERMAKING WAS DEVELOPED TO SUIT EUROPEAN WRITING STYLES AND LATER, PRINTING. IN RECENT YEARS ARTISTS AND CRAFTSPEOPLE HAVE BECOME INCREASINGLY INTERESTED IN THE RICH QUALITIES OF HANDMADE PAPER.

The word "paper" is derived from the papyrus used in Ancient Egypt, although the technique used then was quite different from techniques employed in modern papermaking. The stems of the papyrus plant, which grew abundantly by the banks of the River Nile, were cut and split, then laid at right angles to each other like a woven mat of reeds. This was wetted with muddy water from the Nile, then pounded together to form a hard, thin sheet and left to dry in the sun. Perfectly preserved documents dating from 3500BC have been discovered in the tombs of the Pharoahs, and the works of Greek and Roman scholars were also written on papyrus.

The earliest evidence of papermaking as we know it has been traced to China in about AD105. Its inventor, Ts'ai Lun, was searching for an alternative writing medium to replace the carved strips of bamboo or silk then in use. He experimented with various materials, including old rags, fishing nets and plants such as hemp and mulberry. He also discovered that macerating and beating these materials produced a substance that could be suspended in water and collected on a woven fabric stretched across a frame. The matted material was left to dry in the sun to form a sheet of paper. Ts'ai Lun was imprisoned so that the Chinese government could keep the secret of papermaking and he eventually committed suicide.

China kept his invention hidden for over 600 years until the Arabs conquered Samarkand in the eighth century. Ts'ai Lun's technique spread along the trade routes,

reaching Central Asia by AD751 and Baghdad by AD793. It reached Japan through Buddhist monks, who carried books made of mulberry leaf paper, and developed into a very refined activity and an essential part of Japanese culture.

Historians believe that the Moorish invasion of Spain brought papermakers to Europe. The first recorded paper mill was established in Cordoba in 1036, over 900 years after Ts'ai Lun's original discovery. From Spain papermaking spread throughout Europe and the technique was improved in Germany, which produced the finest papers at that time. With Johann Gutenberg's invention of the printing press in 1453, the demand for books, and therefore paper, greatly increased.

Above: Papyrus Book of the Dead of the Scribe Ani with large figures of the deceased and his wife with garlands of flowers, 19th Dynasty, c.1250BC, British Museum, London.

Below: Page from the Koran, 9th century, Tunisian (vellum), Bibliothèque Nationale, Tunis.

Above: Print showing the process of couching and pressing sheets in Chinese papermaking.

stone plate. This greatly shortened the time required to reduce rags to pulp and was a major step forward.

By 1719 the demand for paper was so great that there was a critical shortage of cotton and linen rags. Réné Antoine Ferchault de Reamur, a French naturalist who had studied wasps building their nests, thought that it was possible to grind wood fine enough to produce cellulose for papermaking. Refined wood pulp, to which chemicals are added, is used for industrially produced paper to this day.

The final step to revolutionize industrial papermaking was a continuous rotating machine invented in 1798 by an Englishman, Nicholas Robert. It was perfected by the Fourdrinier brothers in 1806 and, even though they did not use their invention, all papermaking machines bear their name. They produced rolls of paper, replacing the hand-papermaker's craft and making the industry into the highly mechanized process it is today.

Making paper by hand remains a similar process to that used by the early papermakers. Most professional hand-papermakers use prepared fibres called cotton linters, which are cotton lengths too short for spinning into cloth. The fibres are beaten until they intertwine, or "felt", when shaken by the "vatman", who then dips a mould and deckle into the vat of pulp. The mould is a hardwood frame with crossbars at intervals to which a fine wire screen is sewn. The deckle, a similar frame but without the screen, stops the pulp from running off the mould.

After dipping, the mould is passed to the "coucher", who presses the sheets of paper face downward, sandwiching each between white wool felts. Pressure is applied to remove the water, then the sheets are separated and hung or laid out to dry naturally for 4–5 days. The sheets are then sized and left to settle. The best handmade papers are thus completely free from any chemicals or additives.

Oriental papers were made from plant fibres, producing a soft, flexible paper that was ideal for Chinese calligraphy. A tougher paper was needed in Europe, where writers used sharp quill pens. The idea of making paper from old clothes, cotton rags and linen was introduced, as was sealing the surface with a gelatine solution to give a non-absorbent surface. Paper mills were always located near a supply of flowing water, used in the production of the pulp and as an energy source.

Initially the materials were beaten by hand but this was replaced by a stamping machine, with heavy hammers moving up and down continually to break up the fibres. In 1680 the Dutch invented the Hollander Beating Machine, which consisted of a large tub with a revolving roller which chopped, pounded and pulverized the rags against a

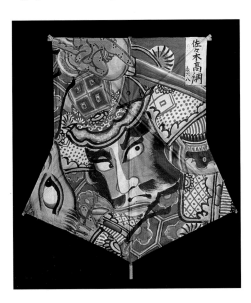

Above: This seven-sided kite is made from paper and bamboo, Japanese, 20th century, Oriental Museum, Durham University, England.

Above: The continuing tradition of papermaking; hanging up pieces of paper to dry at the Two Rivers Paper Company, Somerset, England.

GALLERY

PAPERMAKING IS A TREMENDOUSLY VERSATILE CRAFT. AS WELL AS ALLOWING US TO CREATE BEAUTIFUL TEXTURED SURFACES FOR WRITING PAPER, WRAPPING PAPER OR JUST FOR FRAMING, THERE IS ALSO AN ABUNDANCE OF WAYS TO DECORATE AND EMBELLISH THE SURFACES DURING OR AFTER THE PAPERMAKING PROCESS, AND TO MANIPULATE IT TO CREATE MORE THREE-DIMENSIONAL WORK. THIS GLIMPSE OF THE WORK OF CONTEMPORARY PAPERMAKERS REFLECTS THE ASTONISHING POSSIBILITIES OF WHAT CAN BE ACHIEVED.

Left: HOARD
10–30 cm (4–12 in) diameter
A series of paper vessels made from hand beaten Kozo paper, incorporating knitted copper wire, cotton scrims, paper yarn and unbeaten plant fibres. The pieces represent the uncovering and rebuilding of ancient fragments and were inspired by research into Ancient Roman archaeological sites.
ANNE JOHNSON

Below: WISH YOU WERE HERE
175 x 114 cm (69 x 45 in)
This piece was made with cotton linters, using small paper pieces laminated together while the pieces were still wet. Washes of acrylic and wax were then added, creating a rich and painterly effect.
CAROL FARROW

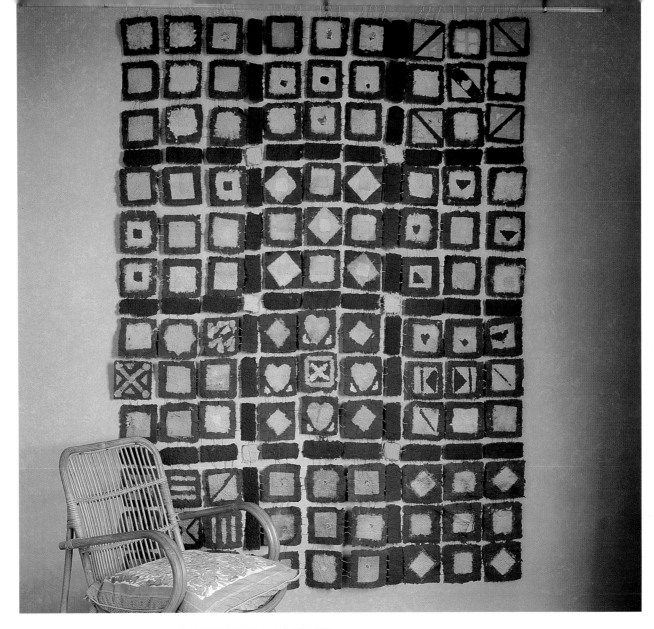

Right: PAPER QUILT
140 x 192 cm (55 x 75 in)
This paper quilt was made
from recycled, dyed paper
pulp, working on a nine
square block. The piece
was made by amateurs at a
drop-in workshop run by
paper artist Anne Johnson
at the Shipley Art Gallery
(Gateshead, England) in
conjunction with an
exhibition of
contemporary quilts.
ANNE JOHNSON

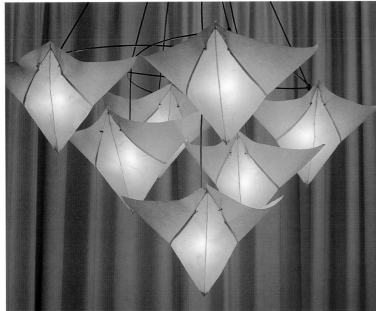

Left: ARROW
CHANDELIER
80 x 100 cm x 100 cm
(31½ x 39½ x 39½ in)
Dramatic lighting is a
powerful way of enhancing
large public spaces. This
chandelier directs light
upwards, creating a warm,
ambient environment. The
piece is made from
laminated paper and fabric
folded into sculptural
forms, and is compatible
with compact fluorescent
and tungsten bulbs.
LINDSAY BLOXAM

Above: ISHTAR
48 x 61 cm (19 x 24 in)
This piece combines
different casting
techniques with decorative
surface treatments. Ishtar
is an ancient goddess of
love and war and the piece
is abstracted to suggest
strength and sexuality.
The underwear may also
represent armour.
ELIZABETH COUZINS-SCOTT

Right: STILETTO
Detail of 100 pairs of
stiletto shoes in adult
sizes. Abaca pulp is made
into thin sheets of paper
which are then layered,
whilst in wet sheet form,
on to a shoe mould. Glue
and armatures are not
used in the finished pieces.
SUSAN CUTTS

Right: FLEUR DU MAL
45 x 45 cm (18 x 18 in)
Incorporating dyed cotton
linters, plant fibres and
horse hair, this form was
created by tearing, shaping
and casting sheets of paper
while wet. Once dry, the
paper is removed from the
armature. Part of a series
exploring the affinity
between seeds and flowers
and elements of the
human anatomy, such as
nerve and blood cells.
WENDY CARLTON-
DEWHIRST

Left: STRATA (detail)
520 x 120 cm (205 x 47 in)
Inspired by layers of rock
strata, this paper is made
from recycled brown craft
paper poured as a very thin
pulp onto a large 520 cm
(205 in) screen. This piece is
a combination of many
sheets built up in layers.
The various colour shades
were obtained by adding
pulped coloured paper to
the main pulp stock.
DAVID WATSON

EQUIPMENT

CREATING HANDMADE PAPERS AT HOME REQUIRES VERY LITTLE SPECIALIST EQUIPMENT APART FROM THE MOULD AND DECKLE. THIS ESSENTIAL ITEM CAN BE PURCHASED FROM CRAFT SHOPS, OR YOU CAN MAKE ONE YOURSELF. ALL THE OTHER EQUIPMENT CAN EASILY BE OBTAINED OR ADAPTED FROM ITEMS IN DAILY DOMESTIC USE, BUT KEEP THESE SEPARATE FROM EVERYDAY KITCHEN UTENSILS.

Bowls and buckets Soak the torn paper scraps in a plastic bowl or bucket to help break down the fibres. It may be necessary to keep different pulps in separate bowls. Also useful for draining pulp for drying or adding colour to the pulp.

Liquidizer After soaking, paper is made into pulp by beating the torn scraps to break down the fibres, using an electric liquidizer or blender. Start by mixing a small handful of torn paper with the liquidizer two-thirds full of water, otherwise it may overheat.

Sieve A sieve is very useful for draining pulp to make it thicker or for drying pulp to use later. Do not pour pulp down the sink as it may block the drain.

Vat The vat can be any rectangular-shaped plastic container, large enough to accommodate the mould and deckle – a large plastic bowl or storage box would be suitable. The pulp is added to clean water in the vat and the mould and deckle are dipped into the pulp to lift a sheet out.

Measuring jug (cups) Used to measure how much water to add to the vat, to dilute glues and size, and for chemicals.

Mould and deckle This essential piece of equipment can be purchased from specialist suppliers, or you can easily make your own (see Basic Techniques). The mould is a wooden frame across which a layer of mesh is stretched; the deckle is another frame the same size but without the mesh. Any robust, flat-sided picture frames would serve the purpose. Net curtaining, silk-screen fabric, aluminium mesh from car accessory suppliers or fibreglass window screening can be used for the mesh as long as it is tautly stretched across the frame. Experiment with different fabrics and plastic garden nets to create interesting surfaces.

Couching cloths or felts These hold each sheet of pulp after it is lifted out of the vat, and absorb some of the water. Originally a white wool felt was used, but vilene or smooth disposable kitchen cloths (dish towels) make a good substitute. The first sheet of paper is "couched" on to a "couching mound", a curved surface made from folded cloths or newspaper. When making a "post" of papers (several sheets couched on top of each other), place a felt between each sheet.

Newspaper Used for absorbing water during pressing and can be used to make a couching mound (see Basic Techniques).

Pressing boards Once a "post" of papers is completed, the sheets are pressed between boards to remove as much water as possible and help the fibres to bond. Make your own pressing boards out of plywood, sealed with two coats of acrylic varnish. The boards should be larger than the paper sheets. Some papermakers stand on the boards, others use bricks as weights or G-clamps to press the boards together.

Drying board A smooth surface such as perspex (Plexiglas ®) or formica is useful for drying out the formed sheets of paper evenly and will make the paper smooth.

Iron To obtain a smooth, even surface, iron the sheets of paper while still damp. Iron over a kitchen cloth (dish towel) and then carefully peel the sheet off the cloth.

Protective equipment Wear rubber gloves and plastic goggles or a face mask (respirator) when handling chemicals such as caustic soda or dyes.

Stainless steel or enamel saucepan For boiling plant material. Do not use aluminium as it will react with the alkaline solution used and damage the saucepan.

Brushes A range of brush sizes is useful for applying paint.

Wide water-proof adhesive tape (duct tape) If you plan to make up a mould and deckle, this will secure the mesh to the mould.

KEY

1 Mould and deckle	**8** Measuring jug
2 Liquidizer	**9** Stainless steel saucepan
3 Vat	**10** Rubber gloves
4 Kitchen cloths	**11** Pressing boards
(dish towels)	**12** Perspex (plastic) board
5 Sieve	**13** Iron
6 Bucket	**14** Brushes
7 Bowl	

MATERIALS

HANDMADE PAPER CAN BE MADE OUT OF MANY DIFFERENT KINDS OF SCRAP PAPER OR PLANTS, SO THE MATERIALS YOU NEED ARE READY TO HAND AND VERY INEXPENSIVE. THE IDEA OF RECYCLING WASTE PAPER APPEALS TO MANY PEOPLE, AND IT IS EASY TO ADD CHARACTER AND TEXTURE WITH PETALS, LEAVES, THREADS OR FABRIC SCRAPS, AS WELL AS COLOUR USING PAINTS AND DYES.

Discarded paper Suitable papers for recycling are computer paper, photocopy paper, shredded paper, brown parcel paper, cartridge (white construction) paper, tissue paper, writing paper, old envelopes and good-quality watercolour paper. The final quality of the recycled sheets will depend on the original paper. Experiment by combining different papers. Newspaper can be used, but it is poor-quality and prone to discolour and break down due to its high acid content; the newsprint will also affect the colour. Glossy magazine paper and papers with shiny surfaces are difficult to recycle because they are chemically treated.

Cotton linters These are plant fibres that have already been partly processed. They come in sheet form and can be bought from specialist suppliers. Use them to make a basic white pulp or add them to recycled paper pulp to give extra strength.

Rags Paper can be made from cotton and linen rags because of their high cellulose content. Long-lasting linen papers are still used to make paper currency today. Old linen or cotton tea towels (dish cloths), tablecloths, shirts and handkerchiefs are all suitable items, especially if they are well-worn. It is necessary to add chemicals to break down the fibres before liquidizing them into pulp.

Extra decorative materials A range of small materials can be added to the basic pulp to add interest. Experiment with torn scraps of other paper (such as glossy paper and newspaper), short lengths of wool (yarn) or thread, flower petals, dried leaves, and scraps of lace or fabric.

Kaolin china clay Added to the vat of pulp, this helps to give the paper a shiny surface on which to write.

Glues and size If to be used for writing or painting, the recycled sheets of paper should be made less absorbent by adding size to the vat when forming the sheets, or afterwards when they are dry. Suitable products are PVA (white) glue, household starch, gelatine, agar-agar (a gelatine made from seaweed, available from health food shops) or cold-water (wallpaper) paste.

Paints and dyes Any water-based paints, such as powder colours, inks and watercolour, can be added to the liquidized pulp before adding it to the vat. Paper pulp can also be coloured with cold- or hot-water dyes. When dyeing you should protect your surface with a polythene sheet and wear rubber gloves and an apron. If you are mixing dye powder, wear a protective face mask (respirator) to prevent inhalation of the fine powder.

The surface of the paper can also be decorated after sizing by using any artist's materials, for example acrylic paints, pastels or coloured pencils.

Plants It is possible to make pulp entirely from plant fibres, or you can add them to recycled paper pulp. First soften the fibres and release the cellulose by boiling the plants in water and adding an alkaline solution such as wood ash, soda ash (anhydrous sodium carbonate) or washing soda (sodium carbonate). Boiling time will vary with different plants, and if after 2–3 hours the material is still not soft, it can be rinsed and reboiled in a fresh solution.

For tougher, woody plants, caustic soda (lye or sodium hydroxide) will be necessary. When working with chemicals such as these, ensure that you start by following a recipe with associated safety instructions. Always work in a well-ventilated room when using chemicals and wear rubber gloves and plastic goggles to protect your hands and face.

Different plants produce papers of great individuality and character, with a wide variety of colours and textures. Suitable plants include wild flowers, straw, seaweed, potato, cabbage leaves, leeks, daffodils, cow parsley and nettles.

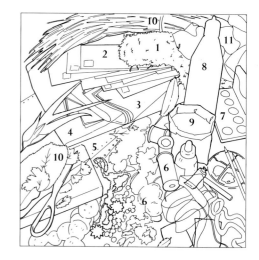

KEY

1 Shredded paper	**7** Paints and dyes
2 Old envelopes	**8** PVA (white) glue
3 Tissue paper	**9** Wallpaper paste
4 Brown paper	**10** Plant materials
5 Computer paper	**11** Cotton tea towel
6 Decorative materials	(dish cloth)

BASIC TECHNIQUES

MAKING HANDMADE PAPER IS QUITE SIMPLE, AND MASTERING THE BASIC TECHNIQUES WILL ENABLE YOU TO COMPLETE ALL THE PROJECTS IN THIS SECTION AND CREATE YOUR OWN DESIGNS. THE MORE YOU PRACTISE THE MORE PROFESSIONAL THE RESULTS WILL BE.

MAKING A MOULD AND DECKLE

Mould and deckles are easily available and it is also possible to improvise with existing frames by adding an aluminium mesh. However, if you need one at an exact size, the construction method shown here is really very simple.

1 For the mould, cut four pieces of wood to frame the paper size you require, checking that the dimensions will fit comfortably inside your vat. Lay pieces in position on a flat surface and where they join mark screw holes for the L-shaped brackets. Drill a small hole at each mark.

2 Glue together at the corners and when dry screw on the brackets.

3 Cut aluminium (or other) mesh to size and stretch it very tightly across the mould. Attach it with staples or nails.

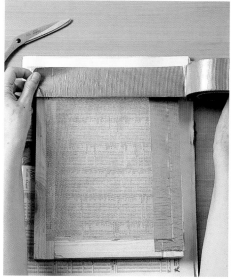

4 Place strips of thick, wide, waterproof adhesive tape (duct tape) over the stapled or nailed edges to secure the mesh completely. Repeat steps 1–2 to make the deckle. Varnish the mould and deckle before use.

THE PAPERMAKING PROCESS

There are several stages to the craft of papermaking – preparing the pulp and vat, making a sheet of paper, couching it and finally pressing and drying.

Preparing the pulp

Pulp can be prepared immediately before papermaking, or alternatively it can be dried and stored for future use. Note that when selecting paper to use for the pulp, the colour of the original paper will always affect the sheets.

1 Tear the paper into postage-stamp-sized pieces. Use 12–15 sheets of A4 (8½ x 11 in) paper to experiment with. Soak the paper scraps for at least 2 hours.

3 Pour the pulp through a sieve. Excess pulp can be dried and saved, or added to the pulp you are using if you want to make it thicker.

5 To dry pulp for later use, pour it through a cloth with a sieve and bowl underneath. Do not pour pulp down the sink as it may block the drain.

2 Place a small handful of torn paper in a liquidizer and fill it two-thirds with water. Liquidize for short periods only (10–15 seconds) until the paper is broken down into pulp.

4 If you wish to colour the paper, add dye or water-based paint at this stage, when the pulp is thick.

6 Remove all excess water by rolling the cloth round the pulp and then squeeze it. The dried pulp can then be stored in an airtight container. To re-use, just dissolve the dried pulp in water.

Preparing the vat and couching mound

Prepare the vat and couching mound to your satisfaction before starting to make paper sheets. This is because it is necessary to work quickly and confidently as soon as you have started to draw the first sheet.

1 Pour approximately 3–5 litres (5–9 pints) of clean water into a plastic bowl that is big enough to take the mould and deckle easily. Add the prepared pulp, until the pulp and water mixture is the consistency of soup. For a first attempt, start with 1 litre (2 pints) of pulp. To make thick sheets of paper, add more pulp; if the sheets are too thick, add more water.

2 Extra decorative materials, such as flower petals or threads, can be added to the vat now or later. This is also the time to add any prepared plant fibres.

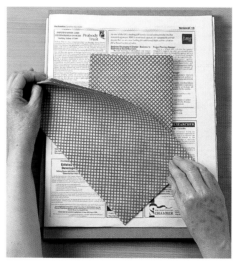

3 A slightly curved couching mound, will make it easier to transfer the pulp sheet. First make two pressing boards, reserving one for later use (see Equipment) and cover with some sheets of newspaper. Fold three smooth cloths into small, medium and large shapes to serve as "felts". Place them on top of each other on one board, the smallest at the bottom and the largest on top. Moisten the mound with water and cover with another cloth.

Making a sheet of paper

It is essential to work quickly when drawing the first sheet of paper. However, if you are not happy with the result, just immerse the mould and deckle in the vat and start again.

1 Place the deckle squarely over the mesh side of the mould.

2 Agitate the pulp with your hand or a wooden spoon in case it has settled.

4 Pull up the mould and deckle and allow to drain, keeping it level. Shake from side to side and up and down to settle the fibres.

6 Extra decorative materials, such as flower petals, can be sprinkled on the newly drawn sheet if desired.

3 Quickly and confidently dip the mould and deckle into the vat, using a scooping movement. Keep the mould and deckle level under the surface.

5 Remove the deckle from the mould. A sheet of pulp should be evenly deposited on the mesh.

Couching a sheet of paper

When couching, you can decide either to make a single sheet, or produce a whole sequence of sheets at the same size. When piling them on top of one another, insert cloths in between each sheet.

2 With one continuous movement, press the mould and pulp down firmly on to the mound.

1 Work quickly when couching. Place the long left-hand edge of the mould on to the long right-hand side of the couching mound at a 90° angle.

3 Lift the opposite edge of the mould, depositing the sheet of pulp on to the kitchen cloth (dish towel) or "felt".

4 Place another damp cloth on top of the sheet of pulp, making sure there are no wrinkles. Continue in this way until you have up to six sheets, known as a "post". Add more pulp to the vat as you continue, otherwise the sheets will become too thin.

Pressing

This process is only necessary if you require a smooth surface to the paper. Beautiful sheets can be created without pressing, where the natural texture of the paper, and of any added materials, can be seen.

1 Each post of papers needs to be pressed to remove some of the water. Place folded newspapers on top of the final felt and then place the second pressing board on top of the newspapers.

2 Turn the "sandwich" over. Remove the base board and couching mound and replace with more folded newspapers then place the base board back in position. Stand on the boards or use heavy weights to expel the water.

Drying

The paper sheets will dry surprisingly quickly, often within a few hours, although more time should be allowed for thicker sheets.

1 Carefully remove the top board and newspapers. The sheets can be carefully peeled away from the felts and allowed to dry naturally.

2 Alternatively, place the sheets on a flat perspex (Plexiglas ®) board and leave to dry, first sponging them to remove excess water. This will give a smoother quality. It is also possible to smooth them carefully with an iron.

Sizing

Sizing paper is not an essential requirement, but it will protect the paper and is important if you are intending to write on the surface.

1 Dissolve one teaspoon of gelatine or agar-agar with approximately 1 litre (2 pints) of hot water in a shallow bowl. Working quickly before the mixture hardens, dip each sheet of paper in the bowl, then lay it on a cloth. Put the sized papers on a perspex (Plexiglas ®) board.

2 Alternatively brush each sheet with PVA (white) glue diluted with water (1 tablespoon of glue to 750 ml/1¼ pints water) then lay on a kitchen cloth on a perspex (Plexiglas ®) board.

3 You can also add household starch or PVA (white) glue to the vat before forming sheets. Use 1–2 tablespoons starch or glue to 4 litres (7 pints) water.

STRAW PAPER

INTERESTING PAPER CAN BE MADE FROM ALMOST ANY GARDEN OR COUNTRYSIDE PLANT. GRASS, IRISES, MONTBRETIA, GLADIOLI, PAMPAS GRASS, YUCCA, DAFFODILS, FOXGLOVES AND EVEN HAY AND STRAW CAN ALL BE USED. RECORD EACH PLANT YOU USE IN A NOTE-BOOK, WITH A SMALL SAMPLE OF THE PAPER ATTACHED. MAKE A NOTE OF WHICH PART OF THE PLANT WAS USED, THE TIME OF YEAR IT WAS GATHERED AND HOW LONG THE FIBRES WERE BEATEN. BE CAREFUL NOT TO COLLECT RARE OR PROTECTED WILD PLANTS.

1 Select your plant materials. If using plants other than straw, firstly remove any tough woody stalks and plant debris.

2 Cut the straw into short lengths. 115g (4oz) of straw was used here. Other plant material should be cut into small lengths of about 2.5cm (1 in).

3 Half-fill a saucepan with straw, then add water so it is two-thirds full. Leave overnight. Wearing rubber gloves, add 4–5 tablespoons of washing soda (sodium carbonate) crystals and bring to the boil, stirring occasionally. Simmer gently for 1–2 hours until soft. Test the plant matter by rubbing it between your gloved fingers – if it feels soft and separates easily it is ready.

4 Leave the mixture to cool or add cold water. Place the net curtain fabric in a sieve supported over a bowl and pour the straw mixture through. Rinse with running water until the water runs clear. The most effective way of doing this is by knotting the two opposite corners of the net fabric together then hang the loop over a tap. ▶

SAFETY NOTE
Tough, woody plants may need to be boiled in a solution of caustic soda (lye or sodium hydroxide) instead of washing soda (sodium carbonate) crystals. Use caustic soda with great caution. Wear rubber gloves and plastic goggles and always add the caustic soda to a generous amount of water. Never add the water to the caustic soda or it will cause a chemical reaction and may splash into your face.

MATERIALS AND EQUIPMENT YOU WILL NEED
STRAW OR OTHER PLANT MATERIAL • LARGE SCISSORS • LARGE STAINLESS STEEL OR ENAMEL SAUCEPAN • RUBBER GLOVES • SAFETY GOGGLES • TABLESPOON • WASHING SODA (SODIUM CARBONATE) CRYSTALS • SQUARE OF NET CURTAIN FABRIC • SIEVE • PLASTIC BOWL OR BUCKET • PLASTIC OR GLASS MEASURING JUG (CUPS) • LIQUIDIZER OR HEAVY-DUTY POLYTHENE (PLASTIC) AND FLAT PIECE OF WOOD OR MALLET • JAM JAR • LARGE RECTANGULAR PLASTIC BOWL • MOULD AND DECKLE • PRESSING BOARDS • COUCHING CLOTHS • PALETTE KNIFE (OPTIONAL)

5 Put a small amount of straw fibres in a liquidizer, fill with water and liquidize in short bursts. Alternatively, you can beat the fibres by hand. Wrap a small amount in heavy-duty polythene (plastic) and beat it with a flat piece of wood, opening the polythene occasionally to add water. Save some of the unbeaten straw to add texture to the paper.

6 Test the fibres by placing a pinch in a jam jar. Cover with your hand or the lid and shake vigorously. The separated fibres should float freely. If there are still clumps of fibre stuck together, you need to continue the beating process.

7 Pour enough clean water into the large plastic bowl to accommodate your mould and deckle easily. Add the straw pulp. You will need less pulp than for recycled paper as the fibres are longer.

8 Make a sheet of paper (see Basic Techniques). As you lift the mould and deckle out of the vat, rock it from side to side as the water drains off to spread the fibres evenly over the surface.

9 Couch the sheet (see Basic Techniques). Alternatively, leave it to air dry naturally on the mould, in which case it will have one textured side and one smooth side.

10 When the couched sheet is completely dry, press and dry it (see Basic Techniques). If air-dried on the mould, remove by rubbing the back of the mesh with your fingertips. Use a palette knife if necessary to lift the edge.

DYED PLANT PAPER

DYEING PLANT FIBRES PRODUCES INTERESTING EFFECTS AS THE DYE MIXES WITH THE PLANT'S NATURAL COLOUR. BLEACHING THE FIBRES FIRST WILL RESULT IN BRIGHTER COLOURS. EXPERIMENT BY USING DIFFERENTLY DYED FIBRES TOGETHER TO PRODUCE PAPER THAT LOOKS ONE COLOUR, BUT IN CLOSE-UP CONTAINS DIFFERENT-COLOURED FIBRES. THE PAPER HERE IS MADE FROM YUCCA LEAVES BOILED WITH SODA ASH (ANHYDROUS SODIUM CARBONATE). THEY MAKE AN ATTRACTIVE STRONG AND TEXTURED COLOURED PAPER.

1 Weigh the dry plant fibres and calculate the amount of warm water that is needed to allow them to move around freely in the dye bowl (approximately 1.5 litres (2½ pints) water to 115 g (4 oz) dry fibres). Place the fibres in the bowl and add 500 ml (17 fl oz) of the total amount of water.

2 To prepare the dye bath, and wearing rubber gloves, an apron and a face mask (respirator), dissolve 1 tablespoon of dye powder in a small amount of warm water. Stir thoroughly and check that no grains of powder remain. Pour half of the remaining water into the second bowl. Add the dissolved dye and stir well.

3 Weigh 10 g (¼ oz) washing soda (sodium carbonate) crystals and dissolve in the remaining water. Then weigh out 60 g (2½ oz) salt. ▶

MATERIALS AND EQUIPMENT YOU WILL NEED

POLYTHENE (PLASTIC) SHEET, TO COVER WORK SURFACE • MEASURING SCALES • PLANT FIBRES • PLASTIC OR GLASS MEASURING JUG (CUPS) •
2 PLASTIC OR GLASS BOWLS • RUBBER GLOVES • PLASTIC APRON • FACE MASK (RESPIRATOR) • TABLESPOON • DYE POWDER •
WASHING SODA (SODIUM CARBONATE) CRYSTALS • WOODEN SPOON • SALT • PIECE OF NET CURTAIN FABRIC • COLANDER •
LARGE RECTANGULAR PLASTIC BOWL • MOULD AND DECKLE • 2 PRESSING BOARDS • COUCHING CLOTHS

4 Add the plant fibres to the dye bath and stir for 5 minutes. Add half the salt and stir well for another 5 minutes. Leave to stand for 5 minutes, then add the remaining salt and stir for 5 minutes. Stir regularly for another 15 minutes. Add half the dissolved washing soda (sodium carbonate) crystals over 5 minutes, stirring well. Stir for 15 minutes. Add the remaining soda and stir well. Continue to stir regularly for 30 minutes for pale shades, or 45 minutes for deep shades.

6 Use the fibre pulp to form sheets of paper (see Basic Techniques). Press the sheets for a smoother finish, or air-dry them to emphasize the natural textures.

5 Carefully drain the dyed plant fibres through a piece of net curtain fabric placed inside a colander. Rinse under running water until the water runs clear.

DYEING INSTRUCTIONS
Protect your work area with a sheet of polythene (plastic). At all times during the dyeing, wear rubber gloves and a plastic apron. Also wear a face mask (respirator) when mixing the dye powder as it is very fine and should not be inhaled. Use only plastic or glass equipment as these materials can easily be washed and will not affect the dye. Keep your dyeing equipment separate and don't use it for other purposes. The quantity of dye quoted is for a mid-shade; increase or decrease the amount to alter the depth of colour. Use warm, not hot, water at all stages.

GREETINGS CARD

SEVERAL INTERESTING HANDMADE PAPERS ARE USED TO MAKE THIS CARD. THE ORANGE PAPER HAS SCRAPS OF FABRIC AND THREAD INCORPORATED IN THE PULP, AS WELL AS NATURAL DYE FROM BOILED ONION SKINS. THE CONTRAST PAPERS ARE DECORATED WITH VETCH AND CLOVER LEAVES. EXTRA TEXTURE AND DETAIL IS ADDED WITH A SILK EMBROIDERY THREAD (FLOSS), STITCHING THROUGH THE PAPER AS YOU WOULD STITCH FABRIC. THE INGENIOUSLY FOLDED ENVELOPE CREATES A PERFECT FINISHING TOUCH.

1 Neatly tear a 19 x 14 cm (7½ x 5½ in) rectangle from the thick paper. Fold in half to make a card shape.

3 Tear small squares, strips and triangles from the other papers. Arrange and glue in place on the card to make an attractive design. Using silk thread (floss), decorate the design with stitches.

5 Fold in the other two corners to form an envelope for the card.

2 Tear a 7 x 6 cm (2¾ x 2½ in) rectangle from contrasting paper. Position it centrally on the front of the card and glue in place.

4 Sign the card and place diagonally in the centre of the A4 (8½ x 11 in) sheet. Then fold in the opposite corners.

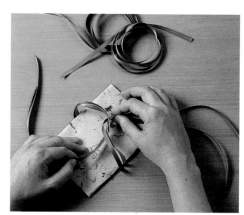

6 Tie decorative securing ribbons around the envelope to match the colours in the papers.

MATERIALS AND EQUIPMENT YOU WILL NEED

THICK HANDMADE PAPER • ASSORTED HANDMADE PAPERS, IN CONTRASTING COLOURS (SEE BASIC TECHNIQUES) • PAPER GLUE •
SILK EMBROIDERY THREAD (FLOSS) • SEWING NEEDLE • SCISSORS • A4 (8½ X 11 IN) SHEET OF HANDMADE PAPER, FOR THE ENVELOPE • RIBBON

EMBEDDED FIBRES

IN THIS ELEGANT TRIPTYCH, LEAVES OR GRASSES ARE TRAPPED BETWEEN TWO LAYERS OF PULP. ALUMINIUM MESH, AVAILABLE FROM CAR ACCESSORY SHOPS OR HARDWARE STORES FOR REPAIRING HOLES IN BODYWORK, IS USED AS A TEMPORARY MOULD. AS A VARIATION, YOU CAN MAKE A PARTIAL LIFT OF PULP FROM THE VAT; THIS GIVES A SOFTER, TEXTURED EFFECT AND LEAVES MORE OF THE PLANTS EXPOSED. ANOTHER POSSIBILITY IS TO CUT GEOMETRIC MESH SHAPES AND EMBED THEM IN THE PULP AS A CONTRAST TO THE PLANT MATERIAL. THE FINISHED TRIPTYCH LOOKS BEST DISPLAYED IN A DOUBLE PERSPEX (PLEXIGLAS ®) FREE-STANDING FRAME.

1 Gather leaves and grasses with interestingly shaped leaves or textured stems, and attractive colours.

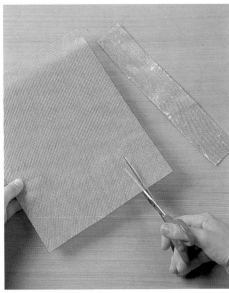

2 Cut a strip of aluminium mesh 4.5 x 25 cm (1¾ x 10 in), taking care to avoid the sharp, serrated edges. Place the pulp in the plastic bowl (see Basic Techniques).

3 Holding the mesh by the edges as shown, carefully lift a strip of pulp out of the bowl. ▶

MATERIALS AND EQUIPMENT YOU WILL NEED

SELECTION OF LEAVES AND GRASSES • STRONG SCISSORS • ALUMINIUM MESH • FINELY BEATEN WHITE RECYCLED PAPER PULP •
LARGE RECTANGULAR PLASTIC BOWL • COUCHING CLOTHS • 2 PRESSING BOARDS

4 Couch the pulp on the cloths (see Basic Techniques). Repeat to make three narrow sheets altogether, couching them side by side with 1–1.5 cm (½–⅝ in) gap between them.

6 Lift three more strips of pulp in the same way. Place on top of the first strips, covering the plant material. Place a pressing board on top and press (see Basic Techniques).

7 Having arranged the plant material on a wet sheet, an alternative is to lift a partial strip of pulp. Dip the edge of the mesh furthest from you back in the vat and move the mesh towards you, lifting it out at the same time. This will wash off some of the pulp. Couch this over the top of the strips. Leave to dry naturally.

5 Arrange the plant material on the wet pulp, extending it over the edge of the paper or on to the next strip of pulp.

8 Another suggestion is to cut geometric shapes out of aluminium mesh and use them to couch pulp on top of the plant material, leaving gaps. Press the sheets well to incorporate the mesh.

LEAF COLLAGE

THIS BEAUTIFUL DESIGN ORIGINATES WITH SMALL SHEETS OF WHITE PAPER CAST OVER LEAF SHAPES, USING A SMALL MOULD AND DECKLE MADE FROM TWO PICTURE FRAMES. THE LEAF SHAPES USED HERE ARE FABRIC RELIEF FORMS, BUT ACTUAL LEAVES ARE JUST AS EFFECTIVE. THE LEAF-EMBOSSED SHEETS ARE ARRANGED ON A BACKING SHEET SPRINKLED WITH ROSE PETALS AND THE DESIGN IS PAINTED WITH WATERCOLOURS IN PINK, GREY AND PURPLE. FRAYED STRIPS OF FABRIC, DYED LEAVES AND SCRAPS OF OTHER HANDMADE PAPERS ADD TO THE EFFECT.

1 Tear the white paper into postage-stamp-sized pieces. Soak for 2 hours in a bucket of water, then liquidize into pulp (see Basic Techniques).

2 Place the pulp in a glass or plastic bowl that will accommodate the small mould and deckle easily.

3 Place six leaf shapes on to cloths on top of a pressing board. Using the small deckle and mould, couch a sheet of pulp over each shape (see Basic Techniques). ▶

MATERIALS AND EQUIPMENT YOU WILL NEED

PIECES OF WHITE PAPER • PLASTIC BUCKET • LIQUIDIZER • GLASS OR PLASTIC BOWL • LEAF SHAPES • COUCHING CLOTHS •
PRESSING BOARD • SMALL MOULD AND DECKLE • A4 (8½ x 11 IN) SIZE MOULD AND DECKLE • FLOWER PETALS •
SELECTION OF HANDMADE INDIAN PAPERS AND FABRIC REMNANTS • INCENSE STICK • PVA (WHITE) GLUE • BRUSH, FOR APPLYING GLUE •
WATERCOLOUR PAINTS, IN PINK, GREY AND PURPLE • ARTIST'S PAINTBRUSH • DYED HONESTY LEAVES

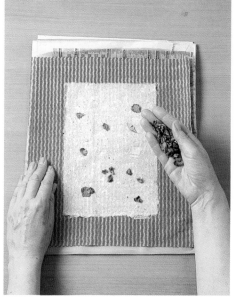

4 When you have made the six small sheets, leave them to dry naturally.

6 Sprinkle flower petals over the A4 (8½ x 11 in) sheet while the pulp is still wet. Leave to dry.

8 When dry, seal all the pieces of paper with diluted PVA (white) glue (1 part water to 1 part glue). Leave to dry, then paint with watercolour paints.

9 Group the leaf papers into a formal arrangement and glue to the A4 (8½ x 11 in) base paper. Attach dyed honesty leaves to the centre panel with dots of PVA (white) glue.

5 Make an A4 (8½ x 11 in) sheet of paper, using the larger mould and deckle. You may then need to use a larger bowl for the pulp.

7 From your collection of handmade papers and fabric remnants, tear two long strips 38 x 5 cm (15 x 2 in) and 38 x 6 cm (15 x 2½ in). Fray the edges of the fabric and burn the edges of the paper strip with an incense stick.

EMBOSSED WRITING PAPER

EMBOSSING IS A VERY EFFECTIVE WAY OF DECORATING HAND-MADE PAPER. A SIMPLE MOTIF OR INITIALS CUT INTO THICK CARD OR A DESIGN MADE OUT OF COILED STRING IS PRESSED INTO THE SURFACE OF THE PAPER. SIZE, IN THE FORM OF GELATINE, IS ADDED TO THE PAPER PULP SO THAT INK WILL NOT SEEP INTO THE PAPER FIBRES. DRYING THE SHEETS ON A SMOOTH SURFACE SUCH AS A KITCHEN WORKTOP (COUNTER) WILL GIVE A SUITABLE FLAT SURFACE FOR WRITING. YOU CAN ALSO IRON THE SHEETS WHEN DRY.

1 Make a mould and deckle for the writing paper, with inner measurements 21 x 15 cm (8¼ x 6 in) (see Basic Techniques). The envelope mould is 21 x 29 cm (8¼ x 11½ in). For the deckle cut a piece of fibreboard the same size as the mould, place the envelope template from the back of the book in the centre and draw round it. Cut the shape out, using a craft knife. Varnish the deckle.

2 Draw a simple shape on thick card and cut out with the craft knife.

3 Prepare the vat (see Basic Techniques). Dissolve the gelatine in 50 ml (2 fl oz) cup of warm water and stir it into the water in the vat. Mix in the paper pulp. Using the writing paper mould and deckle, make a fairly thick sheet of paper and couch it on to cloths on a pressing board (see Basic Techniques).

4 Place your chosen embossing shape on the sheet of paper, positioning it as desired.

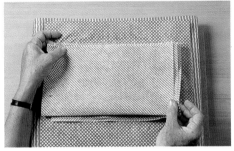

5 Cover the sheet with several layers of cloths. Place the second pressing board on top and press (see Basic Techniques).

6 Remove the top cloths. Turn over the embossed sheet of paper, still on the base cloth, and place on a smooth surface to dry. Repeat steps 4–6 as many times as required. ▶

MATERIALS AND EQUIPMENT YOU WILL NEED

MOULD AND DECKLE, FOR THE PAPER • MOULD AND FIBREBOARD DECKLE, FOR THE ENVELOPE • ENVELOPE • CRAFT KNIFE • CUTTING MAT • ACRYLIC VARNISH • DECORATOR'S BRUSH, FOR APPLYING VARNISH • PENCIL • THICK CARD (CARD STOCK) • LARGE RECTANGULAR PLASTIC BOWL • ½ PACKET OF GELATINE • WHITE RECYCLED PAPER PULP • COUCHING CLOTHS • 2 PRESSING BOARDS • METAL RULER • BONE FOLDER OR STRAIGHT EDGE • PAPER GLUE • SCISSORS • DOUBLE-SIDED ADHESIVE TAPE

7 Using the envelope mould and fibreboard deckle, make a sheet of paper. Carefully wipe away any pulp on the edges of the deckle.

8 After draining, lift off the deckle, couch the sheet and position the embossing shape. Make as many envelope sheets as required and leave to dry.

9 Crease and fold the envelope sheets, using a ruler and the flat side of a bone folder or straight edge. Score along the line of the fold using the flat side of the bone folder. Lay the ruler along the line of the fold and holding the ruler firmly, crease upwards. Repeat on all four sides of the envelope. Crease firmly using the flat side of the bone folder through a protective paper, so that the envelope does not become shiny.

10 Turn in the side flaps, then glue the deep flap to the side flaps.

11 Cut a piece of double-sided tape to fit the remaining flap and place along the edge. Peel off the protective strip to seal the envelope.

PATTERNED PULP

THIS STUNNING SHEET OF PAPER IS BUILT UP IN SEVERAL LAYERS, USING FOUR DIFFERENT COLOURS OF RECYCLED PAPER PULP. THE CHEQUERBOARD SQUARES AND STRIPES AND THE LARGE SPIRAL MOTIF ARE ALL CREATED WITH SIMPLE HANDMADE STENCILS.

THE DIFFERENTLY COLOURED LAYERS OF PULP FUSE WITH THE BACKGROUND SHEET DURING THE PRESSING PROCESS. EXPERIMENT WITH YOUR OWN STENCIL SHAPES AND CHOICE OF COLOURS TO MAKE A PAPER SHEET THAT IS DECORATIVE ENOUGH TO HANG ON THE WALL.

1 Liquidize the white paper into pulp (see Basic Techniques). Make four differently coloured pulps by adding a teaspoon of each colour powder to a small quantity of pulp.

2 Using the red pulp, make a sheet of paper and couch it on to the cloths (see Basic Techniques).

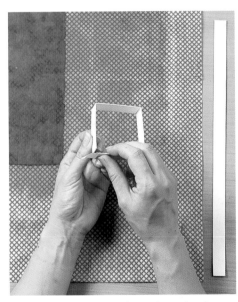

3 Cut a strip of card (card stock) the same length as the longest edge of the red sheet. Bend it into four equal sections to form a square stencil, then tape the ends together. Place the stencil on the mould. ▶

MATERIALS AND EQUIPMENT YOU WILL NEED

LIQUIDIZER • PIECES OF WHITE PAPER • TEASPOON • WATER-BASED POWDER COLOURS, IN YELLOW, RED, BLUE AND PURPLE •
LARGE RECTANGULAR PLASTIC BOWL • MOULD AND DECKLE • COUCHING CLOTHS • 2 PRESSING BOARDS • SCISSORS • CARD (CARD STOCK)•
ADHESIVE TAPE • 4 PLASTIC CUPS • PENCIL • CRAFT KNIFE • CUTTING MAT

4 Using a plastic cup, pour some yellow pulp into the stencil. Remove the stencil and couch the yellow square on top of the red sheet, starting in one corner. Make six yellow squares, couching them on the red sheet in a chequered pattern.

6 Remove the stencil and couch a blue stripe on to the chequered sheet, positioning it as shown. Repeat to make four blue stripes altogether.

8 Place the spiral stencil on the mould and pour in some purple pulp. Remove the stencil and couch the purple spiral on to the centre of the patterned sheet. Press the sheet using the second pressing board until dry (see Basic Techniques).

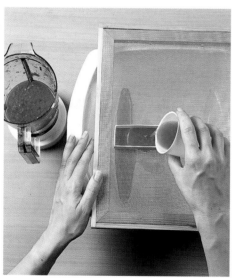

5 Cut a second strip of card (card stock) and bend to make a rectangular stencil. Place it on the mould and pour in some blue pulp.

7 Cut a piece of card (card stock) the same size as the wet sheet. Draw a spiral shape using the template at the back of the book. Using a craft knife and cutting mat, cut out and remove the shape. The remaining card forms a stencil.

TEXTURED SURFACE

ONE OF THE MOST EXCITING THINGS ABOUT MAKING YOUR OWN PAPER IS THAT YOU CAN MANIPULATE IT WHEN IT IS WET. FOR THIS DESIGN, DECIDE WHAT YOUR BASE COLOUR WILL BE AND MAKE THIS SHEET TWICE AS THICK AS USUAL, EITHER BY USING VERY THICK PULP OR BY COUCHING TWO NORMAL SHEETS ON TOP OF EACH OTHER. THE TEXTURED EFFECT IS CREATED VERY SIMPLY WITH A PLASTIC SPRAY CONTAINER. A MOULD IS USED WITHOUT THE DECKLE TO SUPPORT THE PAPER WHILE YOU ARE WORKING ON IT.

1 Place the thick base paper sheet on the cloth. Carefully place the other two sheets on top. Place a second piece of cloth over these and lightly iron.

2 Cut a piece of net curtain at least 10 cm (4 in) larger all round than the mould. Place the mould in the tray, then place the net curtain on top. Remove the pressed paper from the cloth and place on the net, centred over the mould.

3 Set the spray container to produce a jet of water rather than a mist. Starting in the centre, squirt water on to the paper so that it makes a hole, pushing away the top two layers to reveal the colours of the base papers.

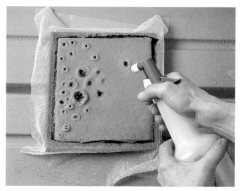

4 Make more holes all over the paper, stopping at regular intervals to let the water drain away. Be careful not to use the spray too vigorously or it may blow a hole right through the paper.

5 When the design is finished, allow the excess water to drain away. Remove the paper from the mould by picking up the net curtain. Leave the paper on the net curtain in a warm place to dry.

MATERIALS AND EQUIPMENT YOU WILL NEED

1 THICK AND 2 NORMAL SHEETS OF NEWLY FORMED PRESSED PAPER, IN DIFFERENT COLOURS • COUCHING CLOTHS • IRON • SCISSORS •
NET CURTAIN FABRIC • MOULD • SHALLOW PLASTIC TRAY, LARGER THAN YOUR MOULD • PLASTIC SPRAY CONTAINER

LAMINATED PAPER

TISSUE PAPER AND PVA (WHITE) GLUE ARE BUILT UP IN LAYERS TO MAKE THIS LAMINATED PAPER. TO ADD TEXTURAL INTEREST YOU CAN INCORPORATE THREADS AND WIRE, OR LEAVES, PRESSED FLOWERS AND OTHER FLAT OBJECTS. USE A THICKER GLUE SOLUTION TO LAMINATE HEAVIER OBJECTS. THE PAPER HAS A TRANSLUCENT QUALITY AND IS SUITABLE FOR DISPLAYING IN FRONT OF A WINDOW.

1 Prepare piles of yellow and turquoise tissue paper squares, approximately 10 x 10 cm (4 x 4 in). Tear circles out of the yellow squares and set aside. Tear another set of squares, approximately **8 x 8 cm (3¼ x 3¼ in).**

2 Cut squares of scrim, approximately 8 x 8 cm (3¼ x 3¼ in). Clamp the brass wire into a small pair of pliers and twist it round the outer edge to form flat spiral shapes.

3 Dilute 2 parts PVA (white) glue with 1 part water and brush over a sheet of green tissue paper on a polythene (plastic) sheet. Place a large yellow square on the background sheet in the top left-hand corner. Put a turquoise square next to the yellow one, overlapping and brushing them with glue. Alternate the colours and the squares with circular holes on top, to create a chequerboard pattern.

4 Glue the smaller tissue squares on top of the squares without holes, placing them diagonally. Glue the scrim squares diagonally over the squares with holes.

5 Glue the yellow circles on to the turquoise squares.

6 Place the brass wire spirals on the scrim squares and cover with a generous coat of thicker glue. Leave the finished laminated sheet on a flat surface to dry overnight. When completely dry, peel off the polythene (plastic) backing.

MATERIALS AND EQUIPMENT YOU WILL NEED

TISSUE PAPER, IN GREEN, YELLOW AND TURQUOISE • SCISSORS • SCRIM • THIN BRASS WIRE • SMALL PAIR OF PLIERS •
PVA (WHITE) GLUE • CONTAINER, FOR DILUTING GLUE • BRUSH, FOR APPLYING GLUE • LARGE SHEET OF PALE YELLOW TISSUE PAPER,
APPROXIMATELY 50 x 38 CM (20 x 15 IN) • POLYTHENE (PLASTIC) SHEET

ROSE PETAL RELIEF

THIS PROJECT FOCUSES ON FINDING INTERESTING SHAPES TO USE AS MOULDS FOR CAST PAPER PULP. THE PLASTIC FORM USED HERE HAS A REGULAR RELIEF PATTERN DEEP ENOUGH TO CONTAIN DECORATIVE MATERIALS SUCH AS ROSE PETALS. THERE ARE MANY SUCH PLASTIC FORMS, SUCH AS DETACHABLE PLASTIC SHELF SUPPORTS OR RAWL-PLUGS. FRAMING THIS IN A MATCHING PAPER FRAME ADDS AN EXTRA DIMENSION. THE SHAPE NEEDS TO FIT INSIDE A PLASTIC LIGHT SWITCH PLATE, FROM WHICH THE FRAME IS CAST.

1 Make the paper into pulp (see Basic Techniques). Drain it through a sieve to remove water and make the pulp thicker.

2 Place the plastic form and the light switch plate face down on a couching cloth laid on a flat surface. Spoon pulp over the edges of the light switch plate to make a square frame. Spoon more pulp over the whole of the plastic form.

3 Press the pulp flat with a small sponge to compress it and remove water. Leave to dry naturally. ▶

MATERIALS AND EQUIPMENT YOU WILL NEED

PIECES OF CREAM OR WHITE PAPER • LIQUIDIZER • PLASTIC MEASURING JUG (CUPS) • SIEVE • SMALL PLASTIC RELIEF FORM • PLASTIC LIGHT SWITCH PLATE • COUCHING CLOTHS • DESSERT SPOON • SMALL SPONGE • PVA (WHITE) GLUE CONTAINER • BRUSH, FOR APPLYING GLUE • VARNISHED WOODEN FRAME • WATERCOLOUR PAINTS • ARTIST'S PAINTBRUSH • DRIED ROSE PETALS OR OTHER DECORATIVE MATERIALS

4 Remove the two paper shapes from the forms. Seal with diluted PVA (white) glue (1 part water to 1 part glue).

6 Seal the paper form again with dilute PVA (white) glue, then paint with watercolours. Use colours to complement the rose petals, using delicately blended watercolour paints. Paint the paper frame made from the finger plate in a similar colour scheme.

7 Glue rose petals or other materials into the recesses of the paper form, using dots of PVA (white) glue.

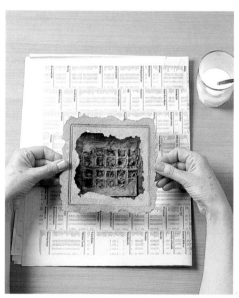

5 Place the cast paper form face down on a couching cloth, then place a small wooden frame over it. Using thicker pulp, spoon it over the edges of the paper form to make a square shape that is contained by the frame. Leave to dry naturally, then carefully remove the paper form and the wooden frame.

8 Decide which way up you want the paper frame to be, then carefully glue it on to the paper form.

PAPER BOWLS

THESE LITTLE BOWLS ARE A DELIGHTFUL WAY TO PRESENT SMALL GIFTS, OR TO HOLD CHOCOLATES ON A DINNER TABLE. THEY ARE VERY SIMPLE TO MAKE AND ALLOW FOR ANY NUMBER OF VARIATIONS AT EACH STAGE. YOU COULD OMIT THE RIBBON AND USE JUST ONE SHEET OF PAPER, OR THE RIBBON COULD BE REPLACED BY FEATHERS. AFTER PRESSING THE CIRCLES TOGETHER, YOU COULD REMOVE SMALL PIECES FROM THE TOP LAYER OF PAPER TO REVEAL THE PAPER AND RIBBON UNDERNEATH.

1 Cut a paper circle large enough to cover three-quarters of the orange. Cut a circle in card (card stock) to this size, and a second circle smaller than the first. Cut eight equal lengths of curling ribbon.

2 Place the green paper on a couching cloth, with the large card circle on top. Holding it down firmly, tear away the green paper up to the edge of the card.

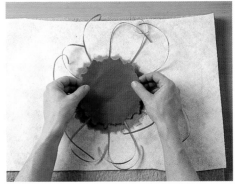

3 Place the eight lengths of curling ribbon across the paper circle like the spokes of a wheel.

4 Using the small card circle, tear out a red paper circle in the same way, following the instructions in Step 2.

5 Carefully lift up the red circle and place it on top of the green circle. Place a couching cloth on top then press the circles together, using a rolling pin. The cloth will absorb some moisture from the damp paper.

6 Remove the wet cloth. Carefully pick up both paper circles together and, turning them over, place them on a dry piece of couching cloth. ▶

MATERIALS AND EQUIPMENT YOU WILL NEED

PAPER • ORANGE • SCISSORS • CARD (CARD STOCK) • NARROW CURLING RIBBON •
SHEETS OF NEWLY FORMED AND LIGHTLY PRESSED PAPER IN GREEN AND RED • 4 LARGE COUCHING CLOTHS • ROLLING PIN

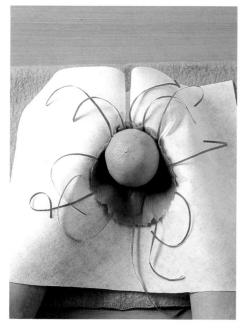

7 Place an orange in the centre of the circles. Using the cloth for support, draw up the paper circles and form them around the orange.

9 Remove the cloth and leave the paper bowl in a warm place until it is completely dry. Ease the bowl away from the orange by opening up the paper a little without it tearing or losing its shape. Finally, curl the ribbons.

8 Bunch the cloth very tightly at the top. Squeeze to remove more moisture and press the paper around the orange.

NOTEPAPER CASE

THIS SEA-BLUE FOLDER IS MADE FROM A SHEET OF PAPER VERY SIMPLY EMBOSSED WITH THE DISTINCTIVE SHAPE OF A SHELL. THE PAPER IS LINED AND COATED WITH GLUE TO GIVE IT EXTRA STRENGTH. IN A PROJECT SUCH AS THIS IT IS IMPORTANT TO FOLD THE PAPER WELL, USING EITHER A TRADITIONAL BONE FOLDER OR THE BACK OF A SCISSOR BLADE. THE DIMENSIONS QUOTED HERE WILL FIT NOTEPAPER 11 x 15 CM (4¼ x 6 IN) AND ENVELOPES 11.5 x 16 CM (4½ x 6¼ IN).

1 Wipe the shell with a little petroleum jelly and place in position on a cloth. Make a sheet of paper at least 36 x 30 cm (14 x 12 in), using blue pulp and couch it on to the cloth, covering the shell (see Basic Techniques).

3 When the paper is dry, line the embossed sheet with thin plant paper, brushing it sparingly with glue. When completely dry, cut out a rectangle 32 x 26 cm (12½ x 10¼ in). Following the template at the back of the book, mark the fold lines and cut the corners using a craft knife and cutting mat.

4 Score along all the fold lines, using a bone folder or the back of a scissor blade and a ruler. Fold the paper inwards along the scored lines.

2 Leave to dry, then remove the shell. Dilute 1 part PVA (white) glue with 5 parts water and brush over the paper.

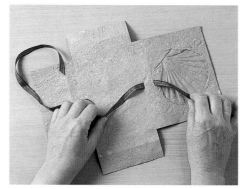

5 Cut slots for the ribbon as marked on the template and thread it through. Tie the ribbon to hold the case shut.

MATERIALS AND EQUIPMENT YOU WILL NEED

SHELL • PETROLEUM JELLY • COUCHING CLOTH • RECYCLED PAPER PULP, DYED BLUE • LARGE RECTANGULAR PLASTIC BOWL • MOULD AND DECKLE • PVA (WHITE) GLUE • CONTAINER, FOR DILUTING GLUE • BRUSH, FOR APPLYING GLUE • THIN PLANT PAPER • SCISSORS • CRAFT KNIFE • CUTTING MAT • BONE FOLDER OR STRAIGHT EDGE (OPTIONAL) • RULER • PURPLE RIBBON

MOULDED FINGER PLATE

FINGER PLATES (PUSH PLATES) WERE DESIGNED TO PROTECT DOORS FROM FINGER MARKS. THEY CAN ALSO BE USED AS AN EFFECTIVE DECORATIVE FOCUS ON A DOOR. THIS PLAIN PERSPEX (PLEXIGLAS ®) PLATE HAS BEEN TRANSFORMED BY A THREE-DIMENSIONAL REPEAT DESIGN. THICK PAPER PULP IS USED TO TAKE CASTS OF THE SHAPE, WHICH CAN BE ANY SUITABLY SIZED RAISED MOTIF.

1 Make the scrap paper into pulp (see Basic Techniques). Drain it through a sieve to remove water and make a thicker pulp.

2 Spoon the thick pulp on to your raised shape to make a cast, squeezing the pulp to remove water. Make three casts and leave to dry naturally.

3 Place a cloth on a flat surface and draw round the perspex (Plexiglas ®) finger plate (push plate), using a pencil.

4 Place the paper shapes face down in the centre of the plate outline. ▶

MATERIALS AND EQUIPMENT YOU WILL NEED

CREAM OR WHITE SCRAP PAPER • LIQUIDIZER • SIEVE • PLASTIC MEASURING JUG (CUPS) • GLASS OR PLASTIC BOWL • DESSERT SPOON •
DECORATIVE RAISED SHAPE • COUCHING CLOTH • PENCIL • PERSPEX (PLEXIGLAS ®) FINGER PLATE (PUSH PLATE) • 4 PIECES OF WOOD • SCISSORS •
PVA (WHITE) GLUE • CONTAINER, FOR GLUE • SOFT PAINTBRUSH, FOR GLUE • WATERCOLOUR PAINTS OR COLOURED INKS •
ARTIST'S PAINTBRUSH • BRASS SCREWS

5 Cut and position four pieces of wood to form a frame slightly larger than the plate outline to allow for shrinkage.

7 Remove the pieces of wood to reveal the long rectangle of dry paper.

9 Cut the paper along the drawn line. Dampen the ends of the paper and press on to the screw holes of the finger plate (push plate) for a perfect fit.

6 Spoon pulp into the wooden mould, covering the cast shapes and the pencil outline. Leave to dry.

8 Place the perspex (Plexiglas ®) finger plate (push plate) over the dry paper and draw round it.

10 Using a soft paintbrush, seal the paper with diluted PVA (white) glue (1 part water to 1 part glue) then decorate with watercolours or inks. Place the paper under the perspex plate and attach to the door with brass screws.

STATIONERY FOLDER

THIS COLOURFUL FOLDER IS SIMPLY DECORATED WITH BRIGHT RED SPOTS, USING DIFFERENTLY SIZED RINGS CUT FROM A PLASTIC CUP AS STENCILS. THE FASTENING TIES ARE TRAPPED BETWEEN TWO SHEETS OF PULP, SO IT IS STURDY AND PRACTICAL. THE A3 (11 x 17 IN) SHEET FOLDS IN HALF TO MAKE AN IDEAL FOLDER FOR A4 (8½ x 11 IN) DOCUMENTS.

1 Using dark blue pulp, make an A3 (11 x 17 in) sheet of paper and couch onto cloths on a pressing board (see Basic Techniques).

2 Cut three lengths of cord, to make ties. Lay them on the wet sheet, one in the centre of each short side and two equally spaced on each long side.

4 Cut a plastic cup into rings to make simple stencils. ▶

3 Cover with a second layer of dark blue pulp. Press lightly with a cloth to remove any air bubbles.

MATERIALS AND EQUIPMENT YOU WILL NEED

RECYCLED PAPER PULPS, COLOURED DARK BLUE AND RED • MOULD AND DECKLE • LARGE RECTANGULAR PLASTIC BOWL • COUCHING CLOTHS • 2 PRESSING BOARDS • SCISSORS • THIN CORD • PLASTIC CUPS • METAL RULER • BLUNT KNIFE

5 Place the stencils randomly on a mould and pour in some red pulp.

6 Couch the red circles on to the dark blue sheet. Repeat until the sheet is covered with circles. Press and dry the decorated sheet (see Basic Techniques).

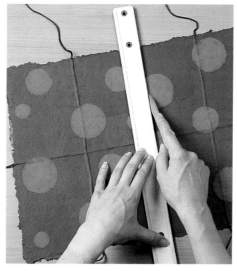

7 Using a metal ruler and a blunt knife, lightly score across the centre of the dry sheet to make the fold line.

8 Fold the sheet of decorated paper in half and fasten with the ties.

LAMINATED CIRCLES

THIS LAMINATED PAPER INCORPORATES SEVERAL INTERESTING TECHNIQUES, INCLUDING WAX RESIST AND INK. INSTEAD OF CANDLE WAX, YOU COULD USE MASKING FLUID OR MASKING TAPE. ONCE LAMINATED WITH GLUE, THE FINISHED PAPER IS QUITE STRONG AND WOULD BE SUITABLE FOR COVERING A BOOK OR AS A SPECIAL GIFT WRAP. STRANDS OF RED EMBROIDERY THREADS (FLOSS) ARE ADDED AT THE END TO CREATE ACCENTS OF COLOUR IN CONTRAST TO THE BLURRED, PAINTERLY EFFECT OF THE INKED CIRCLES.

1 Using a pencil, mark small dots on the pale yellow tissue paper approximately 8 cm (3¼ in) apart. Circle round each mark with the round end of the candle, pressing it quite hard but without tearing the paper.

3 Tear circles of turquoise tissue paper, approximately 4 cm (1½ in) diameter. Cut lengths of red embroidery thread (floss), approximately 6 cm (2½ in) long.

5 Place the embroidery threads (floss) on the turquoise circles, to make informal crosses. Cover with a generous coat of glue.

2 Place a polythene (plastic) sheet under the tissue paper. Using a paintbrush and with the pencil marks as a guide, brush the ink inside and slightly overlapping the candle wax circles. Leave on a flat surface out of direct sunlight.

4 Dilute 2 parts PVA (white) glue with 1 part water and brush all over the dry sheet of tissue paper. Place the turquoise circles in the gaps between the inked circles and brush over with some more glue.

6 Leave the finished paper on a flat surface to dry overnight. When it is completely dry, peel off the polythene (plastic) backing.

MATERIALS AND EQUIPMENT YOU WILL NEED

PENCIL • SHEET OF PALE YELLOW TISSUE PAPER, APPROXIMATELY 50 x 38 CM (20 x 15 IN) • PLAIN WHITE CANDLE, DIAMETER APPROXIMATELY 4 CM (1½ IN) •
LARGE SHEET OF POLYTHENE (PLASTIC) • LARGE ARTIST'S PAINTBRUSH • BLUE OR BLACK INK • TURQUOISE TISSUE PAPER • SCISSORS •
RED EMBROIDERY THREAD (FLOSS) • PVA (WHITE) GLUE • CONTAINER, FOR DILUTING GLUE • BRUSH, FOR APPLYING GLUE

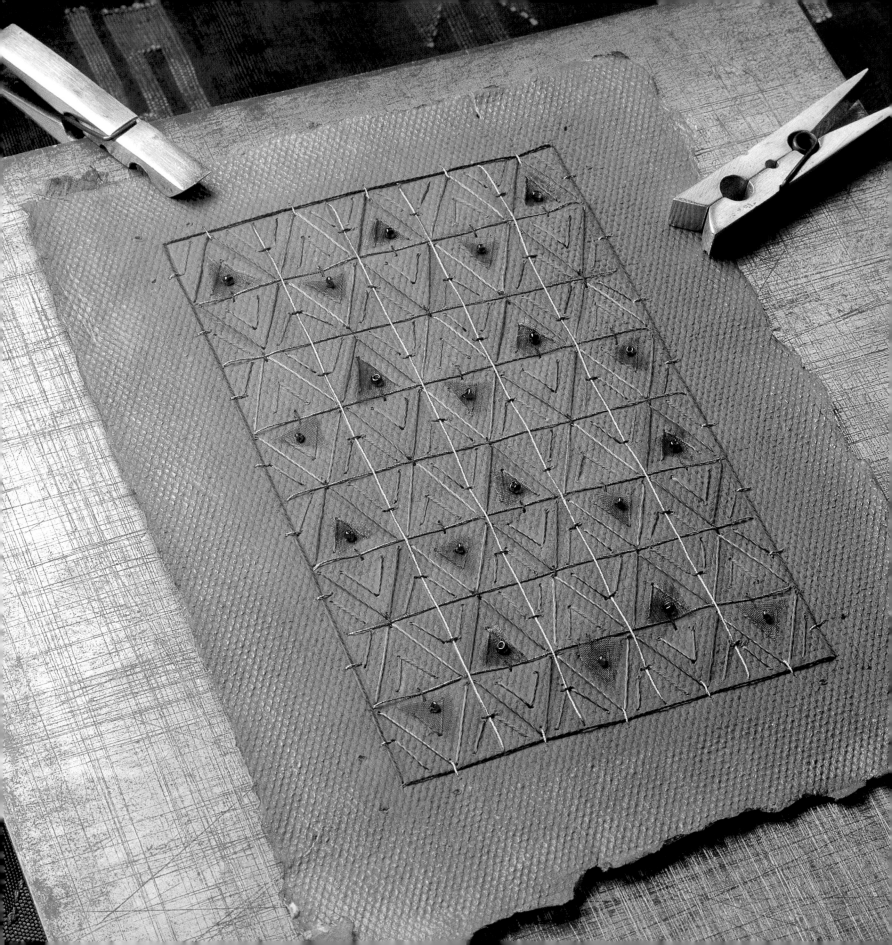

EMBROIDERED TRIANGLES

THIS RICHLY TEXTURED SHEET OF PAPER IS MADE USING A MOULD ON ITS OWN WITHOUT THE DECKLE TO GIVE AN ATTRACTIVE UNEVEN EDGE. IT IS THEN PAINTED A BRIGHT BACKGROUND COLOUR AND DECORATED WITH VARIOUS EMBROIDERY THREADS (FLOSSES), GAUZE TRIANGLES AND TINY BEADS. VILENE ATTACHED TO THE BACK OF THE PAPER PREVENTS IT FROM TEARING DURING THE STITCHING. TRY USING A DIFFERENT COLOUR FOR THE PAINTED BACKGROUND OR DRAW YOUR OWN DESIGN.

1 Make a sheet of paper, approximately 16 x 22 cm (6¼ x 8½ in), using a mould without the deckle (see Basic Techniques). Leave to dry thoroughly then peel off the mould, using a knife to lift the edge.

2 Paint one side of the paper with turquoise acrylic paint diluted with water. Leave to dry then iron between two sheets of tissue paper.

3 Using a ruler and pencil, draw a rectangle 10 x 16 cm (4 x 6¼ in) on the painted paper. Divide this into a grid of 2 cm (¾ in) squares.

▶

MATERIALS AND EQUIPMENT YOU WILL NEED

WHITE PAPER PULP • MOULD • LARGE PLASTIC BOWL • KNIFE • TURQUOISE ACRYLIC PAINT • LARGE PAINTBRUSH • CONTAINER FOR DILUTING PAINT • IRON •
2 SHEETS OF TISSUE PAPER • RULER • PENCIL • PASTEL COLOURED PENCILS (DARK BLUE, GREEN, ORANGE AND CERISE) • SCISSORS • VILENE OR BACKING CLOTH •
DRESSMAKER'S PINS • EMBROIDERY NEEDLES • THICK THREADS (FLOSS) FOR COUCHING, IN DARK BLUE AND METALLICGOLD •
MATT AND SHINY EMBROIDERY THREADS, IN DARK BLUE, METALLIC GOLD, GREEN, ORANGE AND CERISE • ORGANZA, IN BLUE AND RED • SMALL BEADS •
THIN PLASTIC GLOVES • ANTIQUE GOLD FINISH • MOUNTING BOARD, CUT TO SIZE • STRONG DARK BLUE THREAD

4 Using pastel pencils, colour the squares to form a multicoloured triangular grid.

6 Cut small triangles of blue and red organza. Stitch in place, adding a small bead in the centre.

8 Stitch the finished piece to the mounting board using a strong dark blue thread.

COUCHING

Lay a thick thread along one of the drawn lines. Hold it in place at regular intervals with small stitches through the paper and backing cloth (see Diagram 1). Use sewing thread for the straight stitching, matching the colour to the couching thread or alternatively using a contrasting colour thread.

5 Cut a piece of backing cloth larger than the design and pin to the back of the paper. Couch the thick dark blue thread (floss) along the lines outlining the rectangle (see Diagram 1). Couch all the grid lines in metallic gold, stitching along the horizontal lines first, then the vertical lines. Remove the pins and stitch the rest of the design in straight stitch, matching the thread colours to the pastel colours.

7 Wearing plastic gloves, rub the edges of the paper outside the design with antique gold paint.

DIAGRAM 1

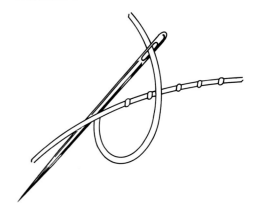

JAPANESE-BOUND BOOK

THIS ATTRACTIVE LITTLE BOOK USES THE TRADITIONAL JAPANESE FOUR-HOLE BINDING TECHNIQUE TO ENCLOSE VARIOUS SOFT PLANT PAPERS FOR THE "LEAVES", OR PAGES. THE TEXTURED PAPER FOR THE FRONT AND BACK COVERS WAS MADE BY INCORPORATING CHOPPED-UP PLANT MATERIALS AND FRESH HERBS IN THE PAPER PULP BEFORE FORMING THE SHEETS.

1 Fold the two sheets of plant paper in half, as shown, for the front and back covers. Individually fold the other sheets in the same way.

2 Place all the sheets with the folded edges together, and the front and back covers in position. Hold the folded edges in place with two bulldog clips.

3 Place the paper sheets on a cutting mat. Then, using a metal ruler or other straight edge, trim the edge opposite the folds with a craft knife. This will be the spine of the book.

4 Mark four equidistant points 1.5 cm (⅝ in) in from the spine, starting 1.5 cm (⅝ in) from the top and bottom of the book. Using a bradawl, make a hole at each marked point through all thicknesses of the paper.

5 Thread a length of raffia in the needle. Insert it between the "leaves" of the spine, leaving about 6 cm (2½ in) for tying later. Bring the needle up through the second hole from the bottom, then take it round the spine and back through the same hole, pulling gently. ▶

MATERIALS AND EQUIPMENT YOU WILL NEED

2 A4 (8½ x 11 IN) SHEETS OF HANDMADE PLANT PAPER • 8 A4 (8½ x 11 IN) SHEETS OF ASSORTED HANDMADE PAPERS •
2 BULLDOG CLIPS • CUTTING MAT • METAL RULER • CRAFT KNIFE • PENCIL • BRADAWL • LARGE-EYED NEEDLE • NATURAL RAFFIA

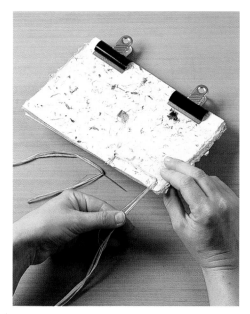

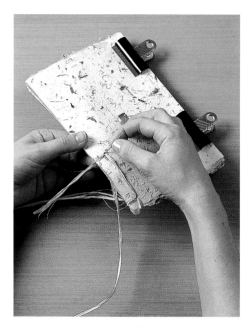

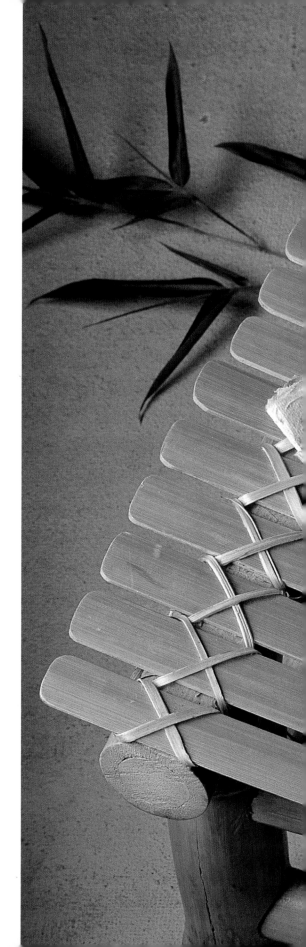

6 Take the needle down the spine to the bottom hole and repeat.

7 Now take the needle round the lower edge of the book and back through the bottom hole, then back up the spine on the opposite side and through the original hole.

8 Repeat with the remaining two holes until you are back at the starting point. Remove the bulldog clips.

9 Take the needle back between the "leaves" to the original end of raffia. Tie the two ends securely, then tuck the knot into the spine.

EASTERN MOBILE

T HE NATURAL COLOURS AND TEXTURES OF WOODEN STICKS AND WHITE HANDMADE PAPER BLEND HARMONIOUSLY IN THIS MOBILE. A STYLIZED PAPER LEAF SHAPE IS GLUED TO THE FRAME, AND THIS SIMPLE MOTIF IS REPEATED IN THE LARGE LEAVES WHICH HANG BELOW. IF YOU PLACE THE MOBILE NEAR AN OPEN WINDOW, THE SUSPENDED LEAVES WILL MOVE GENTLY IN THE BREEZE.

1 Using white scrap paper, make a batch of pulp (see Basic Techniques). Add 2 teaspoons of PVA (white) glue and stir in.

3 Cut reasonably even wooden sticks into gradually shorter lengths. Cut 9–10 lengths altogether.

5 Lay out the sticks to form a triangle. Thread the wire through the holes, wrapping the ends of the wire around the first and last sticks to secure them.

2 Couch plenty of white paper sheets on to couching cloths (see Basic Techniques).

4 Drill a small hole through the centre of each of the sticks. Hold each one firmly as you work.

6 Cover your work surface with a sheet of polythene (plastic). Tear up some of the white paper to make a simple leaf shape which will fit on to the triangle. Paint the paper lightly with diluted PVA (white) glue and press on to the sticks. ▶

MATERIALS AND EQUIPMENT YOU WILL NEED

WHITE SCRAP PAPER • LIQUIDIZER • LARGE RECTANGULAR PLASTIC BOWL • PLASTIC TEASPOON • PVA (WHITE) GLUE • MOULD AND DECKLE • COUCHING CLOTHS • HACKSAW • WOODEN STICKS • HAND DRILL • SOFT WIRE • LARGE POLYTHENE (PLASTIC) SHEET • CONTAINER, FOR DILUTING GLUE • BRUSH, FOR APPLYING GLUE • THIN, PLIABLE TWIGS • SEWING NEEDLE • WHITE SEWING COTTON • SCREW EYE OR HOOK

7 Wire pairs of thin twigs together to form five large leaf shapes.

9 Using a needle, thread long lengths of white cotton through the tip of each leaf.

10 Tie the leaves to the wooden sticks, using varying lengths of cotton thread.

8 Tear up more white paper. Paint lightly with PVA (white) glue and wrap around the twig leaf shapes. Leave all the shapes to dry.

11 Attach a screw eye or hook near the top of the mobile, in the centre, for hanging.

MIXED-PULP NOTEBOOK

USE A SPECIAL DECORATIVE OR EXPERIMENTAL SHEET OF YOUR OWN HANDMADE PAPER TO MAKE THE COVER OF THIS NOTEBOOK. THE BRIGHTLY COLOURED PAPER USED HERE WAS CREATED BY POURING FIVE DIFFERENTLY COLOURED PULPS SEPARATELY ON TO THE MOULD. THE SHEET WAS COUCHED AS NORMAL, THEN HUNG UP TO DRY TO KEEP THE RAISED TEXTURE. THE "LEAVES" OF THE NOTEBOOK ARE MADE FROM A SINGLE LARGE SHEET OF INGRES PAPER, FOLDED SEVERAL TIMES. STITCH THE LEAVES WITH STRONG THREAD.

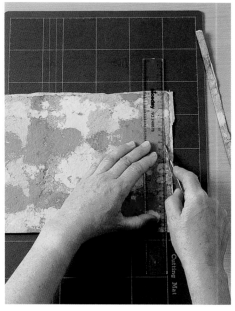

1 Dilute 1 part PVA (white) glue with 5 parts water. Brush the diluted glue all over the decorative handmade paper which will be the cover, to give it extra strength. Leave to dry.

2 Line the cover with the Indian plant paper, using a thin layer of PVA (white) glue. Leave to dry completely.

3 Using a craft knife and cutting mat and a ruler, trim the cover to make a rectangle approximately 26 x 19 cm (10¼ x 7½ in). ▶

MATERIALS AND EQUIPMENT YOU WILL NEED

PVA (WHITE) GLUE • CONTAINER, FOR DILUTING GLUE • BRUSH, FOR APPLYING GLUE • DECORATIVE SHEET OF HANDMADE PAPER, A4 SIZE (8½ X 11 IN) OR LARGER AND THIN ENOUGH TO FOLD • SHEET OF THIN INDIAN PLANT PAPER • CRAFT KNIFE • CUTTING MAT • RULER • SHEET OF THIN INGRES PAPER, 50 X 70 CM (20 X 27½ IN) • BLUNT KITCHEN KNIFE • PENCIL • LONG, STRONG, THICK NEEDLE • SCISSORS • THICK LINEN OR POLYESTER THREAD (FLOSS), IN A COLOUR TO MATCH YOUR COVER • LARGE BUTTON OR BEAD • BRADAWL • THIN CORD OR LEATHER THONG

4 Fold the sheet of Ingres paper in half, lining up the corners exactly. Slice carefully along the fold for two-thirds of its length, using a blunt knife. Fold the sheet in half and cut again. Repeat until it is slightly smaller than the cover.

6 Place the "leaves" inside the cover. Mark matching points inside the cover on the fold line and pierce holes in the same way as before.

8 Take the needle back through one of the outside holes, then right across the inside to the far hole, back through the outside and return through the centre hole. Pull the two ends tight and knot over the central inside thread (floss). Trim the thread (floss) ends.

5 Using a pencil, mark the centre on the folded edge of the Ingres paper and a point 2 cm (¾ in) from each end. Open out the "leaves" and pierce a hole through each mark with a needle, through to the inside fold.

7 Cut a length of thread (floss) three times the length of the notebook. Thread the needle and begin sewing from the inside, through the centre hole of the "leaves" and the cover.

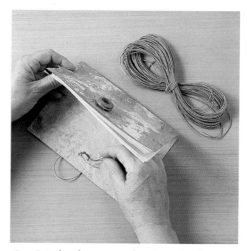

9 Stitch a button or bead to the front cover, near the edge. Keep the stitches wide apart for extra strength. Make two corresponding holes on the back cover with a bradawl. Cut a length of cord or leather to make a loop for the button or bead. Thread this by hand through the holes, then knot the ends on the inside of the cover.

WALL-HUNG MEMORY QUILT

THIS IS A LOVELY WAY TO DISPLAY A PERSONAL COLLECTION OF PHOTOGRAPHS, POSTCARDS, TICKETS, PROGRAMMES AND OTHER MEMORABILIA, BY INCORPORATING THEM INTO A PAPER WALL-HANGING. IF YOU PLAN TO INCLUDE HANDWRITTEN TEXTS, USE A PHOTOCOPY, OTHERWISE THE INK WILL "BLEED" ON CONTACT WITH THE WET PULP. ADAPT THE SIZE AND NUMBER OF THE SQUARES TO SUIT YOUR OWN MATERIAL. THE PATCHWORK SQUARES ARE HELD TOGETHER WITH PAPER STRING OR EMBROIDERY THREAD (FLOSS).

1 With your collection of materials in front of you, decide on a standard size for each patch and the number of patches that are required.

2 Make temporary moulds from aluminium mesh. Cut a square 2.5 cm (1 in) larger all round than the size of the objects, and a strip 13 x 4 cm (5 x 1½ in). Fold strips of masking tape 13 cm (5 in) long over each edge of the mesh to cover the sharp edges.

3 Dye two or three batches of pulp, slightly thicker than normal (see Basic Techniques). Place in separate bowls. Holding the mesh by the edges, lift a square of pulp out of the first bowl. ▶

MATERIALS AND EQUIPMENT YOU WILL NEED

COLLECTION OF PHOTOGRAPHS, TICKETS, SOUVENIRS, ETC. • ALUMINIUM MESH • STRONG SCISSORS • MASKING TAPE • RECYCLED PAPER PULP, DYED IN 2–3 COLOURS • 2–3 LARGE RECTANGULAR PLASTIC BOWLS • COUCHING CLOTHS • PAPER STRING OR EMBROIDERY THREAD (FLOSS) • DOWELLING ROD, 3 MM (⅛ IN) DIAMETER

4 Couch nine squares of one colour of pulp on to kitchen cloth, laying them in three rows of three squares (see Basic Techniques). Use the masking tape on the mesh as a guide for the spacing.

6 Lay nine more squares of the same coloured pulp on top of the first set, to hold the strings or threads in place.

7 Arrange your collection of materials on the squares of wet pulp.

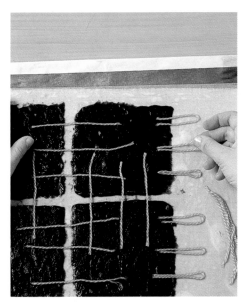

5 Cut 36 lengths of paper string or embroidery thread (floss) 6 cm (2½ in) long, to join the squares. Cut nine lengths 9 cm (3½ in) long, for the hanging loops. Arrange these on the paper squares.

8 Using a different-coloured pulp and the aluminium mesh as a mould, couch strips of pulp over the edges of the materials to hold them in place. Add extra colours at this stage, if desired. Leave the finished piece for several days to dry naturally. Thread the dowelling rod through the loops for hanging.

ACCORDION BOOK

THIS ATTRACTIVE LITTLE ACCORDION BOOK USES A FOLDING TECHNIQUE DEVELOPED IN JAPAN TO STORE LONG SCROLLS OF PAPER. THE COVER PAPER IS MADE BY ADDING FRAGMENTS OF COLOURED SILK AND THREADS TO THE PAPER PULP BEFORE FORMING THE SHEETS. YOU CAN TIE THE RIBBONS AT ONE END TO CREATE A BOOK, OR UNDO BOTH ENDS TO DISPLAY THE ACCORDION FOLDS.

1 To make the covers, apply glue to one side of each piece of mounting board. Place the board centrally on the wrong side of each piece of handmade paper.

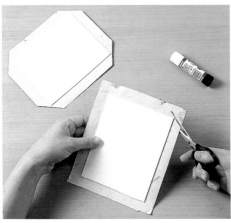

2 Cut across the corners of each paper, close to the corner of the board.

3 Fold the paper over the board and glue in place to finish the covers.

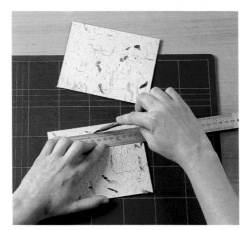

4 Using a craft knife and cutting mat, cut a small slit in the centre of each long side on both covers, about 1 cm (½ in) in from the edge.

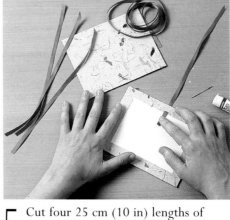

5 Cut four 25 cm (10 in) lengths of ribbon. Using a tapestry needle, push a piece of ribbon through each slit for about 2 cm (¾ in) and glue on to the inside of the board.

6 Divide the cartridge (white construction) paper into eight equal sections. Fold along the length as shown. ▶

MATERIALS AND EQUIPMENT YOU WILL NEED

PAPER GLUE • 2 PIECES OF MOUNTING BOARD, 12 x 15 CM (4¾ x 6 IN) • 2 SHEETS OF HANDMADE PAPER, 16 x 19 CM (6¼ x 7½ IN) • SCISSORS • CRAFT KNIFE • CUTTING MAT • THIN RIBBON • TAPESTRY NEEDLE • STRIP OF CARTRIDGE (WHITE CONSTRUCTION) PAPER, 14 x 84 CM (5½ x 33¼ IN)

7 Glue one end section of the accordion and place centrally on the inside of one cover. Repeat at the other end, making sure the two covers line up.

8 Tie one pair of ribbons to create a book with turning pages.

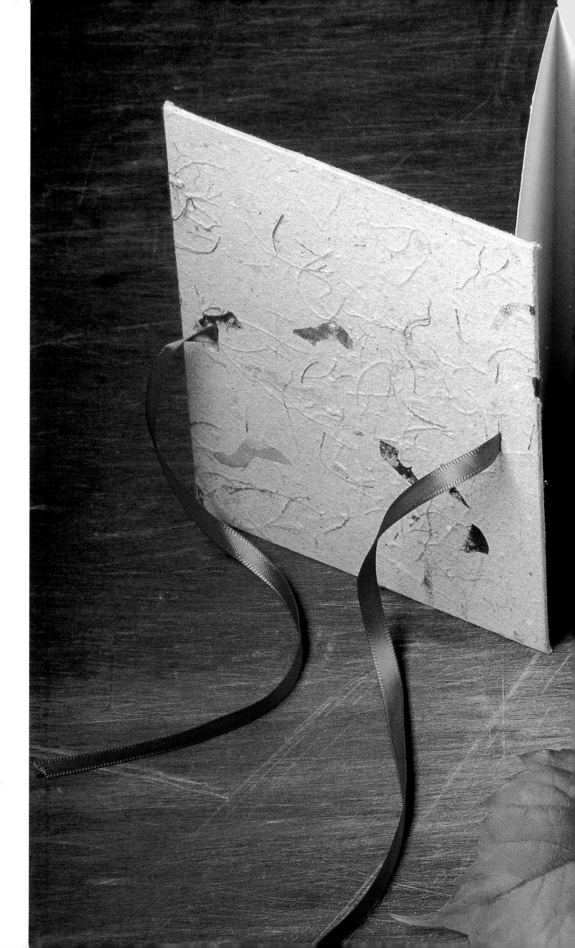

SPIRAL SWIRLS

IN THIS DECORATIVE PANEL, HANDMADE SPIRALS ARE EMBEDDED IN A THICK PULP MADE FROM PURPLE TISSUE PAPER. THE SPIRALS ARE MADE FROM PAINTED PAPER AND SHINY FOIL, AND ARE DECORATED WITH BRIGHT COLOURS TO GIVE A VERY RICH EFFECT. THIS TECHNIQUE CAN ALSO BE USED WITH BEADS OR BUTTONS, AND NATURAL MATERIALS SUCH AS SHELLS AND PEBBLES. VARNISHING THE INNER EDGE OF THE MOULD PREVENTS THE PULP FROM STICKING. IN THIS PROJECT, NINE SPIRALS ARE ARRANGED IN THREE ROWS, BUT YOU CAN MAKE AS MANY SHAPES AS YOU NEED TO FIT YOUR MOULD AND ARRANGE THEM IN A DIFFERENT PATTERN.

1 Fold long strips of painted paper and foil and wind each length round in a flat coil. Secure with coloured wire or thread then decorate with sealing wax. Make a number of different-sized spirals.

3 Using the tissue paper, make a coloured pulp (see Basic Techniques). Drain the pulp through a sieve to remove water and make a thicker pulp.

5 Leave the pulp in the frame to dry naturally, then carefully remove the pulp and spirals.

2 Varnish the inside of the frame. Place it mesh side down over a cloth laid on a flat surface. Arrange the spirals face down inside the frame.

4 Spoon the thick pulp over the spirals until the frame is filled. Using a small sponge, press the pulp gently to remove water.

6 Seal the piece with PVA (white) glue, using a soft brush.

MATERIALS AND EQUIPMENT YOU WILL NEED

PAINTED PAPER • ALUMINIUM FOIL • THIN COLOURED WIRE OR COLOURED SEWING THREADS (FLOSS) • SEALING WAX • WOOD VARNISH • DECORATOR'S BRUSH, FOR APPLYING VARNISH • SMALL FRAME OR MOULD, WITH REMOVABLE BASE • COUCHING CLOTH • COLOURED TISSUE PAPER • LIQUIDIZER • SIEVE • PLASTIC OR GLASS BOWL • DESSERT SPOON • SMALL SPONGE • PVA (WHITE) GLUE • BRUSH, FOR APPLYING GLUE

EMBROIDERED BIRD

THIS DELIGHTFUL BIRD WAS COPIED FROM A FRAGMENT OF AN OLD INDIAN SKIRT AND IT IS EMBROIDERED IN A RICH VARIETY OF THREADS. MICA PAINT GIVES A SLIGHTLY METALLIC EFFECT, AND ORMOLINE STOPS THE GOLD METALLIC POWDER FROM TARNISHING.

1 Fold two sheets of paper and tear them against a ruler to measure 16 x 16 cm (6¼ x 6¼ in) and 11 x 12 cm (4¼ x4 ¼ in). Paint the first with blue paint mixed with water and black mica and the second with red paint mixed similarly. Leave to dry and iron between two sheets of tissue paper.

2 Trace the bird template at the back of the book. Transfer it on to the third piece of paper, using dressmaker's carbon paper. Cut out the bird shape.

3 Paint the bird with dark turquoise and rust paints. Wearing a protective face mask (respirator), apply gold powder mixed with ormoline.

4 Pin the red paper over the blue. Glue the bird in the centre and leave to dry. Using a face mask, paint the square and arch in gold powder with ormoline.

NOTE: refer to couching diagram in the Embroidered Triangles project.

5 Cut a piece of backing fabric slightly smaller than the largest piece of paper and pin to the back. Couch dark-blue thread along the square and arch.

6 Remove the pins. Straight stitch the diamond patterns and borders, using different threads. Couch the outline of the bird in gold thread, then stitch tiny beads for its eye and crown. Add the spangles. Stitch the finished piece to the mounting board, using a strong dark-blue thread.

MATERIALS AND EQUIPMENT YOU WILL NEED

3 SHEETS HANDMADE PAPER • RULER • ARTIST'S PAINTBRUSH • BLUE, RED, DARK TURQUOISE AND RUST ACRYLIC PAINTS • BLACK MICA MEDIUM • CONTAINERS, FOR PAINTS • IRON • 2 SHEETS TISSUE PAPER • PENCIL • TRACING PAPER • DRESSMAKER'S CARBON PAPER • SCISSORS • FACE MASK (RESPIRATOR) • GOLD METALLIC POWDER • ORMOLINE MEDIUM • DRESSMAKER'S PINS • PVA (WHITE) GLUE • BRUSH • VILENE OR BACKING FABRIC • EMBROIDERY NEEDLES • THICK METALLIC GOLD EMBROIDERY THREAD (FLOSS) • EMBROIDERY THREADS (FLOSSES), IN DARK BLUE, ROYAL BLUE, RED, DARK TURQUOISE AND METALLIC GOLD • SMALL BEADS • SPANGLES • MOUNTING BOARD • STRONG DARK BLUE THREAD

CONFETTI ALBUM

T HE HAND-MADE COVER OF THIS LOVELY WEDDING PHOTOGRAPH ALBUM, IS SPRINKLED WITH CONFETTI. THE PAPER FOR THE PAGES NEEDS TO BE QUITE THICK TO SUPPORT THE WEIGHT OF THE PHOTOGRAPHS. THE SPINE AND OPENING EDGES ARE COVERED WITH BOOK CLOTH, FROM SPECIALIST SUPPLIERS. TO MAKE YOUR OWN, GLUE THIN LAYOUT PAPER TO LIGHT-OR MEDIUM-WEIGHT FABRIC.

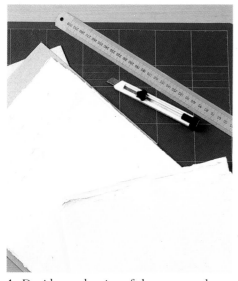

1 Decide on the size of the pages and covers for your album according to the size of the photographs. The pages need to be at least 5 cm (2 in) wider than required, to allow for the "guards" which will accommodate the thickness of the photographs. Between 16–20 pages is an average number.

2 The handmade cover paper should be longer than the cover card, to allow for turnings. Using white pulp, make a sheet of paper (see Basic Techniques). While the sheet is draining over the vat, sprinkle confetti evenly over the surface.

4 Using a craft knife and cutting mat, cut the pages to size. Make a light pencil mark at the top and bottom of each page, 2.5 cm (1 in) from the left-hand edge. Lay the ruler to touch both marks then score along this line with a bone folder or other straight edge. Fold upwards to make a "guard".

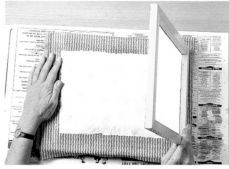

3 Couch the sheet on to cloths (see Basic Techniques). Make at least four confetti sheets to give you a choice. The extra sheets will be used to line the cover. Leave for several days to dry completely.

MATERIALS AND EQUIPMENT YOU WILL NEED

THICK HANDMADE PAPER (SEE BASIC TECHNIQUES) • METAL RULER • THICK COVER CARD (CARD STOCK) • MOULD AND DECKLE •
WHITE RECYCLED PAPER PULP • LARGE RECTANGULAR PLASTIC BOWL • CONFETTI • COUCHING CLOTHS • CRAFT KNIFE • CUTTING MAT • PENCIL •
BONE FOLDER • BOOK CLOTH • PVA (WHITE) GLUE • BRUSH, FOR GLUE • SCISSORS • CLAMP • HAND DRILL OR HOLE PUNCH • WHITE CORD

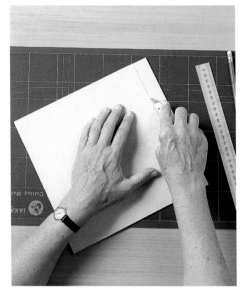

5 Cut two pieces of thick card (card stock) for the covers, 12 mm (½ in) longer than the page height and 6 mm (¼ in) wider than their width. Cut a 2.5 cm (1 in) strip off both pieces and reserve.

7 Working on one cover at a time, take the reserved strip of card (stock) and brush with glue. Place on the larger piece of book cloth, equidistant from the top and bottom and touching the marked line.

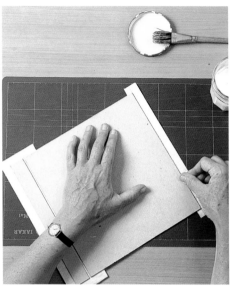

9 Take one of the smaller pieces of book cloth. Brush glue on the narrow edge and stick this edge to the opposite edge of the cover.

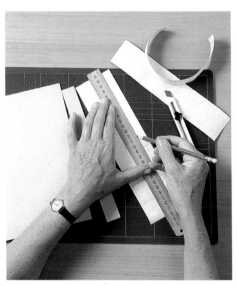

6 Cut two pieces of book cloth, 3 cm (1 ¼ in) longer than the covers and 9 cm (3½ in) wide. Cut two more pieces the same length and 2.5 cm (1 in) wide. On each piece, draw a line 1.5 cm (⅝ in) from one long side, to be turned in later.

8 Draw another line on the book cloth 3 mm (⅛ in) from the strip of card (card stock), on the side farthest from the turn-in. Place the book cloth wrong side up and brush with glue. Aligning the top and bottom edges with the strip of card, glue the cover against the marked line.

10 Cut diagonally across all the corners of the cover, 6 mm (¼ in) from each corner. Place waste paper underneath then apply glue to the long turn-ins. Smoothing it with the bone folder, press the book cloth up, over the edge and down on the card (card stock). ▶

11 Press down the excess at the corners. Glue the remaining turn-ins and press carefully into place.

12 Cut another piece of book cloth a little shorter than the height of the cover, to go over the inside of the spine and overlap on to the cover, as on the outside. Glue it to the spine, down into the gap, then on to the cover, smoothing the cloth with the bone folder. Make the other cover to match.

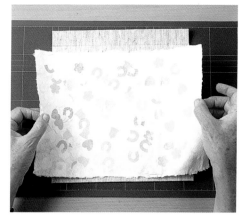

13 Use the best sheet of confetti paper for the front. If it is too wide, put a metal ruler on the paper and tear against the edge, creating another deckle. Trim the turn-ins to 1.5 cm (⅝ in) and glue down. Do the same for the back.

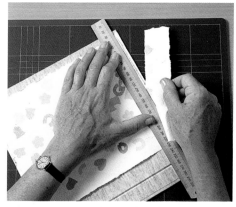

14 Measure the inside of the covers and tear two pieces of decorative paper which are slightly smaller all round. Glue one inside each cover, using the bone folder over a piece of clean paper to ensure the paper is stuck at the edges.

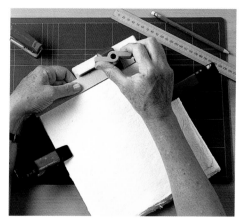

15 To assemble the album, stack all the pages and sandwich them between the covers. Take a strip of card (card stock) the same size as the spine and lay it on top then clamp the album together. Make evenly spaced marks along the centre of the card (card stock) strip then drill holes at these points. The larger the album, the more holes will be needed. You can use a hole punch, but you will need to punch each sheet separately.

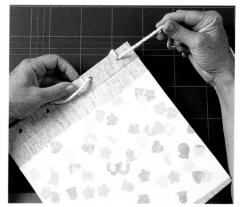

16 Discard the card (card stock) strip. Cut a length of cord and thread through the holes in the spine to hold the album together (see Diagram 1). Tie the ends securely together, fray and fluff them out and trim neatly.

DIAGRAM 1

tie ends together securely

INTRODUCTION

THE BEAUTY OF PAPER CUTTING LIES IN THE SIMPLICITY OF THE CRAFT — YOU ONLY REALLY NEED A SHEET OF PAPER AND A PAIR OF SCISSORS. IN FACT THE POLISH FOLK ARTISTS, WHO BECAME FAMOUS FOR THE CHARM OF THEIR INTRICATE COLOURFUL PAPER-CUTS, ACTUALLY USED SHEEP SHEARS TO CUT THEM OUT. WE HAVE SUGGESTED USING A COMBINATION OF SMALL, SHARP SCISSORS AND A CRAFT KNIFE FOR THE CUTS IN OUR PROJECTS, AND THERE IS SOMETHING TO SUIT ALL LEVELS OF SKILL.

THE DISTINCTIVE LOOK OF A SHAPE THAT HAS BEEN CUT OUT RATHER THAN PAINTED, DRAWN OR PRINTED, COMES FROM THE FACT THAT IT HAS AN ABSOLUTE EDGE — NO FUZZY LINES, FADING OR SHADING. ONCE YOU PICK UP THE SCISSORS OR CRAFT KNIFE TO MAKE SOMETHING FROM PAPER, YOU HAVE TO COMMIT YOURSELF AND CUT — AND ONCE YOU'VE DONE IT, THERE IS NO GOING BACK.

IN THE FIRST PART OF THIS SECTION WE EXPLORE THE LONG HISTORY OF PAPER CUTTING AND THE WAYS IT HAS BEEN USED IN DIFFERENT CULTURES. THE GALLERY SHOWS A VARIETY OF INTERPRETATIONS OF THE CRAFT. WE ALSO SHOW USEFUL EQUIPMENT AND AN ASSORTMENT OF SUITABLE PAPERS, AND EXPLAIN THE SIMPLE TECHNIQUES THAT WILL HELP YOU TO PROGRESS QUICKLY.

Opposite: Paper cutting produces a wonderfully wide range of results, depending upon the type of paper used, the number of times it is folded, the skill of the cutter and the delicacy or robustness of the design.

HISTORY OF PAPER CUTTING

PAPER WAS INVENTED BY THE CHINESE IN THE 2ND CENTURY BC AND THE KNOWLEDGE OF HOW IT WAS MADE PASSED FROM THE ARABS TO EUROPE MANY CENTURIES LATER. IN CHINA THE FIRST PAPERCUTS WERE MADE AS PATTERNS TO TRANSFER EMBROIDERY PATTERNS. PEOPLE BEGAN TO APPRECIATE THE INTRINSIC BEAUTY OF THE PAPERCUT AND PAPER CUTTING DEVELOPED AS A FOLK ART IN ITS OWN RIGHT. UP TO FIFTY LAYERS OF FINE PAPER WOULD BE PLACED IN A FRAME AND CUT OUT AS A BLOCK, USING A VERY SHARP KNIFE. THE IMAGES ON PRESENT-DAY CHINESE PAPERCUTS ARE TRADITIONAL BUT THESE DAYS THEY ARE MORE LIKELY TO BE CUT BY MACHINE. IN JAPAN PAPER CUTTING TOOK THE FORM OF STENCILS THAT WERE USED TO PRINT TEXTILES.

Paper cutting came to European folk art via the trade routes from the Far East through the Middle East and Turkey, where the craft was very popular. Paper itself was a rare commodity and was mostly found in monasteries, where monks incorporated paper cutting into their illuminated manuscripts. A lot of early European paper cutting featured religious subjects, but as paper became more freely available, people began to make papercuts that illustrated everyday life.

The Germans and Swiss made very complicated folded papercuts called "scherenschnitte". These are the famous symmetrical black on white images that were taken up as a popular craft by the communities that settled on the eastern coast of America. Some of the loveliest of these are the Valentines and love letters that featured hearts, flowers, birds, animals and often words as well. Many of the settlers were fleeing religious persecution in Europe and set up strong communities which kept the crafts of their homelands alive. Some of the communities like the Amish and Mennonites still exist and continue their way of life today, and there are fine examples of paper cuttings in their museums and amongst their publications.

Another style of paper cutting, the silhouette portrait, was popular in Britain and France before cameras could capture a likeness in an instant, and most families displayed silhouette portraits in their homes. These were the days when ladies spent hours each day doing embroidery and they found that

Above: The famous Danish author of fairytales, Hans Christian Andersen, was devoted to the craft of paper cutting. This old book contains printed images of some of his favourite papercuts, which are often quite simple and rustic.

Right: In Denmark people herald the arrival of the first snowdrops in February by sending each other papercuts that are folded and intricately cut with a solid block in the middle to hold a cryptic inscription. The recipient has to guess the identity of the sender – or give them a chocolate egg. This one was made by a fourteen-year-old girl for her godmother.

their tiny scissors could be used to make papercuts as well – they made delicate lacy love letters, birth certificates and pictures to commemorate engagements and weddings.

Paper cutting did not die out completely in Europe, and there are places where it is still positively thriving. In Denmark, for instance, people send each other cryptic papercuts when the first snowdrops flower in February – the recipient has to guess the identity of the sender or pay up with a chocolate egg! Denmark's most famous author of fairy tales, Hans Christian Andersen, delighted in paper cutting, and many examples of his cuts can be seen in books about him.

Another country where paper cutting has become part of a popular celebration is Mexico where, on the Day of the Dead, people buy large vibrantly coloured papercut pictures, banners and decorations to parade and then burn in the festival. In the United States people decorate their homes and streets with paper cut into the shapes of pumpkins, witches and skulls at Hallowe'en, and back in the nursery class (school) children still make paper dolls, chains and decorations at Christmas.

There was a time, when the marvel of machines and mass-production was new, when handmade came to mean hard-up, but thankfully that time has passed and attitudes have come full circle. Understanding how easily decorative goods can be churned out by factories has made us value the time and care taken and the unique aesthetic quality of handmade crafts.

Below: The birth record of Peter Gottschalk, which dates from 1769. Decorative paper cutwork of the early date of this birth record are rare.

GALLERY

PAPER CUTTING IS A UNIVERSAL ART AND CRAFT THAT IS PRAC-TISED ALL OVER THE WORLD. IN THIS GALLERY THERE ARE A SELECTION OF PAPERCUTS USING A WIDE RANGE OF MOTIFS WHICH TAKE THEIR INSPIRATION FROM MANY DIFFERENT CULTURES — MEXICO, CHINA, THE UNITED STATES OF AMERICA AND EUROPE. WHEN YOU HAVE TACKLED SOME OF THE PROJECTS IN THE BOOK, TAKE INSPIRATION FROM THE MOTIFS AND TECHNIQUES ILLUSTRATED IN THE GALLERY AND APPLY THEM TO YOUR OWN DESIGNS.

Left: CUTWORK PICTURE
In this intriguing picture, the parade of separate silhouette figures is framed by an elaborate arbor carefully scissored from a single-folded sheet to create a mirror image. To better appreciate the intricate technique, see how many birds you can find!
ABBY ALDRICH ROCKEFELLER FOLK ART CENTER

Left: PAPERCUT SCREEN
This screen was inspired by traditional Polish papercuts made at certain times of the year, such as Easter, to decorate farmhouse walls. The papercuts are nicely set off by the cool Scandinavian colours which have been used on the background of the screen, rather than the more exuberant Polish colours.
DEBORAH SCHNEEBELI-MORRELL

Left: LOVE TOKEN
The cut and folded paper love token originated in Switzerland and Germany. Skilled papercutters elevated this from a pastime to a skilled craft, creating beautiful symmetrical compositions. This charming love token of two parasoled ladies was cut by the author.
STEWART WALTON

Above: CHRISTMAS CARD
This papercut was made using the very latest paper-cutting techniques. The image was designed on computer and then cut by laser into a high-quality black paper.
METRO MODELS

Right: CHINESE PAPERCUTS
Chinese papercuts, like these, are cut from compacted paper blocks – as many as fifty at a time – then peeled off and hand-coloured. The subject matter here is typical: insects, birds, flowers and traditional Chinese motifs such as the lion dog.
CHINA

Left and far left: MEXICAN PAPERCUTS
Papercuts are widely used in Mexico as decoration for festive occasions. They come in a wide range of colours and depict traditional images. White papercuts, such as these two, are used specifically for weddings.
MEXIQUE

Left: LAMPSHADE
The pineapple used to be a symbol of hospitality and was used in many areas of house decoration by our ancestors. American folk artists simplified the shape into stencil designs, and this paper lampshade blends the style of the stencil with the popular folk art of partial cutting and lifting, to produce a surface texture. At night, when the lamp is lit the pineapple shape and texture is revealed.
STEWART WALTON

BASIC TECHNIQUES

PAPER CUTTING IS NOT A COMPLICATED CRAFT, BUT SOME PRAC-
TICE WILL IMPROVE YOUR CUTTING AND FOLDING TECHNIQUE
AND HELP YOU TO PRODUCE NEATER RESULTS. HAVING THE RIGHT
EQUIPMENT IS IMPORTANT — ESPECIALLY A SHARP PAIR OF SCISSORS
OR A CRAFT KNIFE WITH A SUPPLY OF NEW BLADES. SOME PEOPLE
PREFER TO CUT WITH SCISSORS, WHILE OTHERS FIND THAT THEY ARE
MORE COMFORTABLE WITH A CRAFT KNIFE. YOU NEED TO EXPERI-
MENT WITH BOTH TO FIND OUT WHICH SUITS YOU BETTER.

FOLDING PAPER

The number of times you fold the paper will
affect how many times the cut-out image is
reproduced. If you fold once, you get a
mirror image, twice and you get four images
and so on. The Doily and Snowflakes project
make use of more complicated folds, using a
protractor to mark off the angles. This means
that a number of identical cuts will radiate
out from a central point.

Making a single fold

1 Fold the paper in half. Draw half of
your pattern on the fold and cut it out.

2 You will have a perfectly symmetrical
cut-out shape in the middle of the paper.

Making a double fold

1 Fold a sheet of paper in half, then in half
again. Cut a shape out of the middle of the
square, not touching any fold or edge.

2 Open out and you have a shape cut out of
each section. Note that each one is facing
towards the corner of its square.

Concertina (Accordion) folds

It is important to measure the first fold
accurately and keep the other folds the same
size. Check that the right angles remain square.

Folding by hand

If you want a crisp edge, fold the paper
loosely, then run your nail along the crease.

Folding with thumbnail and ruler

Hold a metal ruler firmly and fold the paper
up to its edge and run your nail along it.

Using a bone paper folder

Bone paper folders are bookbinding tools that
give a very crisp edge. Fold the paper loosely,
then run the edge of the bone folder along it.

TRANSFERRING PATTERNS

Patterns have been given for most of the projects. To transfer these to your paper, you can either use a photocopier or tracing paper.

Photocopying patterns

1 Photocopy the pattern from the back of the book, enlarging it if you wish. Cut it out roughly. Spray the back of the copy with spray adhesive and stick it down on the paper that is to be used for the papercut.

2 Carefully cut out the design, following the lines of the pattern.

3 When the cutting is complete, remove the photocopy.

Tracing patterns

Trace the pattern using a pencil. Place the tracing, pencil-side down, on your paper. Rub over the tracing so that the pattern is transferred. Remove the tracing paper and draw over the lines of the pattern.

CUTTING PAPER

Scissors come in a variety of shapes and sizes. When you are cutting paper always turn the paper towards the blades, keeping them in the most comfortable and controllable position.

Making internal cuts with scissors

To start an internal cut, poke the sharp ends of the scissors into the centre of the paper that is to be removed. Do this in a controlled, careful way, then you can withdraw the scissors and insert the lower blade to cut out the shape with the scissors.

Using a craft knife

Always work with a cutting mat to protect your work surface and stop the paper slipping. Hold the knife like a pencil and, if the blade is sharp enough, you should not need to press down hard.

FINISHING OFF (UP)
Flattening the papercuts

The folds that you have made to reproduce the pattern of your papercut will still be visible after you unfold the finished work. You can flatten it by placing it inside a book and applying pressure with a heavy weight for a day or two. Alternatively, cover the papercut with a sheet of paper and smooth the surface with a small steel ruler or the back of a spoon.

Protecting your papercuts

A completed papercut can be protected by folding it inside a sheet of paper.

EQUIPMENT

WE HAVE USED A SELECTION OF DIFFERENT CUTTING AND MEASURING EQUIPMENT TO MAKE THE PROJECTS IN THIS BOOK. THE ESSENTIALS ARE A SHARP PAIR OF SCISSORS AND A SHEET OF PAPER, BUT WITH A FEW EXTRAS YOU CAN EXPAND YOUR PAPER-CUTTING REPERTOIRE AND GET TO GRIPS WITH (MASTER) ALL ASPECTS OF THE CRAFT. WITH THESE SIMPLE TOOLS, YOU CAN MAKE EVERYTHING FROM VERY SIMPLE FOLK IMAGES TO THE MOST ELABORATE AND COMPLICATED OF CUTS.

A bone paper folder is specifically used for folding paper to give a crisp edge (see Basic Techniques). Although very useful, this tool is not strictly essential. As an alternative, you could use a metal ruler.

A fine line black felt-tipped marker pen gives a clear outline when tracing the patterns at the back of the book.

Pencils with hard and soft lead are needed for drawing out shapes and transferring tracings. Soft pencils are best for transferring tracings.

A craft knife is needed for cutting out detailed inner areas. It can be uncomfortable if you grip it tightly, so bind the shaft with masking tape to make a pad that will be easier to hold. You must change the blade of your craft knife quite frequently, otherwise you will be working with a blunt blade that will catch and snag the paper. A sharp blade will give good, clean cuts. When cutting with a craft knife, always work on a cutting mat to prevent the blade from slipping.

Pinking shears are great fun because they give a decorative zigzag edge to papercuts. You can also get scissors with wavy and other decorative edges.

Scissors in various sizes are of course one of the main tools of paper cutting. You will need two or three pairs with different sizes of blade for tackling large and detailed projects. When cutting out delicate and intricate shapes, you should use a small pair of scissors which will give you greater control.

A spoon is useful for smoothing over the back of cut-outs to remove the folds (see Basic Techniques).

A revolving hole punch adjusts to six or more different-sized holes. It is ideal for making a row of even-sized holes for borders.

A metal ruler is needed for cutting straight lines with a craft knife. If you use a perspex (clear plastic) ruler, your craft knife will snag on the plastic and the straight edge will soon become too messy to work with. You can also tear paper against the sharp edge of a metal ruler (see Basic Techniques).

A set square (triangle) with 60 degree and 30 degree corners enables you to accurately divide circles into sixths.

A perspex (clear, plastic) ruler is useful if you need to see the template underneath when you are cutting, such as the clock face numerals of the Star Clock.

A protractor enables you to divide circles into angles.

A pair of compasses (A compass) is useful for drawing accurate circles and it marks the centre of the circle at the same time. If you do not have a pair of compasses (compass), round objects that you find around the home are good substitutes, for example, side plates.

A cutting mat is needed when you are using a craft knife. It protects your work surface, and protects you because it prevents the knife from slipping. A cutting mat is self-healing so it can be used time and time again. The surface of the mat is divided into vertical and horizontal lines to make it easier to check right angles and measurements.

KEY

1	Bone paper folder	**9**	Small scissors with short, very pointed blades
2	Fine line black felt-tipped marker pen	**10**	Spoon to smooth and flatten folded paper
3	Pencil	**11**	Revolving hole punch
4	Craft knife	**12**	Metal ruler
5	Pinking shears	**13**	Set square (triangle)
6	Medium-sized scissors for cutting out large shapes	**14**	Perspex (clear plastic) ruler
7	Small scissors with medium-length blades	**15**	Small steel ruler
		16	Protractor
8	Small scissors with small blades for cutting out intricate shapes	**17**	Pair of compasses (Compass)
		18	Cutting mat

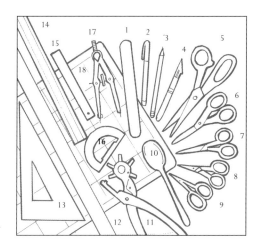

MATERIALS

PAPER IS OF COURSE THE ESSENTIAL MATERIAL IN PAPER CUT-TING. THERE ARE MANY DIFFERENT TYPES OF PAPER THAT ARE SUITABLE FOR PAPER CUTTING AND YOU WILL SOON FIND YOUR OWN PREFERENCES. THE MAIN CONSIDERATION SHOULD ALWAYS BE THE WEIGHT OF THE PAPER — IF IT IS TOO HEAVY AND THICK IT WILL NOT FOLD AND CUT WELL. A THIN PAPER CAN STILL BE CUT OUT BY PLAC-ING IT INSIDE A FOLDED SHEET OF THICKER PAPER AND CUTTING THEM BOTH TOGETHER, BUT GREAT CARE MUST BE TAKEN WHEN HANDLING THE RESULTING PAPERCUT. A VISIT TO A PAPER SPECIALIST (STORE) WILL BE WORTHWHILE.

Most papers are made from wood pulp, although there are some which contain a high proportion of fabrics such as linen and cotton. A lot of paper imported from the Far East is made from tropical plants, like banana, rice and jute, and they often have visible shreds of plant fibres. In India they make a lot of rag paper from recycled clothes — it is high-quality and exceptionally strong. The thinner versions of these papers add a further dimension of texture to the papercuts. Wood pulp needs to be chemically treated to remove the naturally occurring acids. This weakens the paper and causes instability of colour and lack of strength.

The cheapest paper is newsprint. It also happens to be good paper to cut. It creases and folds really well and scissors glide through it. Bond paper is basically wood pulp that has a glue added to bond it together. This is the usual paper for stationery and is also a good paper-cutting material. Laid paper can be recognized by the parallel lines that run through it. This is also a stationery paper, which comes in a range of light colours and is suitable for paper cutting. Woven paper is made with a mesh of fine fibres that you can both feel and see. Coated papers may have a colour added to one side only — as in the brightly coloured or metallic-finish parcel wrap that is currently popular. Experiment with this type of paper before committing yourself to a complex project — the surface colour can crack along the fold, which will spoil the outcome of your work.

Brightly coloured craft papers are available from (at) toy shops (stores) and hobby shops (stores). They are sold in packs and are pre-gummed for a quick lick and stick, although you should use spray adhesive for any sticking. The papers fold and cut with ease.

Handmade Indian papers with visible wood chippings and plant fibres are light-weight but strong and easy to cut. Folding depends upon the "bits" (texture) which may get in the way of a neat crease.

Coloured craft paper has strong solid colour and is easy to work with if the project only requires one or two folds. It cuts crisply.

Coloured laid paper is suitable for using in a photocopier. This paper is crisp and folds and cuts very well. It was used for the Bookmarks.

Crepe paper is crinkly and stretchy. It comes in lots and lots of bright colours and is widely available from newsagents or art and hobby shops.

High-quality tissue paper has a sheen and is quite strong but very thin. It is a lovely paper to cut and can be folded many times over and still be thin enough for accurate cutting.

Handmade Japanese papers are softer to touch than Indian papers but very strong as they contain long threads of fibre. You can buy them from specialist shops (at specialty stores) and they are expensive but worth the money. They cut well but folding is difficult as they spring back.

Foil-coated metallic paper is often coated cellophane paper. It has a tendency to slip and slide and may tear as well. It is, however, the only type to use for real reflective shimmer. Some metallic papers fold well but others are reluctant to unfold once creased. You can buy them as giftwrap in newsagents or art stores.

Glassine paper is a glazed, coloured, heavy tissue-type paper that is mottled and transparent when held up to the light. It folds and cuts beautifully. Get it from a specialist (at a specialty) paper dealer or some art shops (stores).

Coated parcel wrap is the familiar brown parcel (packing) wrapping paper dressed up with a coating of silver (or other colours) on one or two sides. It is a popular gift wrapping paper and cuts and folds very well.

KEY

1	Brightly coloured craft papers	6	Tissue paper
2	Handmade Indian papers	7	Handmade Japanese papers
3	Coloured craft paper	8	Foil-coated, metallic and reflective papers
4	Photocopies on coloured laid paper	9	Glassine paper
5	Crepe paper	10	Coated parcel wrap

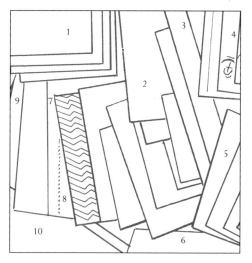

DECORATED LAMPSHADE

THIS IS A VERY SIMPLE BUT EFFECTIVE WAY TO DECORATE A PLAIN LAMPSHADE. WE HAVE USED NATURAL COLOURS, BUT THE PAPER AND SHADE COULD BE BRIGHT OR CONTRASTING IF YOU PRE-FER — THE METHOD IS THE SAME. THERE ARE THREE DIFFERENT PATTERNS TO TRACE (SEE BASIC TECHNIQUES) AND AN INFINITE NUMBER TO INVENT FOR YOURSELF.

1 Draw a circle of paper with an 8 cm (3 in) diameter and cut it out.

3 Fold the circle in half again and crease firmly with your finger.

5 Cut out the edge pattern first. Then do the smaller cuts with a craft knife.

2 Fold the circle in half and make a firm crease with your finger.

4 Fold in half again. Make a tracing of the patterns at the back of the book, then transfer one of them to the folded paper.

6 Open out the papercut. Make several more papercuts, then stick the shapes on to the lampshade at regular intervals.

MATERIALS AND EQUIPMENT YOU WILL NEED

THIN PAPER • PAIR OF COMPASSES (COMPASS) • PENCIL • SCISSORS • TRACING PAPER • CRAFT KNIFE •
CUTTING MAT • PLAIN LAMPSHADE • GLUE STICK OR SPRAY ADHESIVE

CHINESE LANTERNS

THERE WAS A TIME WHEN ALL CHILDREN SPENT THE WEEKS BEFORE CHRISTMAS CUTTING AND STICKING TOGETHER LENGTHS OF PAPER CHAINS AND PRETTY CHINESE LANTERNS LIKE THESE. THE COLOURS USED HERE WILL ADD A TOUCH OF FIESTA TO YOUR CHRISTMAS TREE, ESPECIALLY WHEN LIT BY STRATEGICALLY PLACED TREE LIGHTS. THIS PROJECT CAN INVOLVE ALL THE FAMILY AND THE LANTERNS WOULD ALSO LOOK LOVELY MADE FOR A SUMMER GARDEN PARTY.

SMALL LANTERNS

1 For each small Chinese lantern, draw a rectangle of crepe paper 13 x 12.5 cm (5 x 4¾ in). Cut out.

3 Mark another fold 3 cm (1⅛ in) from the first fold. Cut through the paper up to the guideline. The cuts can be widely or closely spaced to give different effects.

5 Cut the top fold into triangles or decorative fringing.

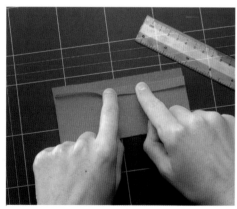

2 Fold in half lengthways, then fold down 1 cm (⅜ in) from both of the top edges.

4 Cut little notches, to add decoration, as shown.

MATERIALS AND EQUIPMENT YOU WILL NEED

DOUBLE-SIDED CREPE PAPER, IN TWO COLOURS • RULER • PENCIL • SHARP SCISSORS • GLUE STICK •
CLOTHES PEGS (CLOTHESPINS) • CHRISTMAS TREE LIGHTS • REVOLVING HOLE PUNCH

LARGE LANTERNS

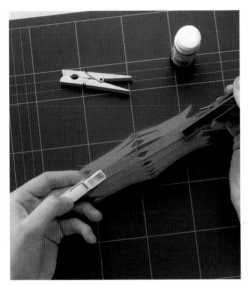

6 Open the lantern and join the short sides with the glue stick. Hold with clothes pegs (clothespins) until dry.

7 Cut a strip of paper to hang over each light bulb on the tree lights, so that the bulb hangs inside the lantern.

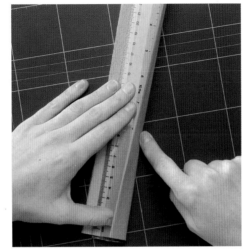

1 To make a large lantern, cut a piece of paper 25 x 23 cm (10 x 9 in) from crepe paper and fold it in half lengthways. Fold down a top strip, as you did for the small lantern, then make a second fold 5 cm (2 in) in from the first fold.

2 Cut two strips in a contrasting colour the same length but only 10 cm (4 in) deep. Fold them in half, then stick each contrasting strip just underneath the folded top edge on either side.

3 Cut slits up to the edge of the added paper, along the whole length of the paper to the second fold.

4 Cut decorative notches along the fold edges between the slits. ▶

5 Scallop the edges of the two coloured
strips, one at a time.

6 Use the hole punch to make a hole in each
scallop shape to reveal the colour below.

7 Unfold the lantern, then join the edges
together using the glue stick. Snip the
scalloped fringing where the glued edges
meet so that you can push out the decorative
fringing. Hold together with a clothes peg
(clothespin) until dry. Add a little strip of
paper to hang it up, as for the small lantern.

PAPER CAFÉ CURTAIN

THIS IS A CLEVER AND VERY ATTRACTIVE WAY TO OBSCURE A WINDOW THAT IS OVERLOOKED, WITHOUT CUTTING OUT THE LIGHT COMPLETELY. THE PAPER NEEDS TO BE QUITE HIGH-QUALITY SO THAT IT WILL NOT CRACK, AND STIFF SO THAT IT WILL HOLD CREASES WELL AND WILL NOT RIP TOO EASILY. VISIT A SPECIALIST PAPER SHOP WHERE YOU WILL BE STRUCK BY THE VARIETY OF PAPERS THAT ARE AVAILABLE TODAY — SOME ARE VERY EXPENSIVE BUT OTHERS THAT LOOK SIMILAR ARE VERY REASONABLY PRICED.

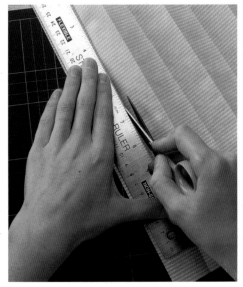  

1 Measure the window to ascertain how many sheets of paper you will need. Remember that the sheet will be half the width once folded. Use the blunt edge of your scissors to score fold lines of equal width along the length of the paper. The width of the pleats can be that of the ruler, as this is an easy way to make sure they are all the same size.

2 Trace the design from the back of the book and transfer one half of the pattern on to a strip of cardboard, enlarging if necessary (see Basic Techniques). Slip it under the pleats and lightly trace the pattern along the fold lines.

3 Using sharp scissors, cut out the pattern along the fold lines. To hang the curtain you can either make holes with a hole punch and run a thread along the top, or you can buy curtain clips, which fasten to the top of the paper curtain.

MATERIALS AND EQUIPMENT YOU WILL NEED

PAPER • SCISSORS • RULER • TRACING PAPER • PENCIL • CARDBOARD • REVOLVING HOLE PUNCH

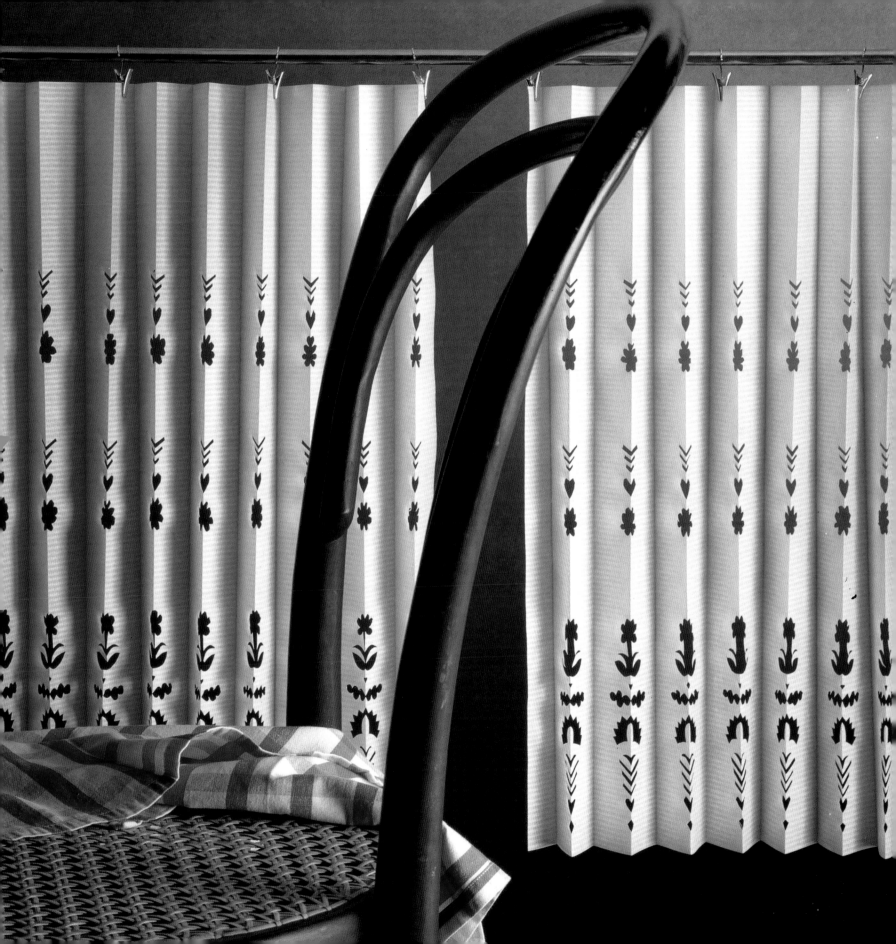

MEXICAN PAPERCUT BUNTING

MEXICAN PAPERCUTS ARE TRADITIONALLY MADE FROM BRIGHTLY COLOURED TISSUE PAPER. THESE ONES ARE CUT FROM STRONG TRANSLUCENT GLASSINE PAPER, BUT YOU CAN USE ANY BRIGHTLY COLOURED LIGHTWEIGHT PAPER CHOSEN FROM THE HUNDREDS OF QUALITIES AVAILABLE. THE FINISHED PAPERCUT CAN BE HUNG UP AS DECORATION AT A WINDOW OR ALONG A SHELF.

1 Enlarge the pattern at the back of the book and trace one half of it on to cartridge (plain) paper (see Basic Techniques). Go over the tracing with black pen so that it will show through easily. The design will fit on to an A4 (letter size) sheet folded in half lengthways. Fold your paper in half and place the tracing along the inside fold. Trace the design on to your paper.

2 Cut out the design, making the internal cuts first by gently piercing a hole and carefully cutting out each shape. Work on alternate ends of the cutting, top and bottom, so that the paper does not become flimsy from overhandling in one place.

3 Finish by cutting a zigzag edge. Fold over the top and glue a length of string inside the fold for hanging.

MATERIALS AND EQUIPMENT YOU WILL NEED

TRACING PAPER • PENCIL • CARTRIDGE (PLAIN) PAPER • BLACK FELT-TIPPED PEN • STRONG TRANSPARENT PAPER SUCH AS GLASSINE OR JAPANESE PAPER • SHARP SCISSORS OR CRAFT KNIFE • FINE STRING • GLUE STICK

SHELF EDGING

Plain paper shelf edgings like this are quickly made and can be replaced every now and then to give a fresh new look. This idea is used all over the world, from the folk art patterns of New England to South Africa where comic strips and newspapers are used to make vibrant zigzag borders. The paper used here is plain newsprint, which is cheap and a pleasure to fold and cut. You can try patterned papers too – gingham patterns look good for kitchen shelves.

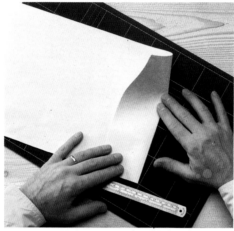

1 Cut a strip of paper 23 cm (9 in) deep and just a little bit longer than the length of the shelf. Make a fold 8 cm (3 in) from one end of the paper.

3 Trace your chosen pattern from the back of the book and transfer it to the folded paper (see Basic Techniques).

5 Cut the edges of the pattern next, being careful not to tear the paper.

2 Turn the paper over and repeat the fold. Continue in this way to make concertina (accordion) folds along the whole length.

4 Make the internal cuts first, using a craft knife and cutting mat.

6 Unfold the paper and press. Fold in half lengthways to fit over the shelf edges.

MATERIALS AND EQUIPMENT YOU WILL NEED

Scissors • Plain newsprint or lining paper • Ruler • Pencil • Tracing paper • Craft knife • Cutting mat

TABLE MAT

MAKE A SET OF THESE STRIKING TABLE MATS AND YOU WILL ASK YOURSELF WHY YOU HAVE NEVER DONE IT BEFORE. ONE OF THE REASONS IS PROBABLY THAT A LAMINATING SERVICE IS NOT SOMETHING YOU USE UNTIL YOU HAVE A REASON — AND THEN YOU DISCOVER JUST HOW STRAIGHTFORWARD IT IS. A PAPERCUT WOULD NOT NORMALLY BE A PRACTICAL IDEA FOR A TABLE MAT, BUT ONCE IT HAS BEEN LAMINATED IT CAN BE WIPED CLEAN AND WILL LAST A LONG TIME. RED AND BLACK PROVIDE A STRIKING CONTRAST, BUT THE PATTERN COULD BE MADE IN ANY COLOUR COMBINATION TO MATCH YOUR DINNER SERVICE OR CURTAINS.

1 Trace the pattern from the back of the book on to a sheet of white paper, then trim the edges, using a craft knife.

3 Spray adhesive on the back of the pattern and stick it on to the trimmed red paper.

5 Carefully peel off the pattern, then open out and flatten the papercut.

2 Fold the red paper in half, then use the pattern to measure the required size and trim the edges to fit.

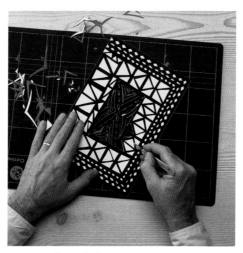

4 Cut through the pattern and the paper. Make the internal cuts first, starting in the middle and working outwards, cutting the edges and along the fold last.

6 Spray adhesive on the back of the papercut and fix on to the black paper. Cover it with a sheet of tracing paper and smooth with your hand to make sure that it has stuck down evenly. Take the mat to a print shop to be laminated.

MATERIALS AND EQUIPMENT YOU WILL NEED

TRACING PAPER • PENCIL • WHITE PAPER • CRAFT KNIFE • METAL RULER • CUTTING MAT • A SHEET EACH OF RED AND BLACK PAPER • SPRAY ADHESIVE

18TH-CENTURY ITALIAN PAPERCUT

CAREFUL WORK WITH A STEADY HAND IS MAGNIFICENTLY REWARDED BY THE COMPLETION OF THIS MOST INTRICATE ITALIAN DESIGN. IT IS MADE FROM A SINGLE SHEET OF THIN BLACK PAPER, FOLDED IN HALF AND CUT OUT WITH A CRAFT KNIFE. THE PHOTOCOPIED PATTERN IS TEMPORARILY GLUED TO THE BLACK PAPER, WHICH MAKES IT EASIER TO CUT ACCURATELY BECAUSE IT IS LESS FLIMSY. THIS PAPERCUT IS VERY DELICATE AND SHOULD BE MOUNTED ON PAPER AND FRAMED.

1 Photocopy the pattern from the back of the book. Fold the piece of black paper in half.

2 Using the spray adhesive, stick the photocopied pattern on to the folded paper.

4 Gently remove the pattern. Press the papercut flat by covering it with a sheet of tracing paper and rubbing with the back of a spoon.

3 Cut out the design carefully, working from the middle out towards the edges.

MATERIALS AND EQUIPMENT YOU WILL NEED

THIN BLACK PAPER (BETWEEN THE WEIGHT OF SUGAR (CONSTRUCTION) PAPER AND TISSUE PAPER) • SPRAY ADHESIVE •
CRAFT KNIFE • CUTTING MAT • TRACING PAPER • METAL SPOON

WHITE LACE SCHERENSCHNITTE

THE CUTTING OF VERY FINE FOLDED PAPER DESIGNS LIKE THIS ONE WAS A POPULAR PASTIME FOR LADIES IN THE 19TH CENTURY. THEY USED SMALL, SHARP EMBROIDERY SCISSORS TO CUT ELABORATE LOVE TOKENS FOR HUSBANDS OR SUITORS. MOST OF THE CUTTING HERE IS DONE WITH A SHARP CRAFT KNIFE; THEN A HOLE PUNCH COMPLETES THE DESIGN WITH PERFORATIONS TO GIVE A LACY EFFECT TO THE BORDER. LAID PAPER, WITH LINES RUNNING THROUGH IT, IS IDEAL FOR THIS DESIGN.

1 Photocopy the pattern from the back of the book. Fold the sheet of paper in half.

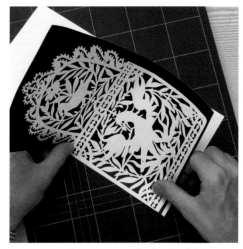

2 Spray adhesive on to the back of the pattern and position it on one half of the folded paper.

3 Using a craft knife and cutting mat, cut out the pattern, beginning in the centre and working out towards the edges. Take your time, there is no rush.

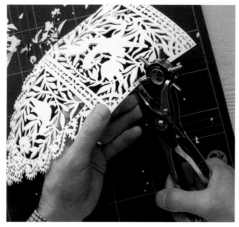

4 Remove the pattern. Using the finest setting on the hole punch, perforate the framework at regular intervals.

5 Open out the papercut and mount it on to a sheet of natural-coloured handmade paper that has a smooth enough texture not to distort the papercut.

MATERIALS AND EQUIPMENT YOU WILL NEED

SPRAY ADHESIVE • SHEET OF WHITE LAID PAPER • CRAFT KNIFE • CUTTING MAT • REVOLVING HOLE PUNCH • SHEET OF NATURAL-COLOURED HANDMADE PAPER

STAR CLOCK

THE BOLD GRAPHIC STYLE OF THIS PAPER CLOCK FACE WILL SUIT ANY CONTEMPORARY ROOM AND IT WILL APPEAL TO ALL AGES. THE BASE IS MOUNTING BOARD, WITH LAYERS OF CUT PAPER FOR THE NUMERALS AND STARBURSTS. BATTERY-OPERATED CLOCK MOVE-MENTS ARE INEXPENSIVE AND YOU CAN CHOOSE FROM A SELECTION OF HANDS — THESE VERY SIMPLE ONES SUIT THIS CLOCK FACE ESPE-CIALLY WELL BECAUSE THE RED SECOND HAND MATCHES THE NUMER-ALS. PRECISION CUTTING IS REQUIRED FOR THIS PROJECT.

1 Cut a 27 cm (10½ in) square of buff paper. Find the centre of the square and use the compasses (compass) to draw two circles, the first with an 11 cm (4⅜ in) radius and the next with a 9.5 cm (3¾ in) radius. Divide the circles into quarters vertically and horizontally, then use the compasses (compass) to divide each quarter into three (thirds). This will give the positions for the 12 numerals.

2 Photocopy the numerals from the back of the book. Enlarge them if necessary, then cut them out using a craft knife, perspex (clear, plastic) ruler and cutting mat.

3 Using spray adhesive, mount each numeral in position around the clock face. The middle of each one should fall on the line that intersects the outer circle. Judge and adjust by eye.

▶

MATERIALS AND EQUIPMENT YOU WILL NEED

BUFF, RED, GREY AND YELLOW PAPER • PAIR OF COMPASSES (COMPASS) • PENCIL • CRAFT KNIFE • PERSPEX (CLEAR, PLASTIC) RULER • CUTTING MAT • SPRAY ADHESIVE • GREY MOUNTING BOARD • METAL RULER • BATTERY-OPERATED CLOCK MOVEMENT

4 Carefully cut out the numerals through both layers, then remove the paper.

6 Stick the buff and red paper centrally on to the grey mounting board.

8 Position and stick the grey and yellow stars on the centre of the clock face.

5 Cut a 27.5 cm (10¾ in) square of red paper and a 29 cm (11½ in) square of grey mounting board using a craft knife, metal ruler and cutting mat.

7 Fold squares of grey and yellow paper in half and half again, then draw star patterns on to them, as shown (the yellow star should be slightly smaller than the grey star). Cut out both stars.

9 Cut a hole for the clock movement in the centre and install it according to the manufacturer's instructions.

VALENTINES

THE TRADITION OF MAKING PAPERCUT VALENTINES GOES BACK AT LEAST TWO HUNDRED YEARS. THERE IS A LOT OF PAPER CUTTING IN EUROPEAN FOLK ART AND EMIGRANTS TOOK THEIR CUSTOMS TO AMERICA WHEN THEY SETTLED THERE. BOTH MEN AND WOMEN WOULD CUT ELABORATE LOVE TOKENS DECORATED WITH HEARTS, RIBBONS, BIRDS, FLOWERS AND STARS. WE HAVE USED ROUGH-TEXTURED HANDMADE PAPER FOR THE CARDS, THEN ADDED RED AND SILVER PAPERCUTS FOR THE DECORATION.

1 Fold the red paper in half, then fold the sheet of white paper around it. This will make it easier to cut accurately.

3 Using a craft knife and cutting mat, cut out the pattern. Make the internal cuts first, then those along the fold.

5 Fold the sheet of silver-coated parcel wrap in half and slide it into the fold of the papercut. Draw a half-heart shape around the outside of the papercut.

▶

2 Select one of the patterns from the back of the book and trace it on to the sheet of plain white paper.

4 Turn the paper around as you work so that you always cut at the most comfortable angle.

MATERIALS AND EQUIPMENT YOU WILL NEED

RED FIBROUS HANDMADE PAPER (FLECKED WITH PETALS OR LEAVES) • PLAIN WHITE PAPER • TRACING PAPER • PENCIL • CRAFT KNIFE • CUTTING MAT • SILVER-COATED PARCEL WRAP • METAL RULER • NATURAL-COLOURED HANDMADE PAPER • SPRAY ADHESIVE • TEXTURED SILVER FOIL PAPER (NOT COOKING FOIL) • PINKING SHEARS

6 Using a metal ruler, tear a piece of natural-coloured handmade paper a little bigger than the height of the silver heart.

8 Make the second card by folding the silver foil paper in half inside another sheet of plain white paper. Trace, then cut out the second shape with pinking shears.

7 Using spray adhesive, stick the heart and papercut on to the backing paper.

9 Cut a pattern along the fold, then open out and stick the silver foil cut-out on to another torn backing sheet. Cut out small heart shapes to add further depth to the design.

PICTURE FRAME

HERE IS A VERY SIMPLE BUT EFFECTIVE WAY TO CUSTOMISE AN EXISTING WOODEN PICTURE FRAME. THE PATTERN OF DIAMONDS AND SQUARES HAS BEEN CUT FROM FIBROUS HANDMADE PAPER TO GIVE IT A "WOODY" APPEARANCE. THE PATTERN CAN BE PROTECTED BY A COAT OF CLEAR VARNISH, OR MADE TO LOOK LIKE MARQUETRY BY USING A TINTED VARNISH.

1 Place the frame on the handmade paper and draw round it with a pencil, both inside and outside.

2 Using a craft knife, ruler and cutting mat, cut out just inside both lines, so that it is slightly smaller than the wooden frame.

4 Next, fold the longer side of the folded paper frame in half widthways, neatly along its length.

▶

3 Fold the paper frame in half across its shorter side and then in half again.

MATERIALS AND EQUIPMENT YOU WILL NEED

PLAIN WOODEN PICTURE FRAME • SHEET OF HANDMADE PAPER • PENCIL • CRAFT KNIFE • RULER •
CUTTING MAT • SPRAY ADHESIVE • CLEAR SPRAY VARNISH • TINTED VARNISH (OPTIONAL)

5 Draw triangles along the edge, leaving gaps in between, and a square in the corner.

7 Cut out the inner triangles.

9 Apply a coat of spray adhesive and place the frame on top of the papercut.

6 Cut out the square and the outer triangles using a craft knife and cutting mat. Do one side, then unfold and refold it and draw and cut out the other side.

8 Unfold the papercut carefully and press it flat.

10 Make sure that the papercut is smoothly stuck down, then spray the frame with a clear varnish. If you wish, you can add a tinted varnish at this stage.

BOOKMARKS

T HE IDEA FOR THESE UNUSUAL BOOKMARKS COMES FROM A COLLECTION OF AMERICAN FOLK ART THAT CONTAINS SIMILAR DESIGNS CUT FROM OLD LETTERS AND LEDGERS. CHILDREN WERE KEPT AMUSED FOR MANY HOURS WITH JUST A PAIR OF SCISSORS AND SOME PAPER. PAPER ITSELF WAS HARD TO COME BY, SO OLD LEDGERS, LETTERS AND HOUSEHOLD ACCOUNT BOOKS WERE RECYCLED AS PLAY MATERIAL. TO GET A SIMILAR EFFECT WE PHOTOCOPIED OLD DOCUMENTS ON TO COLOURED PAPER.

1 Trim the coloured paper to A4 (letter-paper) size so that it will fit in the photocopier.

3 Select the most suitable parts of your photocopied papers. Trim them to double the pattern size and fold in half.

5 Cut each pattern in half, spray the backs of the patterns lightly with spray adhesive and carefully stick them along the folds of the coloured papers.

2 Select the best part of your calligraphy and photocopy on to the coloured paper.

4 Make photocopies of the patterns at the back of the book and cut them out.

6 Using a craft knife, make all the inside cuts first.

▶

MATERIALS AND EQUIPMENT YOU WILL NEED

COLOURED PAPER • OLD DOCUMENTS OR LEDGERS • CRAFT KNIFE • RULER • CUTTING MAT • SPRAY ADHESIVE

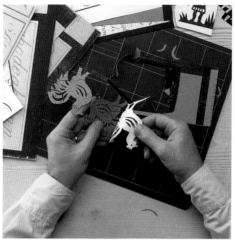

7 To complete the cutting of a pattern, cut around the outside edges.

8 Carefully peel off the pattern and open out the papercut bookmarks.

DOVE LAMPSHADE

CUTTING A PATTERN OUT OF A LAMPSHADE IS AN OLD IDEA, DATING BACK TO THE DAYS OF PIERCED TIN LANTERNS, WHICH HAVE ALSO MADE A RECENT COMEBACK. CANDLE SHADES WOULD HAVE HAD PATTERNS CUT OUT OF THEM, OR PRICKED OUT, TO ALLOW THE LIGHT TO SHINE THROUGH. THIS PROJECT IS MORE ABOUT CUSTOMISING A BOUGHT SHADE RATHER THAN MAKING ONE, AND YOU CAN USE ANY SMALL PAPER SHADE – THE VELLUM LOOK USED HERE IS PARTICULARLY SUITABLE. IF THE LAMPSHADE IS TOO STIFF YOU WILL FIND IT HARD TO CUT THROUGH. THE DOVE PATTERN LOOKS GOOD DURING THE DAY AND EVEN BETTER ONCE THE LAMP IS LIT.

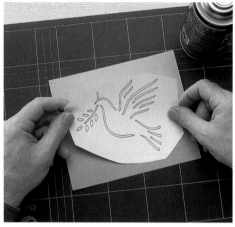

1 Make a photocopy of the dove pattern from the back of the book, enlarging it to fit the size of your lampshade.

3 Peel off the photocopy to reveal the stiff paper stencil of the dove.

5 Carefully draw through the stencil to transfer the pattern on to the lampshade.

2 Using spray adhesive, mount the photocopy on to stiff paper. Cut out the design using a craft knife and cutting mat.

4 Apply a light coating of spray adhesive, then tape the stencil on to the shade.

6 Hold the lampshade firmly with your spare hand and, keeping your fingers out of reach of the knife blade, cut out the pattern. When you cut, poke the point of the blade through first, then make sweeping cuts using the movement of your arm rather than just your wrist.

MATERIALS AND EQUIPMENT YOU WILL NEED

SMALL PAPER LAMPSHADE • SPRAY ADHESIVE • STIFF PAPER • CRAFT KNIFE • CUTTING MAT • MASKING TAPE • PENCIL

DOILY

EVERYONE IS FAMILIAR WITH LACY WHITE PAPER DOILIES AND, THERE IS NO DOUBT ABOUT IT, THEY CAN TURN A HUMBLE PLATE OF BISCUITS (COOKIES) INTO A TEMPTING TEA-TIME TREAT! THIS IS MORE FUNKY THAN FRILLY. IT LOOKS GOOD IN TRADITIONAL WHITE OR YOU COULD CUT DIFFERENT ONES FROM COLOURED PAPER TO SUIT DIFFERENT FESTIVE OCCASIONS — ORANGE FOR HALLOWE'EN, RED AND GREEN FOR CHRISTMAS, SILVER FOR A WEDDING OR BRIGHT MULTI-COLOURS FOR A BIRTHDAY PARTY.

1 Fold the paper diagonally to make a square. Cut off the excess, using a craft knife, ruler and cutting mat.

2 Find the centre of the square by folding it diagonally and pinching.

3 Place the protractor on the centre point and mark off a 36 degree angle. ▶

MATERIALS AND EQUIPMENT YOU WILL NEED

SHEET OF A4 (LETTER-SIZE) PAPER • CRAFT KNIFE • RULER • CUTTING MAT • PROTRACTOR • PENCIL

4 Flip one side of the triangle over along the 36 degree angle and fold.

6 Now flip the paper over and repeat these folds, ending up with four layers of folds.

8 Using a craft knife and cutting mat, cut out the pattern. Cut the internal cuts first, then the outside edge cuts.

5 Fold the outer edge of the piece you have just folded on top to the same line and crease firmly along the fold.

7 Using a pencil, draw a pattern on one side of the folded paper. Keep the pattern within all the unfolded edges of the paper.

9 Open out the papercut carefully and flatten out the doily ready for use.

FRAKTUR-STYLE COLOURED PAPERCUT

BEFORE THE DAYS OF THE PRINTING PRESS, CALLIGRAPHERS WOULD TRAVEL AROUND THE COUNTRY MAKING COMMEMORATIVE CERTIFICATES FOR BIRTHS, MARRIAGES AND DEATHS. THEY USED TRADITIONAL SYMBOLS AND PATTERNS TO DECORATE THE CERTIFI-CATES, THEN FILLED IN THE NAMES IN ELABORATE CALLIGRAPHY OR FRAKTUR WORK. THE PAPERCUT VERSION OF A FRAKTUR WAS MORE LIKELY TO BE MADE BY AN AMATEUR, TO BE GIVEN AS A GIFT OR TOKEN OF LOVE.

1 Photocopy the pattern from the back of the book. Fold the sheet of watercolour paper in half.

2 Spray adhesive on to the back of the pattern and stick it on to the folded paper. Carefully cut out the pattern using a craft knife and cutting mat. Make all the internal cuts first, then cut along the fold.

3 Remove the pattern carefully, open out, then cover with tracing paper and rub with the back of a spoon to flatten.

▶

MATERIALS AND EQUIPMENT YOU WILL NEED

SHEET OF WATERCOLOUR PAPER, NOT TOO THICK • SPRAY ADHESIVE • CRAFT KNIFE • CUTTING MAT • TRACING PAPER • METAL SPOON • PAINT PALETTE •
GUM ARABIC • DISTILLED WATER • GREEN, YELLOW, ORANGE AND BLACK WATERCOLOUR PAINTS • PAINTBRUSHES

4 Using a paint palette, prepare a watercolour medium for diluting the paints by mixing equal parts of gum arabic and distilled water.

5 Mix some green paint using the watercolour medium and paint the green areas of the pattern.

6 Mix yellow paint in the same way and apply, following the illustration.

7 Mix the orange in the same way and apply it where required over the yellow.

8 Mix black some paint and add the details to the illustration with a fine brush.

9 Leave to dry, then press flat under a heavy weight and mount for framing.

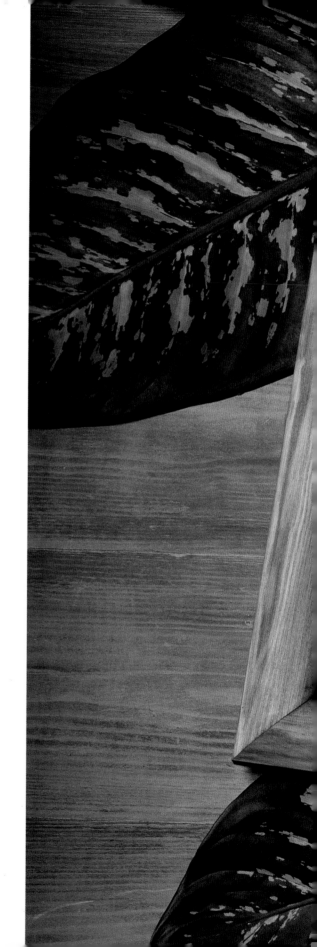

JAM JAR COVERS

PRETTY PAPER CIRCLES LIKE THESE ARE PERFECT FOR DRESSING UP YOUR HOMEMADE JAMS AND CHUTNEYS TO GIVE AS PRESENTS OR TO SELL ON (AT) A PRODUCE STALL (MARKET). THEY MAKE AN ASSORTMENT OF UNMATCHING RECYCLED JARS INTO A SET THAT WILL STAND OUT FROM ALL THE REST WITH THEIR IMITATION LACE EDGINGS. THE PAPER USED HERE IS HANDMADE IN INDIA AND CONTAINS A LOT OF VEGETABLE FIBRES WHICH ADD STRENGTH AND PREVENT IT FROM TEARING EASILY.

1 Cut out a circle of paper that is roughly twice the diameter of the jar lid.

3 Lightly pencil in half-hearts on the edges and cut them out. Mark dotted hearts — one in the middle and two halves either side along the folded edges.

5 Using the small scissors, cut a scalloped edge by snipping out triangles between the bases of the hearts.

2 Fold the circle of paper in half four times.

4 Place the folded paper on a hard surface and use the hole punch and hammer to tap out the dotted holes.

6 Unfold and flatten the cover. Place it over the jam jar and secure it with ribbon tied in a bow.

MATERIALS AND EQUIPMENT YOU WILL NEED

HANDMADE PAPER • SCISSORS — SMALL, POINTED PAIR AND A LARGER PAIR • JAM JAR • PENCIL • SMALL HOLE PUNCH • SMALL HAMMER • RIBBON

DECORATED ELEPHANTS

THIS PROJECT IS PART PAPER CUTTING AND PART PAPER SCULPTURE. THERE IS SOMETHING REALLY MAGICAL ABOUT MAKING A FREE-STANDING ANIMAL OUT OF A FLAT SHEET OF PAPER, AND THEN YOU HAVE THE FUN OF DRESSING IT UP FOR THE PROCESSION. A ROW OF THESE ELEPHANTS WOULD LOOK GREAT ALONG A SHELF OR MANTELPIECE AND ONE ON ITS OWN WOULD MAKE A UNIQUE GREETINGS CARD. CHILDREN WILL ENJOY MAKING THE FANCY BLANKETS AND HEAD-DRESSES, AND ADDING SEQUINS, STARS AND FEATHERS.

1 Fold a sheet of coloured A4 (letter-size) paper in half widthways.

3 Place the paper on a cutting mat and cut out using a craft knife.

5 Holding the elephant firmly, push the head and shoulders towards each other to fold the head and ears back on to the body.

2 Trace, then transfer the elephant pattern from the back of the book, including the dotted and dashed fold lines. The dots indicate inward or valley folds, and the dashes indicate upwards or mountain folds.

4 Make the folds by placing a small ruler along the line and using your thumbnail to fold and crease from the other side.

6 Fold the tail sideways and the tusks upwards.

▶

MATERIALS AND EQUIPMENT YOU WILL NEED

STIFF COLOURED PAPER • PENCIL • CUTTING MAT • CRAFT KNIFE • SMALL METAL RULER • HANDMADE PAPER • DIFFERENT-COLOURED AND TEXTURED PAPER, SUCH AS SCRAPS OF FOIL AND TISSUE PAPER • GLUE AND BRUSH • FEATHERS, SEQUINS AND STARS

7 Cut the under blanket from a piece of natural-coloured handmade paper, tearing the ends to make it look like frayed cloth.

9 Stick these to the elephant, then cut out a triangular headpiece and glue this in place firmly.

11 Glue a coloured feather on top of the headpiece.

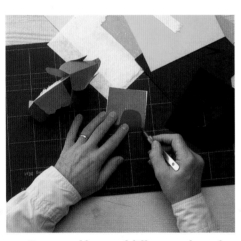

8 Cut several layers of different-coloured and textured paper blankets with zig-zagged, scalloped or rounded edges.

10 Apply small dots of glue and stick on sequins for the eyes and blanket decoration.

12 Apply different-coloured shiny star stickers to the elephant's body. When making a procession of elephants, you can change the order of colours and style of trimmings to add variety.

PAPER FLOWERS

THIS COULD JUST BE THE PERFECT WAY TO SPEND A RAINY DAY AND THE RESULTS WILL CERTAINLY BRIGHTEN UP A DULL CORNER. THE FLOWER PETALS ARE CUT FROM STIFF COLOURED PAPER THAT HOLDS ITS SHAPE WELL, SO YOUR FLOWERS WILL NOT WILT IN THE VASE! CHOOSE YOUR FAVOURITE COLOUR COMBINATIONS AND MAKE THE FLOWERS AS BIG OR AS SMALL AS YOU LIKE — THE FLOWERS IN THIS ARRANGEMENT HAVE BEEN MADE TO ONE SIZE BUT YOU COULD PHOTOCOPY THE PATTERNS TO ANY SIZE.

1 Use the compasses (compass) to draw 12.5 cm (5 in) circles on coloured paper. Cut them out with the larger scissors.

3 Draw on the petal shapes – one complete petal in the middle with a half petal each side into the fold.

5 Draw an 8 cm (3 in) circle for the centre and cut out. Fold the circle as before, then trace and transfer a section of one of the patterns from the back of the book (see Basic Techniques).

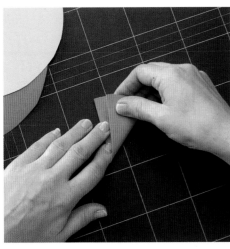

2 Fold each circle of coloured paper in half three times.

4 Cut out around the petals. Open out the paper flowers.

6 Use the craft knife and cutting mat to make the small internal cuts. ▶

MATERIALS AND EQUIPMENT YOU WILL NEED

PAIR OF COMPASSES (COMPASS) • PENCIL • STIFF COLOURED PAPER • SCISSORS – SMALL, POINTED PAIR AND A LARGER PAIR • TRACING PAPER • CRAFT KNIFE • CUTTING MAT • GLUE AND BRUSH • WIRE • MASKING TAPE

7 Use the small, pointed scissors to cut out the rest of the pattern.

9 To make a stem, twist the end of a piece of wire into a loop, then stick it to the back of a flower with masking tape. Arrange your bouquet, or use the flowers as decoration.

8 Apply a dab of glue to the centre of each papercut and stick it in place.

CYCLIST COLLAGE

IN POLAND THERE IS A TRADITION OF MAKING BRIGHTLY COLOURED PAPERCUT PICTURES, USUALLY BASED ON FARMYARD SCENES OR RELIGIOUS THEMES. OUR CYCLIST IS NOT A TRADITIONAL SUBJECT, BUT THE INSPIRATION FOR THE PROJECT COMES FROM ALL THOSE WONDERFUL LIVELY IMAGES. COLOURED PAPER IS SOLD IN PACKS OF DIFFERENT COLOURED SQUARES THAT ARE PRE-GUMMED, BUT WE HAVE ALSO CHOSEN TO USE GLUE FOR STICKING ON THE FRAGILE PIECES.

1 Make tracings of all the pattern pieces, except for the wheels, from the back of the book.

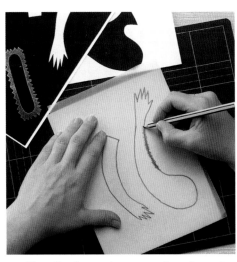

2 Transfer the tracings on to the coloured paper (see Basic Techniques).

4 Cut out the parts of the bicycle, using small, sharp scissors.

▶

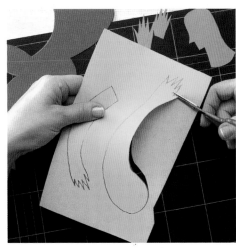

3 Cut out all the pieces of the cyclist using small, sharp scissors.

MATERIALS AND EQUIPMENT YOU WILL NEED

TRACING PAPER • PENCIL • COLOURED GUMMED PAPER SQUARES • SMALL, SHARP SCISSORS • CRAFT KNIFE • CUTTING MAT • PVA (WHITE) GLUE AND BRUSH • BACKGROUND PAPER

5 Fold a piece of grey paper in half and cut out the chain.

6 Draw two circles for the wheels, then fold in half three times.

7 Trace and transfer a section of each wheel pattern from the back of the book. Cut out the pattern. Unfold and flatten.

8 Draw and cut out the fine detailing for the cyclist's arms and legs. Fold up small circles of yellow paper and one green one, then cut out notches to make the wheel centres, bike light and cap badge.

9 Start to assemble the collage by sticking the detail pattern on to the cyclist's clothes. Then do the wheel spokes.

10 Arrange all the pieces on the background paper without sticking them down. When you are happy with the look of your picture, you can systematically stick each piece down. The right foot should be stuck down on top of the bicycle chain, last of all.

SNOWFLAKES

W HEN YOU FOLD A CIRCLE OF PAPER A FEW TIMES AND SNIP OUT NOTCHES, SQUARES, SPIRALS AND TRIANGLES, AND UNFOLD IT, THE RESULTING PATTERN IS ALWAYS MUCH MORE COMPLEX THAN YOU EXPECT — EVEN THE SMALLEST NICK HAS A MATCHING HALF AND THE WHOLE SHAPE IS ECHOED ALL AROUND THE CIRCLE. THERE IS AN INFINITE NUMBER OF PATTERNS THAT YOU CAN MAKE BY COMBINING SIMPLE CUTS, AND BY USING SHINY REFLECTIVE PAPERS YOU CAN MAKE LIGHT-CATCHING HANGING DECORATIONS THAT LOOK LIKE LARGE SPARKLING SNOWFLAKES. THERE ARE PATTERNS TO TRACE IN THE BACK OF THE BOOK THAT WILL HELP YOU TO REPRODUCE THESE SNOWFLAKES, AND THEY WILL NO DOUBT LEAD YOU TO CREATE MANY MORE OF YOUR OWN DESIGNS.

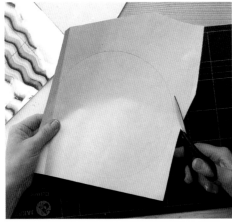

1 Draw a circle on the back of the reflective paper and cut it out with the larger scissors.

3 Photocopy the snowflake patterns from the back of the book, enlarging them to the size you want. Trace one of the segments.

5 Use the small, sharp scissors to snip out the traced pattern shapes. Unfold the circle and flatten.

2 Fold the circle of reflective paper in half three times.

4 Transfer the tracing on to the folded paper.

6 Do the same with the other papers and patterns, using the craft knife and cutting mat to make small, internal cuts.

▶

MATERIALS AND EQUIPMENT YOU WILL NEED

SELECTION OF REFLECTIVE SILVER, GOLD AND SPARKLING PAPERS • TRACING PAPER • PENCIL • PAIR OF COMPASSES (COMPASS) •
SCISSORS — SMALL, SHARP PAIR AND A LARGER PAIR • CRAFT KNIFE • CUTTING MAT • GOLD THREAD

7 For the curved pattern, fold the reflective paper circle as before and cut the first part of the pattern with scissors.

9 Cut several lengths of gold thread and attach each one to a snowflake to hang it up with.

8 Now unfold once and fold in half the other way, then cut out triangular notches along the fold line.

GREETINGS CARDS

EVERYONE ENJOYS RECEIVING A HANDMADE GREETINGS CARD, AND THESE ARE EYE-CATCHING AND GREAT FUN TO MAKE. THE SNOWFLAKE PATTERNS ARE MADE USING THREE DIFFERENT TYPES OF FOLD BEFORE CUTTING. THE WAY YOU FOLD THE PAPER AFFECTS THE NUMBER OF "SPOKES" YOU END UP WITH. THE PAPER USED HERE IS PRE-GUMMED GLOSSY CRAFT PAPER SOLD IN MULTI-COLOURED PACKS. IT IS GREAT FOR FOLDING AND CUTTING, BUT SPRAY ADHESIVE IS STILL BETTER FOR STICKING DOWN THE PAPERCUTS.

THE FOUR FOLD

1 Fold a square of coloured gummed (self-adhesive) paper in half, then in half again to make a square.

2 Trace a section from one of the patterns at the back of the book and transfer it on to the paper square (see Basic Techniques).

3 Begin by cutting out all the shapes along the fold lines, using a craft knife and cutting mat.

MATERIALS AND EQUIPMENT YOU WILL NEED

GLOSSY COLOURED GUMMED (SELF-ADHESIVE) PAPER SQUARES • TRACING PAPER • PENCIL • CRAFT KNIFE • CUTTING MAT • SPRAY ADHESIVE •
STIFF COLOURED CARD (CARD STOCK) • 60/30 DEGREE SET SQUARE (TRIANGLE) • ENVELOPES TO FIT CARDS

THE EIGHT FOLD

THE SIX FOLD

4 Next, make all the internal cuts (see Basic Techniques).

5 Finish off the papercut by cutting the pattern along the edges.

6 Open up the papercut and glue it on to a contrasting coloured card (card stock).

7 Fold a square of paper in the same way as for the four fold, then fold diagonally into a triangle.

8 Trace a quarter section of one of the patterns from the back of the book and transfer the tracing. Cut out the shapes in the same order as before.

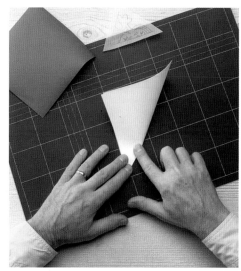

9 Fold the square diagonally once. Fold it in half again but only press down to mark the centre point, then unfold it again.

10 Place the set square (triangle) at the centre point along the fold to get a 60 degree fold. Hold it firmly and fold the paper up around it, marking the crease with your thumbnail. ▶

11 Flip the paper over and flatten it, then fold the other side over to make a symmetrical tulip shape.

12 Transfer the traced pattern on to this folded shape and cut out in the same order as before.

SILHOUETTE

BEFORE THE CAMERA WAS INVENTED, PEOPLE WHO COULD NOT AFFORD TO HAVE A PORTRAIT PAINTED WOULD USE THE SERVICES OF THE SILHOUETTE ARTIST. THE SUBJECT WOULD SIT BY A SCREEN WITH A LIGHT TO PROJECT THE SHADOW OF THEIR PROFILE, OR THE SKILLED ARTIST MIGHT CUT FREEHAND JUST FROM LOOKING AT HIS SUBJECT. OUR METHOD PRODUCES A VERY ACCURATE LIKENESS USING ALL THE TRICKS OF MODERN TECHNOLOGY TO MAKE A CHARMING OLD-FASHIONED PORTRAIT.

1 Enlarge the photograph on a photocopier to a size that will fit your photo mount.

2 Select the best photocopy. Use a pencil to draw in the "bust" shape that is typical on old silhouettes.

3 Using a craft knife and cutting mat, cut very carefully around the face and cut a bit extra around the hair. You may find it easier to cut the profile with small, sharp scissors – it's a personal preference.

4 Turn the cut-out over and colour it with a black marker pen. Be careful not to overwork the edges as every dent will show. ▶

MATERIALS AND EQUIPMENT YOU WILL NEED

PROFILE PHOTOGRAPH • OVAL PHOTO MOUNT • PENCIL • CRAFT KNIFE OR SMALL, SHARP SCISSORS •

CUTTING MAT • BLACK PERMANENT INK MARKER • SPRAY ADHESIVE • CREAM PAPER • RED PAPER • PINKING SHEARS • GLUE AND BRUSH

5 Add the finishing touches to the edges of the hair – this is where the extra allowance is useful. Spray the back of the profile with adhesive and position it in the centre of the cream paper.

6 To make the decorated border, place the oval mount on the back of a sheet of red paper and draw around both the inside and outside edges.

7 Cut out the red paper along the outside outline and fold it in quarters.

8 Cut out the shape just inside the line using pinking shears. Open out flat.

9 Glue the red paper mount on to the cream paper, to frame the silhouette.

10 Leave the silhouette as it is or add the oval photo mount on top.

CAKE TIN

THE RECIPE HERE IS QUITE SIMPLE — TAKE ONE PLAIN TIN (PAN), DO SOME CLEVER SNIPPING AND STICKING AND PRODUCE A MASTERPIECE! THE SECRET OF SUCCESS LIES IN THE STRONG CONTRAST BETWEEN THE TWO COLOURS. DO NOT DESPAIR IF YOU CANNOT FIND A SHINY NEW TIN; JUST SPRAY PAINT AN OLD ONE AND GIVE IT A NEW LEASE OF LIFE. USE THE BEST-QUALITY TISSUE PAPER THAT IS SOLD IN ART AND HOBBY SHOPS BECAUSE IT IS FAR STRONGER AND COMES IN A RANGE OF VIBRANT COLOURS.

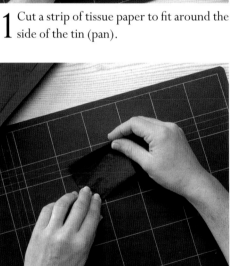

1 Cut a strip of tissue paper to fit around the side of the tin (pan).

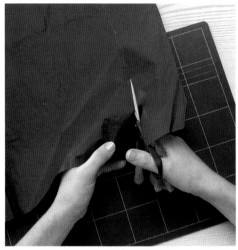

2 Fold the strip in half three times, firming each crease as you go.

3 Photocopy the patterns for this project from the back of the book. Keep the pattern of the figures in front of you and draw it on to the tissue paper — tracing does not really suit fine paper, so rely on observation.

4 Cut out the pattern using small, pointed scissors and turning the paper to meet them, not the other way around.

5 Place the lid of the tin (pan) on another piece of tissue paper and draw around it. ▶

MATERIALS AND EQUIPMENT YOU WILL NEED

SCISSORS — SMALL, POINTED PAIR AND A LARGER PAIR • BRIGHT BLUE TISSUE PAPER • PLAIN CAKE TIN (PAN) WITH LID • PENCIL •
SPRAY ADHESIVE • CLEAR MATT VARNISH • SOFT PAINTBRUSH

6 Cut out the circle and fold it in half three times to form a triangular shape.

8 Unfold the circle, and then, using spray adhesive, mount it on the lid. Apply at least one coat of clear varnish with a soft brush to protect the surface and allow it to be wiped clean.

7 Again keeping the pattern for the lid alongside for reference, draw the pattern on the folded paper, then cut it out.

9 Using spray adhesive, stick the papercut strip around the side of the tin. Seal this with varnish and allow plenty of drying time before placing the lid on the tin (pan).

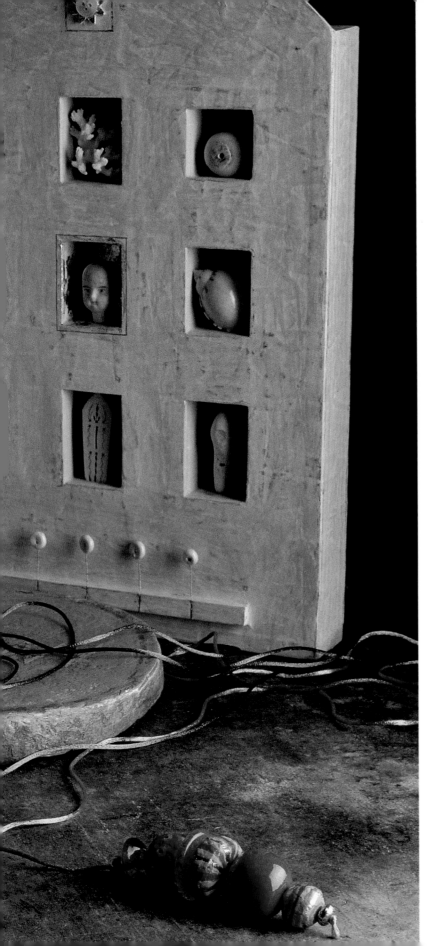

INTRODUCTION

PAPIER MACHE IS A CHAMELEON CRAFT, CAPABLE OF IMITATING MANY DIFFERENT MATERIALS. ITS VERSATILITY AND, OF COURSE, LOW COST, HAS MADE IT ONE OF THE MOST POPULAR METHODS OF MAKING BOTH BEAUTIFUL AND USEFUL OBJECTS FOR MANY CENTURIES. ONCE USED TO MAKE ARTICLES AS DIVERSE AS A HORSE-DRAWN CARRIAGE AND ARCHITECTURAL PANELS, OR MINIATURE DECORATIVE SNUFF BOXES, PAPIER MACHE CAN BE USED TO ENHANCE MODERN INTERIORS IN SIMILARLY INNOVATIVE WAYS. FUN AND EASY TO TACKLE, THE PROJECTS IN THIS SECTION HAVE BEEN DESIGNED TO INSPIRE EVEN THE NOVICE CRAFTSPERSON TO ATTEMPT THIS REWARDING CRAFT.

Left: A surprising variety and quality of objects can be made from papier mâché. Its strength and versatility have made it an ideal technique for household objects.

HISTORY OF PAPIER MACHE

PAPIER MACHE HAS AN EXCITING HISTORY, ORIGINATING IN CHINA EARLY IN THE 2ND CENTURY AD. SINCE THEN IT HAS BEEN USED TO MAKE CHAIRS FOR ROYALTY, PANELS FOR COACHES, JEWELLERY, AND CHINESE SPEARS AND ARMOUR. THROUGHOUT HISTORY IT HAS MADE VARIOUS APPEARANCES AS THE LATEST CRAZE, YET THE BASIC TECHNIQUES REMAIN THE SAME AS IN THE 2ND CENTURY.

Paper was first made by Ts'ai Lun, an official at the Chinese court of the Emperor Ho Ti, who developed an ingenious way of breaking down plants and rags into single fibres. The fibres were pounded to a pulp and collected on a fabric-covered frame, where they matted and dried as paper. The knowledge of paper-making spread to Japan, the Middle East and India, finally reaching Europe via Spain in the 10th century AD. The modern-day practice of recycling waste paper into moulded objects became well established in Persia and India, where craftsmen made extravagantly lacquered and embellished papier mâché pen holders from around the 15th century. Kashmir in Northern India was an important centre of this art; its products were exported to Europe during the 16th and 17th centuries as trade routes developed, and were much admired for the quality of their lacquering and their exquisitely painted decoration.

A flourishing trade in eastern goods developed, as a mania for chinoiserie – objects with oriental motifs executed in a Western style – gripped Europe. Demand far exceeded supply, and workshops were set up, notably in France and England, to produce home-grown imitations of items such as porcelain and lacquerware. French

Above: Painted and lacquered papier mâché pen cases from Qajar, Persia, 1860.

Left and right: Backs of playing cards made from papier mâché from Kashmir, India, c. 1600.

pasted paper sheets rather than pulped paper. The panels were sealed with linseed oil and dried slowly under a low heat, which made them extremely strong. They were used for everyday articles, such as furniture, and the material was ideally suited to japanning (varnishing) and painting. Clay's panels were so strong and resilient that they were also used to make the walls of horse-drawn coaches. Clay patented his invention in 1772, and by the

Left: Painted and lacquered papier mâché chest with ivory fringe, c.1660.

Below: Two French hand-painted papier mâché fans inlaid with mother-of-pearl, c. 1780.

craftsmen were intrigued by oriental papier mâché and experimented with the medium, adding materials such as sand, glue and chalk to the pulped paper. They developed their techniques until capable of producing convincing moulded architectural ornaments in imitation of costly stucco and plasterwork. This practice was also adopted in England, where several papier mâché workshops were established, primarily in London and the Midlands.

The development of a lacquering process that compared favourably with Japanese and Chinese lacquerware also helped to establish papier mâché in Europe. Known as japanning, this quicker, less expensive technique was used widely from the 1740s in the decoration of papier mâché items such as small tables, snuff boxes and hand mirrors. In the mid-18th century Henry Clay, assistant to John Baskerville, a manufacturer from Birmingham, England, took a step forward in papier mâché production, which laid the foundations of a whole industry. He produced laminated panels, made from

Above: Papier mâché chair with split cane seat, embellished with mother-of-pearl, c. 1840–50.

Right: Circus figures made of wood and papier mâché by Schoenhut & Co, Germany, c 1900.

time the patents expired in 1802, he was very wealthy. His Birmingham factory was taken over in 1816 by what was to become the most famous partnership in the papier mâché industry, Jennens and Bettridge.

Jennens and Bettridge raised papier mâché design to new heights, introducing decorative and practical refinements. They developed a distinctive range of japanned goods inlaid with slivers of mother-of-pearl; later they included tortoiseshell, ivory and precious stones. They also patented a method of steam-moulding and pressing papier mâché panels into large-scale architectural features, such as internal walls for steamships. By 1850, Jennens and Bettridge were England's foremost exponents of papier mâché. They had a huge workforce, with ex-employees leaving to set up their own factories. At London's Great Exhibition of 1851 in the Crystal Palace, papier mâché was hailed as an important material with a bright future, and Jennens and Bettridge exhibited a wide range of artefacts, including a child's cot, a chair and a piano. This was the heyday of papier mâché production in Europe. Manufacturing methods had become highly sophisticated, and the resulting objects were indistinguishable from the finest lacquered wood. A huge range of items, from buttons to headboards, was produced; George Jackson and Son made stunningly ornate imitation plaster- and stuccowork ceilings and walls, and Charles Bielefield produced a papier mâché "village" of eleven houses for export to Australia.

Papier mâché was also popular in North America, and Jennens and Bettridge, and other manufacturers, were exporting their wares there before the middle of the 19th century. In 1850, when the United States' first papier mâché factory was established at Litchfield, Connecticut, English workers were brought over to teach their skills. The Litchfield Manufacturing Company was started by English-born Quaker William Allgood, and was successful from the start. The factory initially produced small ornamental items, such as fans and card cases, but then concentrated on making papier mâché versions of the area's main product, decorative clock cases. These were warmly received, and commended at the World Fair in New York in 1854. Litchfield Manufacturing merged with a clock company in 1855, but a nearby

factory, Wadhams Manufacturing Co., continued to produce papier mâché goods, such as desks and gameboards, until the outbreak of the American Civil War.

Although the Western papier mâché industries had run out of steam by the end of the 19th century, cultures who had been consistently using papier mâché continued making boxes, cases, lamp-stands, trays and frames, decorated with extremely intricate traditional designs, such as interlocking flowers, animals and scenes from court life. The tourist economies of Kashmir and Rajasthan benefit to this day.

In Mexico, remarkable papier mâché sculptures and artefacts are made throughout the year to commemorate religious festivals. The best known of these is on All Souls' Day, known as the Day of the Dead, when Mexicans build ornate shrines and prepare meals for departed relatives whom they believe will come to visit. Brightly coloured skeletons going about everyday activities, devils, skulls, angels and various other characters can be seen, all made from papier mâché. Many of the sculptors are anonymous, but a few are well known. The late Pedro Linares, for example, was the head of a papier mâché making family, whose highly original work was collected by admirers including the painters Diego Rivera and Frida Kahlo. His family continues in this tradition, making amazing constructions, many hand-modelled without using moulds, of intricate figures of the dead or of symbolic animals, such as dragons or roosters.

Spain is another contemporary stronghold of papier mâché production, where enormous papier mâché characters with huge heads join the religious Corpus Christi processions, and are later blown up with fireworks.

The craft of papier mâché has recently undergone a huge revival of interest in

Europe and America. This could be because of the current interest in recycling waste paper, the relative low cost and availability of the material, the ease with which the basic skills can be learned, or simply an appreciation of the vitality, versatility and beauty of the medium.

Whatever the reason, this simple material – paper – has inspired ancient and contemporary designers to produce exciting and original work and it looks set to continue well into the 21st century.

Above: A stunning papier mâché dragon made by the Mexican Felipe Linares, using flour and water paste and a layering process, is hand-formed.

Left: Death Figure in a Purple Cape by Saulo Moreno, Mexico. This piece is entirely hand-formed, without using a mould.

GALLERY

PAPIER MACHE IS A POPULAR MEDIUM AMONG CONTEMPORARY ARTISTS AND CRAFTSPEOPLE DUE TO ITS STRENGTH, ITS RELATIVE LOW COST AND THE EASE WITH WHICH IT CAN BE MOULDED.

DRAWING ON INFLUENCES ANCIENT AND MODERN, THE INGENUITY AND SKILL OF THE ARTISTS REPRESENTED HERE HAS TRANSFORMED THIS HUMBLE TECHNIQUE INTO A STYLISH AND MODERN MEDIUM.

Right: BIRD SHRINES
These elegantly shaped shrines are inspired by the natural history displays found in museums. The case is constructed from papier mâché and contains a real bird's skull and a quail's egg. Both shrines include a small papier mâché bird inspired by illustrations from a book of 19th-century natural history engravings.
CAROLINE WAITE

Left: WHITE ICON
An innovative card construction covered with papier mâché. The surface of the case is decorated with a distressed paint surface, simulating an aged plaster wall, and embellished with real shells. The case contains a 19th-century porcelain doll, flanked by two flowers in vases.
CAROLINE WAITE

Left: SUN BOWL
This delicate sun-shaped bowl was made by layering handmade and recycled papers into a mould. A spiral of copper wire was added to each "petal" around the rim. Dried leaves were laid over the interior and exterior.
CLAIRE ATTRIDGE

Above: GOLDEN STAR FRUIT BOWL
This bowl was made by layering strips of paper into an existing fruit bowl mould. Geometric motifs and stars were painted in gold, complementing the rich purple and pink hues of the background.
HANNAH DOWNES

Left: RASPBERRY BOX
The intense colour of
this casket is achieved by
applying hand-coloured
paper over a card
armature. The box's
bronze feet and the knob
on the lid are gilded
wooden balls, and the
heart-shaped finial is
formed from twists of
copper wire.
CLAIRE ATTRIDGE

Left: LEAF BOWL
The main body of this
small, textured bowl is
constructed from layers of
handmade and hand-
coloured papers. Leaf
skeletons stand out in low
relief against the interior.
A delicate filigree effect
around the rim is achieved
with twisted copper wire.
CLAIRE ATTRIDGE

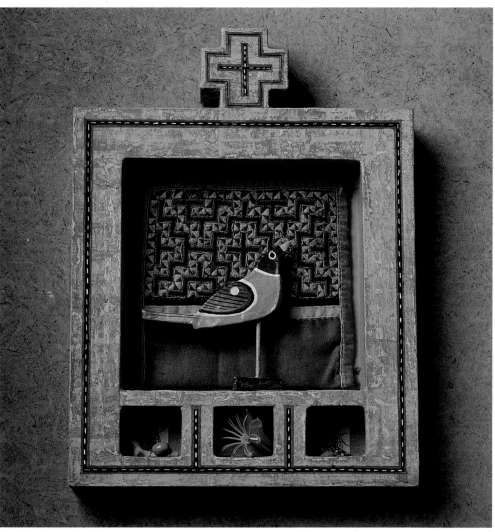

Left: BIRD WALL PANEL
Old fragments of richly
embroidered cloth from
Thailand were used as a
background to this
innovative wall panel.
The bird and exterior
structure are both
constructed from papier
mâché. Found objects have
been placed in the three
recesses at the bottom.
CAROLINE WAITE

Above: HOUSE OF DOLLS
An unusual display case
housing an eccentric
collection of dolls, created
from buttons, jewels and
doll parts, bound together
with papier mâché. The
dolls are decorated with
newspaper collage. Each
doll is fitted with a brooch
back so that it can be worn
as jewellery, if desired.
JULIE ARKELL

Left: ELEGANT CASKETS
Recycled card and paper were used to construct the basic armatures for these caskets. Their elegance is created through a subtle combination of restrained background colours with gold embellishments. Bronze wire and gilded balls form the handles.
CLAIRE ATTRIDGE

Left: WALL BOX
A small door conceals a secret compartment lined with delicately patterned wallpaper, containing a red papier mâché heart. The box has a distressed background, adorned with brightly painted symbols and a blossoming flower. An antique button is used as a small handle for the door.
CAROLINE WAITE

Above: GILDED PLATTERS AND BOWL
These decorative dishes demonstrate the versatility of papier mâché. Formed from plate and bowl moulds, the basecoat paint was slightly distressed with fine sandpaper before a layer of gold paint was applied, giving the impression of opulent gold leaf.
HANNAH DOWNES

EQUIPMENT

PAPIER MACHE CAN BE MESSY, SO IT IS A GOOD IDEA TO COVER YOUR WORK SURFACE WITH A WATERPROOF SHEET. PROTECT YOUR CLOTHES TOO, WITH AN APRON OR OVERALL (SMOCK). YOU MAY HAVE MANY ITEMS OF EQUIPMENT NEEDED TO MAKE PAPIER MACHE IN YOUR KITCHEN ALREADY. IF YOU ARE USING HOUSEHOLD PLATES AND BOWLS, KEEP THEM FOR CRAFT PURPOSES ONLY.

Moulds Old plates are ideal moulds provided that no part of the interior of the mould is wider than the opening through which the papier mâché is to be removed. Balloons are perfect for round shapes; they can be popped with a pin before removal from the dry paper shell. Kitchen items used should not be re-used for food.

Petroleum jelly Grease moulds with a thin layer of petroleum jelly before use, so that the dry papier mâché can easily be removed. Cling film (plastic wrap) is a good alternative for flat surfaces.

Cutting mat Used to protect your surfaces from a sharp craft knife. Special mats can be bought from art supply shops. A thick sheet of plywood is a low-cost, less-permanent alternative.

Craft knife A craft knife is useful for cutting sheets of corrugated cardboard. Most knives have detachable blades, and some have a swivel head to cut out complex shapes with ease. All craft knives are extremely sharp, so it is important always to cut away from your body, and to keep the knife out of the reach of children.

Metal ruler A metal ruler will stand up to a sharp knife, and should be used for accurate cutting.

Scissors These are generally useful.

Masking tape This is a removable paper tape. It is useful for holding glued items in place while they dry. It also secures armatures while papier mâché is applied.

Paintbrushes A 2.5 cm (1 in) paintbrush is ideal for priming and applying varnish, as it covers a large area quickly. Buy a good-quality brush; cheaper brushes will shed hairs, ruining a smooth surface. Sable, sable/nylon, or nylon designer's brushes – flat or pointed – are suitable for decorating papier mâché with gouache or poster paints. Bristle brushes are suitable for applying acrylic paint. Wash, dry and store brushes carefully after use to keep them in good condition.

Fine sandpaper This is used to smooth the surface of dry papier mâché before it is primed. Sanding produces a fine dust, so always protect your face with a mask.

Wire cake rack This is used to support items as they dry. It speeds up the drying time by allowing air to circulate.

Bradawl (Awl) This is a metal point mounted in a wooden handle used for piercing holes. Place the object on a scrap of wood before you pierce it, as the bradawl (awl) is very sharp. Stick the point of the bradawl (awl) into a cork when it is not in use, to keep it safe.

Leather gloves To protect the hands and wrists. Wear them when using materials such as wire mesh and chicken wire.

Rubber (latex) gloves Lightweight, close-fitting gloves should always be worn when using any form of adhesive and pulp.

Wire cutters These are used to clip through wire and wire mesh. A pair with a spring fulcrum is easier to use.

Protective mask A respiratory mask should always be worn when sanding, using powdered materials, and handling paper pulp, to prevent the inhalation of dust. A mask that protects against fumes should be used when working with strong-smelling glues and solvent-based products.

Modelling tool Modelling tools are useful for shaping paper pulp and come in many shapes and widths. Plastic and wooden versions are available from craft, sculptors' and potters' suppliers.

Palette A china palette, with separate compartments, is good for mixing small quantities of paint. An old, white china saucer makes a suitable substitute when no longer needed for food.

Pencil A pencil is needed for marking measurements and guidelines for cuttings.

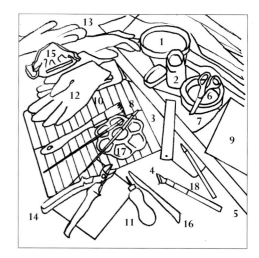

KEY

1 Mould
2 Petroleum jelly
3 Cutting mat
4 Craft knife
5 Metal ruler
6 Scissors
7 Masking tape
8 Paintbrushes
9 Fine sandpaper
10 Wire cake rack
11 Bradawl (awl)
12 Leather gloves
13 Rubber (latex) gloves
14 Wire cutters
15 Protective mask
16 Modelling tool
17 Palette
18 Pencil

MATERIALS

MANY OF THE MATERIALS NEEDED FOR PAPIER MACHE ARE INEXPENSIVE AND EASY TO OBTAIN. MAKING PAPIER MACHE IS A GREAT WAY OF RECYCLING MATERIALS, SO SAVE NEWSPAPERS, OLD GREETINGS CARDS AND PAPERS, READY FOR USE IN PROJECTS. AVOID GLOSSY, WAXED OR LAMINATED SURFACES, WHICH ARE HARD TO MANIPULATE AND NON-POROUS, SO WILL NOT ABSORB GLUE.

Newspaper or newsprint (the raw paper) comes in different weights and qualities; broadsheets are usually printed on finer-quality newsprint than tabloids, and are strong and pliable, so ideal for layering into moulds and on to armatures. Tabloid newsprint is generally more porous and disintegrates readily when wet, so it is useful for making pulped details. Coloured sheets are helpful when building layers.

Corrugated cardboard also comes in different weights. "Double wall" cardboard has two rows of corrugations. This heavy-weight cardboard is ideal for making armatures that can be covered with layered strips to form a strong base. Boxes from electrical equipment are an ideal source. Single wall, or lightweight, corrugated card is good for low-relief details, such as moulding. Corrugated cardboard should be primed with a coat of diluted non-toxic PVA (white) glue and left to dry before the paper is applied, to minimize the risk of warping.

PVA (white) glue is ideal for making papier mâché, because it dries to a strong finish. It can be used undiluted to glue armatures, or diluted with water to the consistency of single cream to apply paper strips. PVA (white) glue dries clear and shiny, so it can also serve as a non-water-proof varnish for finished items. Always choose a non-toxic, and child-safe brand as some brands may irritate your skin. If you have sensitive skin, rub a barrier cream into your skin before using. As an extra precaution, apply the glue with a brush, or wear thin rubber (latex) gloves.

Water-based paste is also suitable, but takes longer to dry than PVA (white) glue. Do not be tempted to use wallpaper paste for papier mâché, as many brands contain fungicides, and should not come into prolonged contact with the skin. Non-toxic granules are the safest.

Tissue paper is ideal for making pulp. Soaked briefly in glue and squeezed out, it breaks down into a pulp that is easy to manipulate. For layering, tissue paper is very difficult to handle when wet as it disintegrates quickly; however, its stunning effects make it worth persevering with.

Recycled paper comes in all colours and textures. It can be used to make whole objects or used as a decorative layer over newspaper. Unlike newsprint, it generally has no grain, and so it is difficult to tear it into strips; the resulting papier mâché is therefore less regular.

Paint is used to prime work. Use two coats of non-toxic white paint to seal the surface and cover the print. Water-based paints, such as acrylic, emulsion (latex), poster and gouache are all suitable top coats. Papier mâché can also be gilded; prime first with two coats of acrylic gesso.

Varnish can be used to seal surfaces. A low-solvent polyurethane varnish is suitable over poster or gouache paints. Apply it in a well-ventilated area. Artist's aerosol varnishes can be used; wear a protective face mask when using these. If you have decorated with acrylic paints, protect with a water-based acrylic varnish.

Paper pulp can be made by shredding and soaking paper, but this is a long process. To make pulp mix rehydrated, store-bought pulp with undiluted PVA (white) glue to a thick paste. Add a filler of whiting (powdered chalk) to thicken. Pulp should be fairly stiff, without being too dry. Always wear a protective face mask and rubber (latex) gloves when preparing and handling pulp.

Wire mesh is useful for making shaped armatures. Fine-gauge wire mesh and chicken wire are the most common. Protective leather gloves are a must when handling the wire. When you cut out a shape, check the edges and remove any sharp spurs, disposing of them safely.

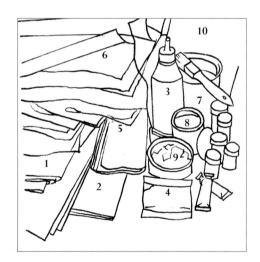

KEY

1 Newspaper	**6** Recycled paper
2 Corrugated cardboard	**7** Paint
3 PVA (white) glue	**8** Varnish
4 Water-based paste	**9** Paper pulp
5 Tissue paper	**10** Wire mesh

BASIC TECHNIQUES

THERE ARE ONLY A FEW TECHNIQUES TO MASTER WHEN MAKING PAPIER MACHE BUT CARE IS NEEDED FOR GOOD RESULTS. THE FINISHED SURFACE IS ALL-IMPORTANT, AND IT TAKES PRACTICE TO ACHIEVE A NEAT, REGULAR APPEARANCE. ONCE YOU HAVE LEARNED THE BASIC SKILLS, YOU WILL PROBABLY DEVELOP YOUR OWN WAY OF WORKING, AND PREFER SOME TYPES OF PAPER OR GLUE TO OTHERS.

TEARING NEWSPAPER

PREPARING A MOULD

1 Tearing rather than cutting newspaper creates less obvious joins between strips. Like fabric, newspaper has a grain and will tear much more easily in one direction than the other. Generally, the grain runs from the top to the bottom of the newspaper. To make paper strips, grasp several folded sheets of newspaper in one hand, and begin a tear about 2.5 cm (1 in) from the edge. Pull directly down, and the paper will tear into long, straight strips. Strips of almost any width can be produced in this way.

2 If you try to tear newspaper across its width, you will be working against the grain, and the paper will be almost impossible to control. Find the grain by making a small tear in the top corner; if it is difficult to achieve this initial tear, turn the newspaper around!

Before papier mâché is applied to it, the surface of the mould must be lightly greased with petroleum jelly, rather like a cake tin (pan). This will create a barrier between the glue and the mould, and prevent the papier mâché from sticking to it. It will then be easy to remove when it has dried. A piece of cling film (plastic wrap) can sometimes be used instead.

LAYERING INTO A MOULD

Large moulds, such as plates and bowls, can be covered using paper strips approximately 2.5 cm (1 in) wide. Five to six layers should suffice. Spread the strips with glue on both sides and lay them in the greased mould. They should be slightly longer than the mould and protrude beyond the edge, so that the whole area is covered. Smooth each strip gently with your fingers and press out any air bubbles under the paper. Each new strip should slightly overlap the last to give a really strong result.

MAKING CARDBOARD ARMATURES

1 To build three-dimensional items without using a mould, make an armature from heavy corrugated cardboard and cover with papier mâché. The cardboard becomes a permanent part of the structure. Measure each piece of the armature carefully, and glue and tape in place to create a sturdy and durable framework.

2 Brush the armature with a coat of diluted PVA (white) glue and leave to dry before applying paper strips or pulp. This will seal the surface of the cardboard, making it less absorbent and preventing it from warping once the strips of glued paper are added.

3 Cover the sealed armature with papier mâché in the usual way. Approximately five layers of paper will make a strong object and disguise the corrugated cardboard underneath. Apply each layer of strips at right angles to the layer beneath for extra strength.

4 When the layers of papier mâché are complete, leave the armature to dry overnight – or longer in cold weather. Place the object on a wire cake rack in a warm, dry place. Do not be tempted to speed up the drying by setting the item close to direct heat, which could warp the papier mâché and the framework.

PREPARING THE SURFACE

1 All papier mâché should be prepared properly if you intend to paint it, especially if it is made from newspaper. First, rub the surface with fine sandpaper to smooth it and disguise the edges of the paper strips. Wear a protective face mask (respirator) when sanding.

2 Prime the papier mâché with two coats of non-toxic paint. This provides a good ground for paint, and conceals the newsprint. Emulsion (latex) paint is ideal, but poster or powder paint also works well. Acrylic paint is suitable if the subseqent decoration is done with acrylic.

PROTECTING YOUR SKIN

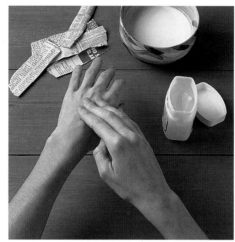

1 Before making papier mâché, it is advisable to rub a thin covering of petroleum jelly or rich moisturizer into your hands. This will protect your hands from dryness and make it much easier to clean your hands when you have finished, especially if you use PVA (white) glue.

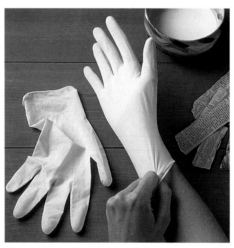

2 Although you should always use non-toxic, fungicide-free glues and pastes, wear a pair of thin rubber (latex) gloves when handling contact adhesive and pulp, and at other times if your skin is sensitive. Do not make papier mâché if you have a skin condition or broken skin.

DRYING FLAT OBJECTS

Objects such as frames and wall panels should be dried flat after sealing and when covered with papier mâché, to prevent warping. Place the object on a wire cake rack or a sheet of thin plastic. Although the glue will stick to the plastic as it dries, the plastic can easily be peeled away once the item is dry.

CUTTING CARDBOARD WITH A RULER

Always use a metal ruler or straight edge and a cutting mat when working with a craft knife. Plastic rulers are not sturdy enough to withstand sharp blades, and will develop nicks along their edges, becoming unusable.

CURVING CORRUGATED CARDBOARD

1 Scoring enables corrugated cardboard to be formed into all sorts of curved shapes. Cut a strip to the required size, making sure that the corrugations run from top to bottom of the shape. Use a craft knife to carefully score down each concave corrugation.

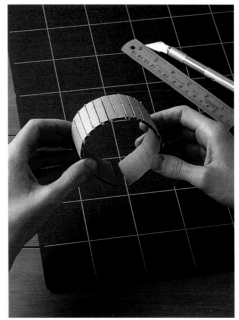

2 When all the score lines have been made, the cardboard will be flexible enough to curve into a variety of shapes.

MAKING PAPER PULP

Always wear a protective face mask (respirator) and thin rubber (latex) gloves, when making paper pulp. Mix rehydrated paper pulp and PVA (white) glue in a container to a thick paste. Sieve whiting (powdered chalk) into the mixture until it is malleable, but not too stiff or too dry.

KALEIDOSCOPIC ROOM DIVIDER

THIS COLOURFUL DIVIDER IS MADE BY LAYERING SIMPLE TISSUE PAPER SHAPES TO CREATE A TRANSLUCENT, KALEIDOSCOPIC EFFECT. EACH SECTION IS FORMED AS A SEPARATE SQUARE, THEN STITCHED TO A BACKGROUND OF JAPANESE HAND-LAID PAPER, WHICH IS SHEER BUT INCREDIBLY STRONG. SEEN AGAINST DAYLIGHT, THE COLOURS GLOW WITH A VIVID INTENSITY. THE DESIGNS MUST BE SIMPLE FOR THE GREATEST IMPACT. AS WATER-BASED GLUE IS USED, CHOOSE BLEEDPROOF TISSUE PAPER, OR THE COLOURS WILL RUN.

1 Cut the required number of backing squares measuring 36 x 36 cm (14 x 14 in) from white tissue paper. Cut a range of coloured tissue paper shapes.

3 When the squares are thoroughly dry, gently peel them from the plastic. Place each one on a cutting mat and carefully trim the edges.

5 Trim the handmade paper to size if necessary, then glue the sheets together using undiluted PVA (white) glue to make the screen as wide and long as necessary.

2 Place a white square on a sheet of plastic. Lay the coloured shapes on top according to the design. Brush diluted PVA (white) glue over the square and apply the first layer of shapes. Build up the design, adding layers. Leave the square to dry. Repeat to decorate the other squares.

4 Place the paper squares in position on the sheets of handmade paper, making sure that they are evenly spaced. Pin the squares to the paper and machine- or hand-stitch them in place, removing the pins before you get to them.

6 Fold over 2.5 cm (1 in) of paper to the back of the screen and crease it into place. Stitch along the edge of the fold to make a casing for a length of dowel, so that the screen can be suspended.

MATERIALS AND EQUIPMENT YOU WILL NEED

BLEEDPROOF TISSUE PAPER, WHITE AND VARIETY OF COLOURS • PINKING SHEARS OR ORDINARY SCISSORS •
SHEET OF PLASTIC • PVA (WHITE) GLUE • PAINTBRUSH • CRAFT KNIFE • CUTTING MAT • METAL RULER •
HANDMADE JAPANESE PAPER • DRESSMAKING PINS • SEWING THREAD AND NEEDLE • SEWING MACHINE (OPTIONAL) • LENGTH OF DOWEL

MEXICAN CARNIVAL DOLL

THIS DOLL IS MADE ENTIRELY FROM PAPER PULP, WHICH DRIES TO A VERY HARD FINISH. HER ARMS AND LEGS ARE PIERCED, AND THE JOINTS MADE WITH PIPE CLEANERS, ALLOWING HER TO MOVE HER LIMBS. PULP IS HERE MOULDED BY HAND USING THE SAME TECHNIQUE USED FOR MOULDING CLAY. ALL THE PIECES ARE SANDED TO MAKE THEM COMPLETELY SMOOTH, WHICH PROVIDES A LOVELY PAINTING SURFACE AND GIVES THE PULP THE APPEARANCE OF PORCELAIN. THIS DOLL IS NOT A TOY, SO IS UNSUITABLE FOR CHILDREN.

1 Wearing rubber (latex) gloves and a face mask (respirator), form the doll's torso and head from a sausage of paper pulp. Make the head by gently pulling a blob of pulp up out of the main mass of the body. Bend a length of thin galvanized wire into a U shape and push it down through the head into the body to strengthen the doll.

2 Use small pellets of pulp to mould the doll's hair and cover up the wire. Allow the doll's body to dry slightly, then place it on a scrap of wood, and gently make a channel through the shoulders and hips with a bradawl (awl). Leave it on an old wire cake rack to dry.

3 Model two arms and legs from pulp. When they have dried out slightly, use a bradawl (awl) to make a hole through the top of each limb so that they can be joined to the doll's body. Leave the limbs on the rack to dry completely. ▶

MATERIALS AND EQUIPMENT YOU WILL NEED

THIN RUBBER (LATEX) GLOVES • FACE MASK (RESPIRATOR) • PAPER PULP (SEE BASIC TECHNIQUES) • THIN GALVANIZED WIRE • WIRE CUTTERS • BRADAWL (AWL) • SCRAP OF WOOD • OLD WIRE CAKE RACK • FINE SANDPAPER • WHITE ACRYLIC GESSO • PAINTBRUSHES • ACRYLIC PAINTS IN A VARIETY OF COLOURS • WATER-BASED MATT ACRYLIC VARNISH • PIPE CLEANERS

4 When all the pieces are completely dry, smooth their surfaces with fine sandpaper. Smooth until the pieces resemble fine porcelain. Wear a protective face mask (respirator) while sanding.

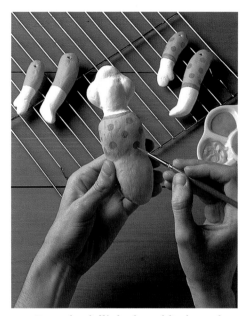

6 Paint the doll's body and limbs with yellow acrylic paint. Add bands of orange around the wrists, ankles and neck, and paint orange spots over the yellow background.

7 Use a fine paintbrush to depict the doll's features. Paint her hair and boots black. When the doll is completely dry, seal the surface with two coats of water-based matt acrylic varnish.

5 Prime the doll's body and limbs with two coats of white acrylic gesso. Allow the first coat to dry thoroughly before applying the second. Leave to dry completely on the wire cake rack.

8 Place the doll flat, and position the arms and legs. Push pipe cleaners all the way through the arms and legs and the body, and twist the ends to keep the limbs securely in place.

GRECIAN VASE

THIS LONG-NECKED VASE IS INSPIRED BY VESSELS PRODUCED IN THE MEDITERRANEAN AREA SINCE ANCIENT TIMES. IT PROVIDES AN EXCELLENT EXAMPLE OF HOW THE HUMBLEST OF OBJECTS CAN BE THE BASIS OF STYLISH PAPIER MACHE. A FINAL LAYER OF BROWN WRAPPING PAPER SHOWING THROUGH THE CHALKY PAINT CREATES A SUN-BLEACHED APPEARANCE. TWO LENGTHS OF CURVED DRIFTWOOD FORM THE VASE HANDLES, AND A SHELL WASHED SMOOTH AND PIERCED BY THE SEA, LENDS AN APPROPRIATE FINISHING TOUCH.

1 Inflate a round balloon and tie the end firmly. Rest the balloon on a small bowl. Tear newspaper into 2.5 cm (1 in) wide strips and dip them into the diluted PVA (white) glue. Cover the balloon with 5–6 layers of papier mâché strips, making sure that it is evenly coated. Suspend the balloon from a length of string to dry.

2 Cut two lengths of cord long enough to fit around the necks of the yogurt containers. Wind the cord around the tops of the containers and keep it in place with small strips of masking tape. Turn the containers upside down and carefully cut out the base of each one, using scissors.

3 Tear some more 2.5 cm (1 in) strips of newspaper. Dip the strips into the diluted PVA (white) glue, and cover each container with three layers. Use thin strips to bind the rims of the containers so that the cord is neatly covered. Leave the containers to dry completely. ▶

MATERIALS AND EQUIPMENT YOU WILL NEED

ROUND BALLOON • SMALL BOWL • NEWSPAPER • DILUTED PVA (WHITE) GLUE • STRING • SCISSORS • COTTON CORD •
TWO CLEAN, DRY YOGURT CONTAINERS OF DIFFERENT SIZES • MASKING TAPE • PIN • PENCIL • BROWN WRAPPING PAPER •
FACE MASK (RESPIRATOR) • FINE SANDPAPER • WHITE EMULSION (LATEX) PAINT • SAND AND FILLING PLASTER • BROAD PAINTBRUSH •
STRONG, CLEAR GLUE • HAIRY TWINE • WORN SHELL OR PEBBLE • TWO PIECES OF CURVED DRIFTWOOD

4 When the papier mâché on the balloon is completely dry, pierce with a pin to pop the balloon within. Position the paper shape centrally on the smaller yogurt container and hold it in place with strips of masking tape. Cover the join with several layers of thin papier mâché strips.

6 When dry, tear some large strips of wrapping paper, dip them into the diluted PVA (white) glue, and apply one layer to the vase. Leave the vase to dry. Then, wearing a protective face mask (respirator), lightly sand the surface.

8 Wind hairy twine around the neck and foot of the vase. Suspend a piece of worn shell or pebble from a length of twine to adorn the neck of the vase.

5 Position the larger tub centrally on top of the paper shape. Draw around the inside of the container and carefully cut away the resulting circle to make the opening of the vase. Replace the container and tape it in place. Cover the join with several layers of papier mâché.

7 Wearing a face mask (respirator), mix some white emulsion (latex) paint with a little sand and filling plaster. Use a broad brush to paint the vase, including the inside of the neck. Allow the brown paper to show through in some areas, to give the vase a slightly patchy appearance. Leave the vase to dry thoroughly.

9 Using strong, clear glue, attach a length of driftwood to either side of the vase to form the handles. Secure them in place with masking tape while they dry.

LEAFY WALL PANELS

PAPIER MACHE PANELS AND OTHER ARCHITECTURAL DETAILS WERE POPULAR DURING THE 19TH CENTURY, WHEN ELABORATE IMITATIONS OF PLASTER- AND STUCCOWORK WERE PRODUCED. THESE PANELS ARE LESS ORNATE THAN THEIR PREDECESSORS, BUT WILL ADD A TOUCH OF ELEGANCE AROUND A DOOR FRAME. THE SURFACE IS RUBBED BACK TO REVEAL A HINT OF UNDERLYING COLOUR. THE PANELS MAY BE TEMPORARILY ATTACHED, USING STICKY PADS OR, FOR MORE PERMANENT DECORATION, USE PVA (WHITE) GLUE.

1 For the side and top of the door, cut three panels of cardboard measuring 61 x 14 cm (24 x 5½ in), or to fit around your door. Brush both sides of each panel with a coat of diluted PVA (white) glue and lay flat on a sheet of plastic to dry.

2 Draw a line down the centre of each panel. Measure and mark a point every 15 cm (6 in) down the line.

3 Dab a spot of undiluted PVA (white) glue at each 15 cm (6 in) mark. Cut a length of cotton cord for each panel, and attach in a wavy line, curving it in and out between the dabs of glue. Use small pieces of masking tape to keep the cord in place. Line the panels up, end to end, to make sure that the ends of the cords form a continuous wavy pattern.

4 Trace the leaf motif from the template at the back of the book, and transfer it four times to a piece of heavy corrugated cardboard for each panel. Place the cardboard on a cutting mat and cut out all the leaves, using a craft knife. Glue the leaves at equal distances down the length of each panel. Tear newspaper into 2.5 cm (1 in) strips, dip them in diluted PVA (white) glue, and cover each panel with three layers. Lay the panels flat on a sheet of plastic to dry. ▶

MATERIALS AND EQUIPMENT YOU WILL NEED

HEAVY CORRUGATED CARDBOARD • SCISSORS • PVA (WHITE) GLUE • PAINTBRUSHES • SHEET OF PLASTIC • METAL RULER • PENCIL • THICK COTTON CORD • MASKING TAPE • TRACING PAPER • CRAFT KNIFE • CUTTING MAT • NEWSPAPER • FACE MASK (RESPIRATOR) • FINE SANDPAPER • EMULSION (LATEX) PAINTS: WHITE AND BLUE • SOFT CLOTH • PETROLEUM JELLY • STICKY PADS (OPTIONAL)

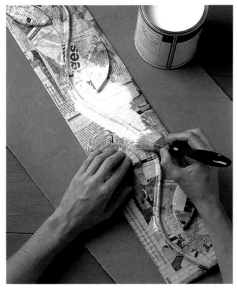

5 Wearing a protective face mask (respirator), gently rub back each panel with fine sandpaper. Prime the panels with two coats of white emulsion (latex) paint and leave to dry thoroughly.

7 Using a soft cloth, apply a very thin coat of petroleum jelly over the front of each panel.

8 Paint each panel with two coats of white emulsion (latex) paint, completely covering the blue surface. Leave the panels to dry thoroughly.

6 Still wearing the protective face mask (respirator), paint the front of each panel with a coat of blue emulsion (latex) paint. Leave them to dry thoroughly.

9 Wearing a mask (respirator), rub back the surface of each panel very lightly so that specks of blue paint are revealed. Attach the panels around the door frame, using undiluted PVA (white) glue, or sticky pads if fixing temporarily.

KEEPSAKE BOX

THIS BOX MAKES A CHARMING HIDING PLACE FOR TREASURED ITEMS. ITS SOPHISTICATED APPEARANCE BELIES ITS SIMPLE CONSTRUCTION; IT IS STRAIGHTFORWARD TO MAKE, BUT THE ELEMENTS MUST BE PRECISELY MEASURED AND CUT TO ENSURE A PERFECT FIT. THE DELICATE, SLIGHTLY WEATHERED SURFACE IS ACHIEVED BY PAINTING THE SURFACE AND THEN RUBBING BACK. SUBTLE PAINTED MOTIFS AND COLLAGED SCRAPS ENHANCE THE LOOK, AND PROVIDE AN OPPORTUNITY TO PERSONALIZE THE BOX.

1 For the base of the box, cut two pieces of mounting board measuring 11.5 x 16.5 cm (4½ x 6½ in), and glue them together. Measure and mark out the positions of the box walls and compartments as follows: Draw a rectangle 1.5 cm (⅝ in) from the edges of the base. Draw a second rectangle inside it that is 2 mm (¹⁄₁₆ in) smaller all round. Divide this rectangle into eight equal sections for the compartments.

2 Cut three strips of mounting board measuring 13.5 x 2.5 cm (5¼ x 1 in). Using the PVA (white) glue, glue and tape one strip along the centre of the base. Glue and tape the other two strips along the edges of the inner rectangle. Cut two further strips of 2.5 cm (1 in) wide board to make the walls for the ends of the inner rectangle, and glue and tape one of these strips into place.

3 Cut four strips of 3 cm (1⅛ in) wide board to make walls for the larger rectangle. Glue and tape three strips in position, as before. Measure and cut eight pieces of 2.5 cm (1 in) wide board to make the compartments, and glue and tape them in place inside the central rectangle. Glue the remaining two board strips in place at the side of the box. ▶

MATERIALS AND EQUIPMENT YOU WILL NEED

A2 SHEET OF MOUNTING BOARD • METAL RULER • SET SQUARE (TRIANGLE) • PENCIL • CRAFT KNIFE • CUTTING MAT • PVA (WHITE) GLUE • MASKING TAPE • NEWSPAPER • PASTE • WHITE EMULSION (LATEX) PAINT • PAINTBRUSHES • GOUACHE PAINTS IN A VARIETY OF COLOURS • FACE MASK (RESPIRATOR) • FINE SANDPAPER • SCRAPS OF INTERESTING PAPER • MATT ACRYLIC VARNISH • ORNAMENTAL BUTTON

4 Cut four 3 cm (1⅛ in) wide strips of board to make the outer walls of the base, and glue and tape them into position. Cut four strips of board to fit over the space between the compartments and the outer walls, and glue and tape them into place.

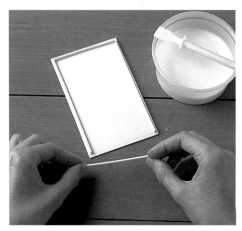

5 To make the lid, measure the opening in the top of the box and cut out two rectangles of mounting board that are 3 mm (⅛ in) smaller all round than the opening. Glue the rectangles together. Draw a line around the lid 2 mm (¹⁄₁₆ in) in from the edge. Cut four 3 mm (⅛ in) pieces of mounting board to fit inside the pencil line and glue them in place to make a lip for the lid.

6 Using a pencil and ruler, divide the top of the lid in four sections to find the central point. Cut a small rectangle of board to make a ledge for the button that forms the handle. Cut a small notch into the rectangle to contain the shank of the button.

7 Cover the entire box and lid with two layers of papier mâché squares, pasted smoothly over the surface. Leave the box and lid to dry thoroughly.

8 Prime the box and lid with a coat of white emulsion (latex) paint. When dry, apply a coat of turquoise paint, mixed from gouache and white emulsion (latex). Follow this with a coat of lighter, blue-green paint, then one of yellow ochre. Apply each colour with a dry brush, and only when the previous coat is dry. When the last coat is dry, lightly rub back the surface of the box and lid with sandpaper, wearing a face mask (respirator).

9 Paste scraps of paper on to the surface of the box and lid. Sketch decorative motifs faintly with a pencil, then fill in using gouache paints. When the box and lid are dry, seal them with a coat of acrylic varnish. Finally, glue the button to the top of the lid to make the handle.

those we love

STAR FRAME

THE WARM TONES OF BROWN WRAPPING PAPER MAKE IT IDEAL FOR PAPIER MACHE, EITHER ON ITS OWN, OR OVER NEWSPAPER. THIS LOW-RELIEF PATTERNED FRAME EXPLOITS THE MATERIAL'S NATURAL QUALITIES IN A SIMPLE, HARMONIOUS DESIGN. BROWN PAPER IS LESS EASY TO HANDLE THAN NEWSPAPER. THE TORN EDGES ALSO TEND TO DARKEN WHEN THE GLUE HAS DRIED, BUT THIS GIVES A LIVELY, INTERESTING SURFACE. SOME PAPERS ARE WAXED TO MAKE THEM WATERPROOF, AND ARE NOT SUITABLE FOR PAPIER MACHE.

1 Use a ruler and set square to draw a square, 38 x 38 cm (15 x 15 in), on to corrugated cardboard. Draw another square within it, measuring 18 x 18 cm (7 x 7 in), to make the frame opening. Place the cardboard on a cutting mat and cut out the frame with a craft knife.

2 Draw a star design and transfer it eight times to corrugated cardboard. Cut out all the stars.

3 Cut four small circles of cardboard and glue them to the centres of four of the stars. Glue all the stars around the frame, with the plain stars at the corners.

4 Measure and cut out a 38 x 38 cm (15 x 15 in) backing board from the cardboard. Draw and cut out a frame spacer from lightweight corrugated cardboard. Prime the frame front, back and spacer with diluted PVA (white) glue and place them flat on a sheet of plastic to dry.

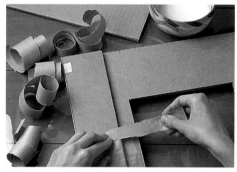

5 Glue the spacer to the back of the frame. Tear wide strips of brown paper and dip into the diluted PVA (white) glue. Cover the frame and backing board with two layers. Lay flat to dry.

6 Glue the backing board to the back of the frame, lining up the edges. Hold the frame together with masking tape and seal the bottom and side edges with two layers of papier mâché strips. When dry, glue a hanger to the back with clear glue.

MATERIALS AND EQUIPMENT YOU WILL NEED

METAL RULER • SET SQUARE (TRIANGLE) • PENCIL • HEAVY CORRUGATED CARDBOARD • CRAFT KNIFE • CUTTING MAT • TRACING PAPER •
PVA (WHITE) GLUE • LIGHTWEIGHT CORRUGATED CARDBOARD, FOR SPACER • PAINTBRUSH • SHEET OF PLASTIC •
BROWN WRAPPING PAPER • MASKING TAPE • STRONG, CLEAR GLUE • PICTURE HANGER

GILDED FINIALS

FINIALS CAN TRANSFORM EVERYDAY CURTAIN POLES INTO STYL-ISH ACCESSORIES. NO ONE WOULD GUESS THAT THE GLISTENING EXAMPLES SHOWN HERE ARE MADE FROM FOAMBOARD, PULP TISSUE PAPER AND BOTTLE CAPS. THE GOLD IS DUTCH METAL LEAF (CHEAP-ER THAN GOLD LEAF); IT CAN BE REPLACED BY GOLD PAINT OR GILT CREAM, BUT THESE DO NOT SPARKLE WITH THE SAME INTENSITY.

1 Trace the finial design from the template at the back of the book, and transfer it twice to a piece of foamboard. Place the foamboard on a cutting mat and cut out the finials using a craft knife.

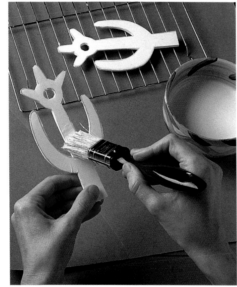

2 Brush the finials on both sides with diluted PVA (white) glue and lay them flat on a wire cake rack to dry thoroughly.

3 Dip pieces of tissue paper into the diluted PVA (white) glue. Squeeze out the excess glue, and work the tissue paper lightly in your hands until it becomes pulpy. Press the pulp on to one side of the finial shapes and smooth the surface. Lay them flat on the cake rack to dry well. ▶

MATERIALS AND EQUIPMENT YOU WILL NEED

TRACING PAPER • PENCIL • 6 MM (¼ IN) THICK FOAMBOARD • CRAFT KNIFE • CUTTING MAT • PVA (WHITE) GLUE • PAINTBRUSHES •
OLD WIRE CAKE RACK • TISSUE PAPER • PLASTIC BOTTLE CAPS • STRONG, CLEAR GLUE • MASKING TAPE • NEWSPAPER • FACE MASK (RESPIRATOR) •
FINE SANDPAPER • WHITE ACRYLIC GESSO • WATER-BASED GOLD SIZE • LARGE SOFT BRUSH • GOLD DUTCH METAL LEAF

4 Draw around the top of a bottle cap twice on to the foamboard and cut out the resulting circles. Glue a circle to the base of each finial.

6 Tear narrow strips of newspaper, dip them into the diluted PVA (white) glue, and cover the dry finials with three layers of papier mâché. Leave the finials to dry thoroughly.

8 Apply a thin coat of water-based gold size to one finial and leave it to become tacky (about 20–30 minutes).

5 Glue the base of a finial to the top of each bottle cap, keeping them in place with small strips of masking tape.

7 Wearing a protective face mask (respirator), lightly sand each finial, and prime with two coats of white acrylic gesso. Allow the first coat to dry before the second coat is added.

9 Using a large, soft brush, apply metal leaf over the tacky gold size, continuing until the whole of the finial is covered. Brush away the excess leaf. Gild the second finial in the same way.

ROCOCO SCREEN

THIS ORNATE BUT GRACEFUL SCREEN IS MADE USING THE SIM-
PLEST OF MATERIALS. THE OUTER EDGES CAN BE AS ELABORATE
AS YOU LIKE, BUT THE DECORATIONS ON THE CENTRAL PANEL MUST
FIT FLUSH TO THE EDGES TO ENABLE THE SCREEN TO BE HINGED.

SCREEN BLANKS CAN BE BOUGHT FROM CRAFT AND HOBBY SHOPS,
OR DIRECTLY FROM A SUPPLIER BY MAIL ORDER. YOU COULD CUT
THEM OUT YOURSELF, OR ASK A CARPENTER TO DO SO, TO GIVE YOU
A SCREEN THAT FITS YOUR DESIGN SPECIFICATIONS EXACTLY.

1 Wearing a protective face mask, lightly rub down both sides of each screen panel with fine sandpaper, then prime each one with acrylic primer.

2 Cut a large piece of thin corrugated cardboard to cover each screen panel. The cardboard for the central panel should fit exactly; the cardboard for the side panels should overlap by 6 cm (2½ in). Draw a fan-shaped section for the top of each panel and cut out.

3 Draw and cut out slender curlicues of cardboard. Position them down one side of the cardboard that will cover the outer panels. Draw around them in pencil, and cut around the outer lines to make the decorative edges of the panels. ▶

MATERIALS AND EQUIPMENT YOU WILL NEED

FACE MASK (RESPIRATOR) • THREE-PANEL SCREEN BLANK • FINE SANDPAPER • WATER-BASED ACRYLIC PRIMER • PAINTBRUSHES • SCISSORS •
THIN CORRUGATED CARDBOARD WITH EXPOSED CORRUGATIONS • METAL RULER • PENCIL • CRAFT KNIFE • CUTTING MAT • THIN RUBBER (LATEX) GLOVES •
CONTACT ADHESIVE • PVA (WHITE) GLUE • WHITE TISSUE PAPER • EMULSION (LATEX) PAINTS: WHITE AND A VARIETY OF PALE COLOURS • GOLD ACRYLIC PAINT •
WATER-BASED ACRYLIC VARNISH • SET OF PIANO HINGES

4 Use the curlicues as templates along the other edge of the side panels. This time, cut out the shapes, using a craft knife, to make indented patterns.

6 Cut smaller swirls and embellishments to fit around the top of each screen as a relief design. Fix them into position with PVA (white) glue. Stick the curlicues in place over the main panels of the screen.

7 When all the additions have dried, tear thick strips of tissue paper and apply two layers over the surface of all three panels, using diluted PVA (white) glue and a wide brush. Make sure that you cover the edges of the screen, to bond the panels firmly. Leave the panels to dry.

5 Wearing a protective face mask (respirator) and thin rubber (latex) gloves, glue the cardboard to the panels, using the contact adhesive.

8 Prime the panels with white emulsion (latex) paint, then decorate them with pale shades of emulsion (latex) paint and gold outlines in acrylic paint. Seal the panels with two coats of acrylic varnish, and hinge the screen together.

PEBBLE CLOCK

NATURAL OBJECTS AND EVERYDAY MATERIALS ARE CHARMINGLY COMBINED IN THIS CLOCK TO ECHO THE PASSAGE OF TIME. THE BASIC ARMATURE IS A DISC OF HEAVY CORRUGATED CARDBOARD, AND THE HOURS ARE PICKED OUT USING SLENDER PEBBLES.

A FRILL OF SHORT TWIGS MAKES A SPIKED CONTRAST TO THE PLAIN WHITE RIM OF THE CLOCK FACE — PIECES OF DRIFTWOOD, SHELLS OR MORE PEBBLES WOULD ALSO LOOK GOOD. QUARTZ CLOCK MOVEMENTS ARE AVAILABLE FROM CRAFT SUPPLIERS OR HOBBY SHOPS.

1 To make the clock face, draw a circle with a diameter of 26 cm (10¼ in) on a sheet of heavy corrugated cardboard. Place the cardboard on a cutting mat, and cut out the circle with a craft knife.

2 Tear newspaper into 2.5 cm (1 in) strips and dip them in diluted PVA (white) glue. Cover the clock face with three layers of strips and lay it on a wire cake rack to dry thoroughly.

3 Using a sharp pencil, make a hole in the exact centre of the clock face wide enough for the clock movement to be inserted. Follow the manufacturer's instructions for operating the movement. ▶

MATERIALS AND EQUIPMENT YOU WILL NEED

PAIR OF COMPASSES (COMPASS) • PENCIL • HEAVY CORRUGATED CARDBOARD • CRAFT KNIFE • CUTTING MAT • NEWSPAPER • PVA (WHITE) GLUE • OLD WIRE CAKE RACK • SHARP PENCIL • CLOCK MOVEMENT AND HANDS • FACE MASK (RESPIRATOR) • FINE SANDPAPER • WHITE EMULSION (LATEX) PAINT • PAINTBRUSH • SCISSORS • BROWN WRAPPING PAPER • MATT GOLD PAPER • STRONG, CLEAR GLUE • PEBBLES • THIN TWIGS

4 Wearing a protective face mask (respirator), lightly rub the surface of the clock face with fine sandpaper and prime it with two coats of white emulsion (latex) paint. Allow the first coat to dry thoroughly before applying the second.

6 Use the pencil to punch through the existing hole into the brown and gold paper. Fix the clock movement and hands to the clock face, following the manufacturer's instructions.

8 Cut the twigs into short lengths. Working on the back of the clock, draw a guideline 2.5cm (1 in) from the edge of the clock. Glue the twigs at equal distances around the edge. Leave the clock face down to dry thoroughly.

5 Cut a circle of brown paper with a diameter of 25 cm (10 in), and a circle of matt gold paper with a diameter of 9 cm (3½ in). Glue both to the centre of the clock face.

7 Turn the hands to 12 o'clock and make a corresponding pencil mark on the clock face. Rotate the hands and mark each hour in the border.

9 Turn the clock over and use strong, clear glue to attach a pebble at each hour mark on the clock face. Cut very short lengths of twig and glue them around the edge of the inner, gold circle. Lay the clock flat until the glue is thoroughly dry.

STARRY DRAWER KNOBS

Decorative knobs can enliven the plainest furniture. These star drawer knobs are made entirely from pulp tissue paper, but are very strong. They are simply finished with spirals of household string, and a touch of gold paint to emphasize their shape. Drawer knobs offer wide scope for embellishing plain furniture: you could make a set with a different motif for each knob, or use coloured tissue paper as a final layer and leave the drawers unpainted.

1 Loosely crumple a sheet of tissue paper into a ball and dip it into diluted PVA (white) glue until completely saturated.

2 Squeeze the excess glue from the paper and work it between your hands for a few seconds, so that it breaks down and becomes pulpy. Form the pulp into a small ball.

3 To make each knob, hold a ball of pulp between your thumbs and forefingers and flatten it into a disc. Gently press the disc between your fingers until the paper is completely smooth. Place the disc on a wire rack to dry slightly. Repeat to make as many knobs as you need. ▶

MATERIALS AND EQUIPMENT YOU WILL NEED
TISSUE PAPER • PVA (WHITE) GLUE • WIRE CAKE RACK • NEWSPAPER • BRADAWL (AWL) • SCRAP OF WOOD • PENCIL •
A 50 X 3 MM (2 X ⅛ IN) MACHINE SCREW AND THREE NUTS FOR EACH KNOB • FACE MASK (RESPIRATOR) • FINE SANDPAPER •
WHITE EMULSION (LATEX) PAINT • PAINTBRUSH • HAIRY STRING • SCISSORS • GOLD ACRYLIC PAINT

4 Tear small pieces of tissue paper and dip them into diluted PVA (white) glue. Squeeze and roll them between finger and thumb to make pointed shapes. Press the points firmly into the edges of the discs to attach them. Leave the knobs to dry thoroughly on a wire rack.

6 Screw a machine screw through the middle of each knob and secure it in place with a matching nut. Cover the head of each screw with two layers of papier mâché strips and leave the knobs to dry.

8 Spread a little undiluted PVA (white) glue in the middle of each knob and coil a length of hairy string on to it to make a decorative centre.

5 Cover the knobs with one layer of small papier mâché strips. When they are dry, place each one on a piece of scrap wood and use a bradawl to make a hole in the centre. Widen each hole with a pencil until a machine screw will fit into it.

7 Wearing a protective face mask (respirator), lightly sand each knob and prime it with two coats of white emulsion (latex) paint, allowing the first coat to dry thoroughly before adding the second.

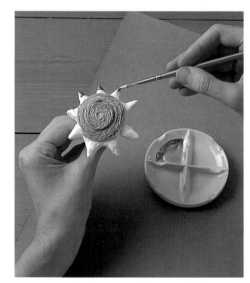

9 Paint the tips of the knobs gold. To fix the knobs, mark the centre point of each drawer. Clamp the drawers firmly and drill a hole in the centre. Wind a nut on to the machine-screw shank of each knob. Push the ends of the shanks through the holes in the drawers and add another nut to each. To secure the knobs, tighten all the nuts.

BAY LEAF HERB STAND

THIS DAINTY STAND, INSPIRED BY FRENCH BAKERY SHELVES, IS PERFECT FOR STORING POTS OF FRESH HERBS OR JARS OF SPICES OR DISPLAYING SMALL ORNAMENTS. ITS DELICATE SPIRALS AND PAPIER MACHE BAY LEAVES DISGUISE ITS STRENGTH. HERE, FLORIST'S WIRE SPIRALS DECORATE THE SHELF TOPS AND SIDES YET OTHER MOTIFS COULD BE USED, SUCH AS HEARTS OR FLOWERS.

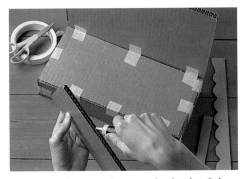

1 Using the templates at the back of the book, measure and mark out all the components, except the border frill, on a sheet of heavy corrugated cardboard. Cut two pieces for the front and sides. Cut a strip of lightweight cardboard, measuring 30 x 2.5 cm (12 x 1 in), and form one long edge into a wavy border. Assemble the stand using PVA (white) glue and masking tape. Cut a thin strip of heavy cardboard and glue it underneath the top shelf to strengthen it. Attach the scalloped trim to the top shelf.

2 Brush diluted PVA (white) glue over all the surfaces of the stand, including underneath. Leave to dry.

3 Tear newspaper into 2.5 cm (1 in) strips. Dip the strips into diluted PVA (white) glue and cover the stand with five layers of papier mâché. Use small, narrow strips to go around the scalloped border on the top shelf. Leave to dry.

4 Using the template at the back of the book, trace and cut out nine leaves from heavy cardboard. Dip thin newspaper strips in diluted PVA (white) glue, and layer each leaf twice. Leave to dry.

5 Using pliers, grasp one end of a length of wire and curl into a spiral, leaving sufficient length to attach to the shelf. Open out the spiral slightly to create a smooth pattern. Repeat to make four matching shelf ends. ▶

MATERIALS AND EQUIPMENT YOU WILL NEED

METAL RULER • PENCIL • HEAVY AND LIGHTWEIGHT CORRUGATED CARDBOARD • CRAFT KNIFE • CUTTING MAT •
PVA (WHITE) GLUE • MASKING TAPE • PAINTBRUSHES • PALETTE • NEWSPAPER • TRACING PAPER • ROUND-NOSED PLIERS • FLORIST'S WIRE • BRADAWL (AWL) •
FACE MASK (RESPIRATOR) • FINE SANDPAPER • EMULSION (LATEX) PAINTS: WHITE AND LIME GREEN •
ACRYLIC PAINTS: LIGHT, MEDIUM AND DARK GREEN • WATER-BASED ACRYLIC VARNISH

6 Position the wire spirals on the shelves and secure them top and bottom with small pieces of masking tape. Tear narrow strips of newspaper and cover the top (non-spiral) ends only with three layers of papier mâché.

8 Remove the masking tape from the bottom of the wire shelf ends. Wearing a face mask (respirator), lightly sand the leaves and the stand. Prime them with two coats of white emulsion (latex) paint, allowing each coat to dry thoroughly.

10 Apply light green acrylic paint to the leaves. Add a second, patchy coat of medium green. Paint veins on the front of each leaf, using the darkest green.

7 Use the pliers to cut 8 cm (3¼ in) lengths of florist's wire for the leaf stems. Pierce a hole through the base of each leaf with a bradawl. Dab a little glue on one end of each piece of wire, and push the wires up into the leaves.

9 Paint the stand with two coats of lime green emulsion (latex) paint. When the paint is thoroughly dry, use undiluted PVA (white) glue to fix the free ends of each piece of wire into place on the shelves.

11 Use a bradawl to make a hole for each leaf along the top edge of the stand. Dab a little undiluted PVA (white) glue on to one end of each piece of wire and push into position to form the stem. Seal the stand with a coat of acrylic varnish.

AFRICAN POT

PAPIER MACHE MIMICS FIRED CLAY TO STRIKING EFFECT IN THIS AFRICAN-INSPIRED POT. THE BODY OF THE POT IS CONSTRUCTED USING A BALLOON MOULD, AND THE NECK AND FOOT ARE MADE OF CARDBOARD. THE SURFACE IS COVERED WITH A GENEROUS LAYER OF PAPER PULP, INCISED WITH DELICATE DESIGNS, THEN TREATED TO A THIN WASH OF PAINT TO GIVE A DISTRESSED APPEARANCE.

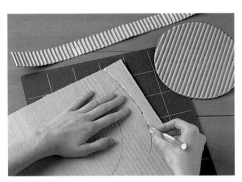

1 Inflate a round balloon and tie the end firmly. Smear a layer of petroleum jelly over the balloon and rest it on a small container. Dip large squares of newspaper into diluted PVA (white) glue and build up four layers of papier mâché, completely covering the balloon. Leave to dry.

2 To make the foot, cut a narrow strip of corrugated cardboard, with the corrugations running crosswise. Then cut a semi-circular strip to form the neck of the pot, and a circle and a long, thin strip of corrugated cardboard to create the lid.

3 Glue and tape the circle and strip together to form the lid. Curve the strip of cardboard that makes the neck, and glue and tape the ends together. Curve the foot and glue and tape this too. Cover all three pieces with strips of brown gummed paper tape to strengthen them. Prick the balloon and invert the pot.

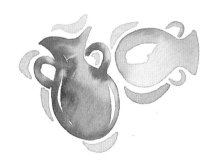

4 Glue and tape the foot in place. Dry, then cover the join with 2–3 layers of papier mâché. Join the neck to the pot and cut an opening in the top of the pot.

▶

MATERIALS AND EQUIPMENT YOU WILL NEED

ROUND BALLOON • PETROLEUM JELLY • SMALL BOWL • NEWSPAPER • PVA (WHITE) GLUE • WIDE BRUSH •
THIN CORRUGATED CARDBOARD • CRAFT KNIFE • CUTTING MAT • MASKING TAPE • BROWN GUMMED PAPER TAPE • SCISSORS •
FACE MASK (RESPIRATOR) • THIN RUBBER (LATEX) GLOVES • PAPER PULP (SEE BASIC TECHNIQUES) • MEDIUM- AND FINE-GRADE SANDPAPER •
METAL SKEWER • POSTER PAINTS: RAW UMBER AND BURNT SIENNA • HOUSEHOLD SPONGE • PALETTE • PAINTBRUSH •
STENCIL CARDBOARD • TWINE • JAPANESE TISSUE PAPER

5 Wearing a face mask (respirator) and gloves, cover the outside of the pot with a generous layer of paper pulp. Leave to dry. Lightly sand the surface, then add a second layer. Cover the outside of the lid in the same way. Leave to dry thoroughly.

7 Mix raw umber and burnt sienna poster paints with water to make thin washes. Dab them on to the pot and lid, using a damp household sponge. Work the paint over the surface to create a patchy, distressed effect.

9 Cut a length of twine that is twice the circumference of the neck of the pot. Fold the twine in half and cover it with thin strips of Japanese tissue paper. Wearing thin rubber (latex) gloves, coat the papered twine with a layer of paper pulp, and allow to dry slightly.

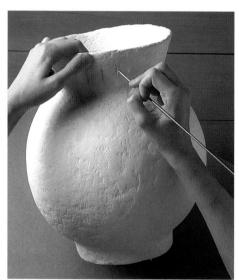

6 Wearing a protective face mask (respirator), rub the surface down lightly with medium-grade sandpaper, and finish with fine sandpaper. Use a metal skewer to incise simple patterns, such as rows of lines, in the pulp.

8 Cut simple designs, such as zigzags and small rectangles, into the stencil cardboard. Place the stencils on the pot and lid, and push paper pulp through the cuts, using a small scrap of corrugated cardboard, to form relief patterns.

10 While the twine is still damp, wrap it around the neck of the pot, pressing it in firmly so that it stays in place when dry.

FOLK ART BOX

THIS ENDEARING LITTLE BOX IS CONSTRUCTED FROM HEAVY CARDBOARD AND PIPE CLEANERS. PAPER PULP IS USED TO MOULD THE HORSE AND BUILD UP AREAS OF LOW RELIEF. THE BOX IS PAINTED A DENSE WHITE TO RESEMBLE FIRED CLAY, AND THE DECO-RATION IS BOLD BUT SPARE, IN BRIGHT PAINTS THAT REINFORCE THE BOX'S FOLK-ART APPEARANCE. HEAVY CORRUGATED CARDBOARD ENSURES A STURDY BOX, WHICH WOULD MAKE AN IDEAL PRESENT, ORNAMENT OR TRINKET BOX, BUT IS UNSUITABLE FOR CHILDREN.

1 Using a craft knife, cutting mat and metal ruler, cut out two pieces of heavy cardboard, 15 x 10 cm (6 x 4 in) for the lid and base. Cut two pieces of heavy cardboard 15 x 6 cm (6 x 2½ in) for the sides, and two pieces 10 x 6 cm (4 x 2½ in) for the ends of the box. Spread a line of undiluted PVA (white) glue around the inside edge of the box base, and glue and tape the four walls in place.

2 To form the lip of the lid, cut a rectangle 13 x 7.5 cm (5¼ x 3 in) from the heavy cardboard and glue to the centre of the underside of the lid.

3 Cut a rectangle of thin cardboard, 8 x 6 cm (3¼ x 2½ in). Place the cardboard on a piece of scrap wood. Using a bradawl (awl), make four holes where the horse's legs will be. For the legs, thread a pipe cleaner through each pair of holes, from the base to the top of the cardboard.

4 To form the horse's body, take a pipe cleaner and thread it around the top of each leg to make a rectangle. Remember to leave an extra loop at the back of the horse for its tail. Use more pipe cleaners to create the neck, head and ears, and to enlarge the main body. ▶

MATERIALS AND EQUIPMENT YOU WILL NEED

CRAFT KNIFE • CUTTING MAT • PENCIL • METAL RULER • HEAVY AND LIGHTWEIGHT CORRUGATED CARDBOARD •
PVA (WHITE) GLUE • MASKING TAPE • BRADAWL (AWL) • SCRAP WOOD • PIPE CLEANERS • PAPER PULP (SEE BASIC TECHNIQUES) •
FACE MASK (RESPIRATOR) • THIN RUBBER (LATEX) GLOVES • RECYCLED PAPER • PASTE • WHITE EMULSION (LATEX) PAINT •
PAINTBRUSHES • ACRYLIC PAINTS IN A VARIETY OF COLOURS

5 Mix a quantity of paper pulp. Wearing a face mask (respirator) and rubber (latex) gloves, mould the shape of the horse over the pipe-cleaner armature, using pieces of pulp. Leave the horse to dry thoroughly.

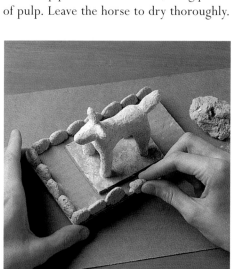

6 Place the horse and stand in the centre of the lid, and mark the positions of the pipe cleaners that run beneath the stand. Cut two small channels in the lid to accommodate the pipe cleaners, and glue the horse to the lid. Brush a coat of diluted PVA (white) glue over the top of the lid to provide a key, then use small discs of pulp to make a decorative edging around it.

7 When the lid is thoroughly dry, tear small squares of recycled paper, coat them with paste glue, and use them to cover the box and lid. Allow them to dry completely.

8 Prime the surface of the box and lid with two coats of white emulsion (latex) paint, allowing the first coat to dry thoroughly before the second is added.

9 When the emulsion (latex) paint is dry, start to decorate the horse and lid, using acrylic paints.

10 Paint the inside of the box. Finally, complete the decoration by adding a simple pattern to each outside wall.

CHEQUERED DOORS

Bathroom or kitchen cabinets are often dull, but you can turn them into striking items at minimal cost, using just a few layers of paper. Tissue and handmade paper in warm, neutral colours, sealed with diluted varnish to make the paper highly practical and create a translucent, interesting texture, convey a stylish effect. Gather a collection of papers that match your existing decor, and experiment with different colours, shapes and designs.

1 Wearing a protective face mask (respirator), lightly sand the front and sides of the door. Apply a coat of acrylic wood primer and leave it to dry thoroughly.

2 Tear pieces of white tissue paper and apply one layer to the front of the door, using diluted PVA (white) glue and a wide brush.

3 Measure the inner recess of the door. With the aid of a metal ruler, tear some squares of yellow ochre and brown handmade paper to fit the space. ▶

MATERIALS AND EQUIPMENT YOU WILL NEED

FACE MASK (RESPIRATOR) • FINE SANDPAPER • WATER-BASED ACRYLIC WOOD PRIMER • PAINTBRUSHES • WHITE TISSUE PAPER • PVA (WHITE) GLUE • WIDE BRUSH •
METAL RULER • YELLOW OCHRE AND BROWN HANDMADE PAPER • SHEET OF JAPANESE TISSUE PAPER •
THIN CORRUGATED CARDBOARD • SCISSORS • COLOURED TISSUE PAPER • THIN RUBBER (LATEX) GLOVES • MATT OIL VARNISH •
WHITE SPIRIT (ALCOHOL)

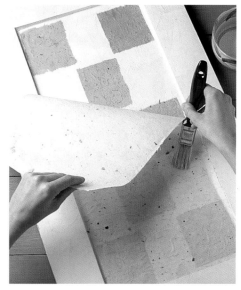

4 Using diluted PVA (white) glue and a brush, attach the yellow squares to the front of the door in a chequerboard pattern. Tear a rectangle of thin Japanese tissue paper the same size as the inner panel, and glue it over the top of the yellow squares to subdue the colour.

6 Tear irregular-sized strips of coloured tissue paper and glue over the cardboard squares and the sides of the door, using diluted PVA (white) glue and a wide brush.

8 Glue the large brown paper squares between the yellow squares in the door recess. Tear narrow strips of the same paper and glue them around the inside of the recess, covering the edges of the squares. Leave the door to dry thoroughly. Then, wearing thin rubber (latex) gloves, and working in a well-ventilated area, dilute two parts of oil varnish with one part of white spirit (alcohol) and seal the door with two coats.

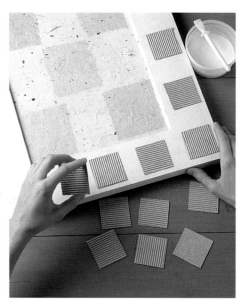

5 Cut small squares from thin cardboard to make a low-relief border, and glue them around the door frame with undiluted PVA (white) glue.

7 Tear tiny squares of brown and yellow handmade paper and, using diluted PVA (white) glue, stick them on to the centres of the cardboard squares, alternating the colours.

DUCK-EGG BOWL

THE WIDE RANGE OF RECYCLED PAPERS NOW AVAILABLE IN EXCITING COLOURS AND TEXTURES MAKES EXCITING PAPIER MACHE. THIS COOL BLUE BOWL CONSISTS OF LAYERS OF THIN, SPECKLED RECYCLED PAPER. THE SIMPLE LINES AND UNPAINTED, ROUGH SURFACE CREATE A PLEASINGLY ANTIQUE FEEL, WHILE A RIM OF WIRE SPIRALS GIVES THE BOWL AN ELEGANT FINISH.

1 Spread a thin layer of petroleum jelly inside the mould. Tear the paper into 2.5 cm (1 in) strips. Dip the strips into diluted PVA (white) glue and lay them inside the bowl, overlapping the edges slightly. Apply five layers and leave to dry.

3 Trim the excess paper from around the rim to neaten the edges. If you are not confident of cutting an even curve, draw a pencil line first to guide you.

5 Attach the spirals at equal distances around the inside of the bowl rim, using strips of masking tape. All the spirals should face the same way.

2 Insert a palette knife between the mould and the paper shell and gently separate. When the sides of the paper bowl are free, carefully lever it from the mould. Place the bowl upside down and leave until the underneath is dry.

4 To make the spirals, grasp the end of a length of florist's wire with a pair of round-nosed pliers. Use an even pressure to curl the wire, then open it out slightly with your fingers to form a uniform pattern. Repeat for as many spirals as you need.

6 Cover the masking tape with small pieces of papier mâché to keep the spirals neatly in place. Leave the bowl to dry thoroughly before you use it.

MATERIALS AND EQUIPMENT YOU WILL NEED

PETROLEUM JELLY • OLD BOWL TO USE AS MOULD • THIN SPECKLED RECYCLED PAPER • DILUTED PVA (WHITE) GLUE •
FLEXIBLE PALETTE KNIFE • SCISSORS • PENCIL (OPTIONAL) • FLORIST'S WIRE • ROUND-NOSED PLIERS • MASKING TAPE

COLLECTOR'S SHOWCASE

DISPLAYING COLLECTIONS OF SMALL OBJECTS WITHOUT CREAT- ING CLUTTER CAN BE TRICKY. THIS PAPIER MACHE SHOWCASE FITS THE BILL PERFECTLY. CONSTRUCTED FROM MOUNTING BOARD FOR SOLIDITY AND EMBELLISHED WITH A PAPIER MACHE FINISH, IT IS PAINTED IN RESTRAINED, SUBTLE COLOURS TO COMPLEMENT THE THEME OF THIS GROUP OF MINIATURE ITEMS.

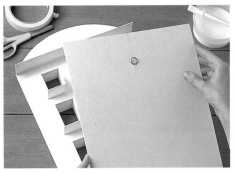

1 Decide on the dimensions of your display case. For the back, cut two identical pieces from a sheet of mounting board. Make a small central slit 4 cm (1½ in) down from the top of one piece. Push the shanks of a split ring (wire) hanger through the slit, open them out, and keep them in place with glue and masking tape. Glue the pieces of board together, with the shanks of the hanger to the inside.

2 Measure out another piece of board the same size. Add an arch at the top and cut out the entire shape. Use this as a template to cut another piece and glue the two pieces together. Mark out the windows on the front.

4 Cut four strips of board 4 cm (1½ in) wide to fit along the top and bottom of the case front on the inside. Glue them together and glue and tape them in place. Glue around the window frames, and glue and tape the back and front together.

3 Place the case front on a cutting mat and carefully cut out each window. Measure the depth of your largest object, and cut strips of board as wide as this, to fit around each window. Glue and tape the strips in place.

5 Cut four strips of board for the sides. Glue them together and glue and tape them in place. Cut two narrow strips of board and glue them together to make a ledge for the front of the case. Glue the ledge centrally, below the windows. ▶

MATERIALS AND EQUIPMENT YOU WILL NEED

TWO SHEETS MOUNTING BOARD • CRAFT KNIFE • CUTTING MAT • METAL RULER • PENCIL • BRASS SPLIT RING (WIRE) HANGER •
PVA (WHITE) GLUE • MASKING TAPE • NEWSPAPER • CARDBOARD • WHITE EMULSION (LATEX) PAINT • PAINTBRUSHES •
GOUACHE PAINTS: BROWN, LIGHT GREY AND SILVER • FACE MASK (RESPIRATOR) • FINE SANDPAPER • BEADING WIRE • PLIERS •
WHITE CHINA BEADS • DUTCH METAL LEAF • ORNAMENTAL BUTTON

6 Cover the entire display case with two layers of papier mâché squares, pasted smoothly over the surface. Make sure that the papier mâché is pushed neatly into the corners of the windows. Support each window frame with strips of cardboard.

7 Prime the display case with a coat of white emulsion (latex) paint and allow it to dry thoroughly.

8 Apply a coat of the brown paint to the display case. Leave to dry. Mix the grey and brown gouache with the white emulsion (latex) paint and re-paint the case. Paint the inside of the central window silver. Cover the surface with a thin coat of white emulsion (latex) paint. Wearing a face mask (respirator), lightly rub it down to reveal the colours beneath.

9 To make supports for the decorative row of beads, cut a short length of fine beading wire for each bead. Thread the bead on to the middle of its wire, and twist the ends of the wire together with small pliers to make "stalks".

10 Paint an outline around the central window and a small square at the top. Apply metal leaf around the central window and glue the button to the centre of the square. Use undiluted PVA (white) glue to fix each object into its window. Stand the display case upright, and leave the glue to dry thoroughly.

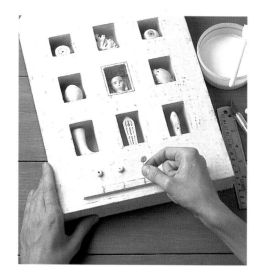

11 Divide the ledge into six equal sections. Using a craft knife and metal ruler, cut a shallow notch at each mark. Spread a little undiluted PVA (white) glue into each notch and press the wire stalks of the beads into them. Leave the case to dry thoroughly.

SCROLLED WALL BRACKET

THIS IMPRESSIVE WALL BRACKET IS FINISHED WITH A LAYER OF CHINESE NEWSPAPER AND LEFT UNPAINTED FOR A MINIMALIST LOOK. FOR AN EXTRA AIR OF CLASSICAL SPLENDOUR, IT COULD BE PAINTED GOLD OR SILVER, OR BE MATCHED TO AN EXISTING COLOUR SCHEME. THE CARDBOARD AND WIRE MESH ARMATURE IS FIRST ENCASED IN A LAYER OF TISSUE PAPER STRIPS, WHICH CONTRACT AS THEY DRY, PULLING THE ARMATURE INTO A TAUT SHAPE THAT IS EASY TO COVER. THE BRACKET IS UNSUITABLE FOR HEAVY OBJECTS.

1 To make the bracket, draw out three rectangles of cardboard measuring 20 x 16 cm (8 x 6¼ in). Draw another three wedge-shaped pieces, measuring 20 cm (8 in) long, and 18 cm (7 in) tapering to 12 cm (4¾ in) wide. Cut out all the pieces, using a craft knife and cutting mat. Glue the three pieces of each size together, using undiluted PVA (white) glue.

2 To assemble the bracket, place the rectangle and wedge-shaped pieces of cardboard at right angles and using undiluted PVA (white) glue, stick and tape them together.

3 Wearing protective leather gloves, cut a rectangle of wire mesh measuring 61 x 23 cm (24 x 9 in). Snip off any spurs of wire and dispose of them safely. Turn over the long edges of the mesh by 5 cm (2 in) at the top and 2 cm (¾ in) at the bottom, so that the resulting shape is slightly tapered. ▶

MATERIALS AND EQUIPMENT YOU WILL NEED

METAL RULER • PENCIL • HEAVY CORRUGATED CARDBOARD • CRAFT KNIFE • CUTTING MAT • PVA (WHITE) GLUE • MASKING TAPE •
PROTECTIVE LEATHER GLOVES • SCISSORS • 6 X 6 MM (¼ X ¼ IN) WIRE MESH • WIRE CUTTERS • NEWSPAPER • TISSUE PAPER •
PASTE • THICK CORD • CHINESE NEWSPAPER • METAL EYELETS • STRONG, CLEAR GLUE

4 Starting at the widest end of the mesh shape, gently roll it into a scroll. Roll the narrower end in the opposite direction to form a second, smaller scroll. The scrolled mesh should sit neatly inside the bracket.

6 Tear wide strips of tissue paper and coat them very lightly with paste glue. Cover the whole scroll with one layer of tissue paper strips, paying special attention to the sides, so that the scroll is a solid shape. Leave the bracket to dry thoroughly.

8 Draw wavy lines down either side of the front of the scroll and a straight line down the centre. Glue lengths of thick cord along the lines to create a low-relief design.

5 Place the scroll inside the bracket and tape it into position. Twist a sheet of newspaper and stuff it inside the larger scroll to pad out the space.

7 Apply three layers of newspaper strips over the whole of the bracket. Run the papier mâché strips from the wire mesh to the cardboard to fill in the gaps. Leave to dry completely.

9 Using squares of Chinese newspaper, cover the entire bracket again. Make sure that the paper is neatly applied, as this is the final layer. Screw two eyelets into the back of the bracket and secure them in place with a dab of strong glue.

EXOTIC BLIND PULLS

THESE GORGEOUS BLIND PULLS, INSPIRED BY THE COSTUMES AND COLOURS OF THE EAST, CAN BE ADAPTED TO A VARIETY OF DESIGNS. THEY ARE MOULDED ON CARDBOARD ARMATURES, USING PAPER PULP PELLETS, THEN COVERED WITH PAPIER MACHE STRIPS TORN FROM NEWSPRINT (UNPRINTED NEWSPAPER). IF NEWSPRINT IS UNAVAILABLE, ORDINARY NEWSPAPER WILL WORK JUST AS WELL.

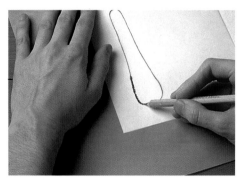

1 Trace the teardrop shape from the template at the back of the book, and transfer it twice to thin white card. Cut out both pieces.

2 Cut a length of string to fit from top to bottom of the teardrop with a generous overlap, and keep it loosely in the centre of the cardboard shape with two small strips of masking tape.

3 Wearing a face mask (respirator) and gloves, use paper pulp pellets to build up the curved shape of each half of the pull. Keep the same depth of pulp on both cardboard pieces, and mould it so that the sides of the teardrop taper gently. Leave both halves to dry on a wire cake rack.

4 Glue the halves together, back to back. Tear small strips of newsprint and dip in diluted PVA (white) glue. Cover the pull with one or two layers of papier mâché strips and leave to dry.

5 Decorate using the acrylic paints. (If using newspaper, first prime with two coats of the emulsion (latex) paint.)

6 Remove the string from the centre of the teardrop. Cut the satin cord to the required length. Bend a piece of wire in half to make a needle, place the cord in the loop, and twist the ends of the wire together. Thread the cord through the teardrop and remove the wire. Add small beads above and below the teardrop to secure the cord. Varnish twice to seal.

MATERIALS AND EQUIPMENT YOU WILL NEED

TRACING PAPER • PENCIL • THIN WHITE CARDBOARD • SCISSORS • STRING • MASKING TAPE • FACE MASK (RESPIRATOR) • THIN RUBBER (LATEX) GLOVES • PAPER PULP (SEE BASIC TECHNIQUES) • OLD WIRE CAKE RACK • PVA (WHITE) GLUE • NEWSPRINT OR NEWSPAPER • WHITE EMULSION (LATEX) PAINT • ACRYLIC PAINTS IN A VARIETY OF COLOURS • PAINTBRUSHES • SATIN CORD • THIN FLORIST'S WIRE • SMALL BEADS • WATER-BASED ACRYLIC VARNISH

CINDERELLA CHAIR

AN EVERYDAY KITCHEN CHAIR BLOSSOMS INTO A ROCOCO PROFUSION OF CURLICUES AND FLAMBOYANT FRILLS — ALL DEVISED FROM CORRUGATED CARDBOARD. WHEN THE MAKEOVER IS COMPLETE, THE CHAIR IS COATED WITH A GENEROUS LAYER OF PAPER PULP THAT HARDENS AND STRENGTHENS THE DETAILS. THE CARDBOARD IS ATTACHED WITH CONTACT ADHESIVE, WHICH IS VERY STRONG SMELLING AND SHOULD BE USED IN THE OPEN AIR IF POSSIBLE. IF NOT, WORK IN A WELL-VENTILATED SPACE.

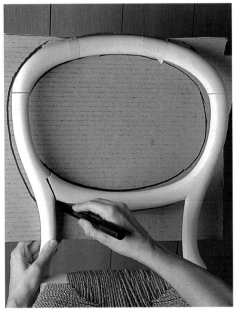

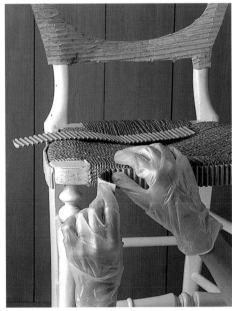

1 Tape a sheet of thin corrugated cardboard to the back of the chair and draw around the outline of the frame, using a marker pen. Remove the cardboard and cut out the shape. Wearing a protective face mask (respirator) and rubber (latex) gloves whilst using the contact adhesive, glue the cardboard to the front of the chair.

2 Cut long thin strips of cardboard with the corrugations running vertically across. Glue the strips round the sides and front of the chair seat. Cut a cover from corrugated cardboard to fit the top of the chair, and glue it in place.

3 Cut two identical strips of 6 cm (2½ in) wide corrugated cardboard, to run around the edge from the chair seat to the centre top of the chair. Cut a piece of thin galvanized wire the same length as the strips, and sandwich it centrally between the two. Glue the strips together. Repeat to make another strip. ▶

MATERIALS AND EQUIPMENT YOU WILL NEED

THIN CORRUGATED CARDBOARD WITH EXPOSED CORRUGATIONS • MASKING TAPE • MARKER PEN • SCISSORS • FACE MASK (RESPIRATOR) •
THIN RUBBER (LATEX) GLOVES • CONTACT ADHESIVE • THIN GALVANIZED WIRE • WIRE CUTTERS • WIDE PAINTBRUSH •
PAPER PULP (SEE BASIC TECHNIQUES)

4 Curve a wired strip of cardboard around one half of the chair-back outline. Roll the top and bottom of the strip into wide curls and glue it in place. Cut a very long, narrow ribbon of cardboard and use it to cover the edges of the strip. Repeat to make the curlicues for the other half of the chair.

6 Cut strips of cardboard to cover the lower portions of the chair back, just above the seat. Cut more narrow strips and glue them to the top edge of the seat.

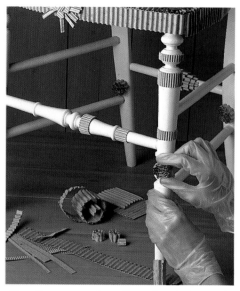

8 Cut strips of cardboard and glue them around the legs and struts of the chair. Form cardboard rosettes and glue them to the front of the chair legs. Make swirls of cardboard for the lower edge of the seat and the front of the legs.

5 Cut a 3 cm (1¼ in) wide strip of cardboard and glue it around the inside edge of the seat back to cover the raw edges of the cardboard cover.

7 Cut spirals, small flowers, bows and other decorations from cardboard, and glue them to the chair back and around the seat as embellishment.

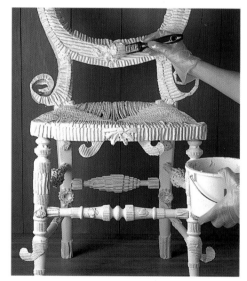

9 Using a wide brush, and wearing rubber (latex) gloves and face mask (respirator), apply a generous coat of paper pulp all over the surface of the chair. Allow it to dry thoroughly, to strengthen the cardboard.

SCALLOPED FRUIT DISH

THIS ELEGANT PEDESTAL DISH IS A CONTEMPORARY INTERPRETATION OF THE PRESSED GLASS AND MOULDED FRUIT PLATES THAT HAVE ADORNED MANY A COUNTRY SIDEBOARD. GRACEFUL AND UNDERSTATED, ITS HARMONIOUS SHAPE AND SMOOTH WHITE SURFACE WILL COMPLEMENT ITS COLOURFUL CONTENTS. THE PLATE'S ARMATURE IS CONSTRUCTED FROM FINE WIRE MESH, MANIPULATED TO MAKE A FLUTED EDGE. THE SEPARATELY MADE STAND IS BUILT UP USING PAPER PULP TO GIVE A CARVED APPEARANCE.

1 Draw a circle with a diameter of 30 cm (12 in) on a sheet of paper and cut it out to make a template for the dish. Tape the template to a piece of wire mesh. Wearing protective leather gloves, carefully cut around the template, using wire cutters. Trim away any sharp spurs of wire around the circle and dispose of them safely.

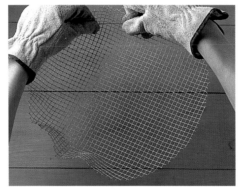

2 Pull and push the rim of the mesh disc into a fluted shape. Make sure that the fluted curves are regular, and that the base of the plate remains flat.

3 Tear wide strips of tissue paper and layer them over both sides of the plate, using paste glue. Use thinner strips of paper to cover the rim. Leave to dry.

4 To make the stand, draw a circle with a diameter of 10 cm (4 in) on a sheet of paper and cut it out to make a template. Cut out four circles from thin cardboard. Draw and cut a wavy edge around two of the circles. Cut a strip of thin cardboard measuring 18 x 5 cm (7 x 2 in). Make sure that the corrugations run from top to bottom of the stand so that you can roll it easily. ▶

MATERIALS AND EQUIPMENT YOU WILL NEED

THIN PAPER • PAIR OF COMPASSES (COMPASS) • PENCIL • SCISSORS • MASKING TAPE • PIECE OF 6 x 6 MM (¼ x ¼ IN) WIRE MESH • PROTECTIVE LEATHER GLOVES • WIRE CUTTERS • TISSUE PAPER • PASTE • TRACING PAPER • THIN CORRUGATED CARDBOARD • PVA (WHITE) GLUE • THIN RUBBER (LATEX) GLOVES • FACE MASK (RESPIRATOR) • PAPER PULP (SEE BASIC TECHNIQUES) • NEWSPAPER • WHITE EMULSION (LATEX) PAINT • PAINTBRUSH • WATER-BASED ACRYLIC VARNISH (OPTIONAL)

5 Glue two of the circles together, using undiluted PVA (white) glue, then glue the two flower shapes on top. Roll the strip of cardboard tightly, and secure the end with a piece of masking tape. Glue and tape the roll in the centre of the flower shapes. Wearing gloves and a face mask, mix a small quantity of paper pulp and use it to build up and shape the base, following the outline of the flower.

7 Tear squares of newspaper and coat them with the paste glue. Cover the entire plate with six to eight layers of papier mâché squares, then leave it to dry thoroughly.

6 Glue the two remaining cardboard circles together. When the pulp covering the base is completely dry, glue and tape the base to the middle of them. Attach the finished stand to the centre of the underside of the plate.

8 When the plate is dry, apply two coats of white emulsion (latex) paint, allowing the first coat to dry completely before the second is added. Seal the fruit dish with two coats of matt acrylic varnish, if desired.

HERALDIC WALL VASE

THIS SMALL WALL VASE HAS A HERALDIC LOOK, DERIVED FROM ITS SHIELD-LIKE SHAPE AND METALLIC FINISH, HIGHLIGHTED BY TOUCHES OF BRONZE. THE AGED METAL APPEARANCE IS ACHIEVED BY APPLYING SEVERAL COATS OF GOUACHE PAINT MIXED WITH WHITE EMULSION (LATEX) PAINT, THEN LIGHTLY RUBBING DOWN THE SURFACE TO REVEAL PATCHES OF DIFFERENT LAYERS OF COLOUR. THE VASE HOLDS AN ANTIQUE THICK-WALLED MEDICINE BOTTLE; ALLOW ENOUGH CLEARANCE AROUND THE BOTTLE FOR EASY REMOVAL.

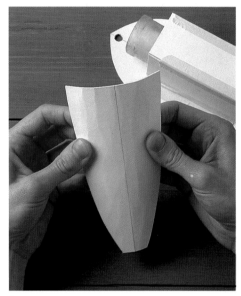

1 Trace the vase shapes from the template at the back of the book, and transfer one back and two fronts to a sheet of mounting cardboard. Place the cardboard on a cutting mat, and cut out one front and one back. Glue them together using undiluted PVA (white) glue, then carefully cut out the hole at the top of the vase back designed for hanging.

2 Measure the height and width of the bottle. Draw a central rectangle on the vase back that is 6 mm (¼ in) larger all round than the bottle. Place the bottle inside the rectangle and measure its depth. Cut three strips of cardboard 6 mm (¼ in) wider than the depth of the bottle to fit around the sides and base of the rectangle, and glue and tape them in place. Cut another rectangle of cardboard to cover the front of the bottle and glue and tape it into position, so that the bottle is boxed in.

3 Cut out the second vase front and draw a central line down it. Using your fingers, carefully bend the front into a shallow curve from the central line outwards. Place the curved front centrally over the vase, resting it against the front wall of the box that contains the bottle. Glue and tape it firmly in place to strengthen the joints. ▶

MATERIALS AND EQUIPMENT YOU WILL NEED

TRACING PAPER • PENCIL • SHEET OF MOUNTING CARDBOARD • MASKING TAPE • CRAFT KNIFE • CUTTING MAT • PVA (WHITE) GLUE •
METAL RULER • SMALL GLASS BOTTLE • SCISSORS • THIN, FLEXIBLE CARDBOARD • NEWSPAPER • POWDERED GLUE PASTE •
WHITE EMULSION (LATEX) PAINT • PAINTBRUSHES • GOUACHE PAINTS: BLUE, GREY, BROWN, BRONZE AND SILVER •
FACE MASK (RESPIRATOR) • FINE SANDPAPER • WATER-BASED GOLD SIZE • BRONZE DUTCH METAL LEAF • SOFT BRUSH • ORNAMENTAL BUTTON

4 To make the top of the vase front, hold scraps of cardboard over the openings around the shoulders of the bottle and draw round the shapes. Cut out the two resulting pieces, and glue and tape them in place. Stand the vase on a scrap of card and draw around it to make the base. Cut it out and glue and tape it in position.

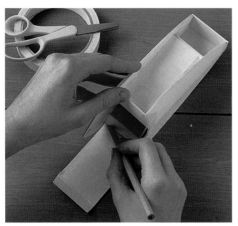

5 Place the vase on a strip of thin, flexible cardboard and draw around the outline to make one side piece. Draw around the other side, then cut out both pieces and glue and tape them in place.

6 Using glue paste, cover the vase with two layers of papier mâché squares. Leave the vase to dry thoroughly in between applying layers. Press the paper right into the areas around the joins to give them extra strength. Leave to dry.

7 Prime the surface inside and out with a coat of white emulsion (latex) paint and allow to dry.

8 Make two tones of bluish grey paint and one of warm brown by mixing gouache with white emulsion (latex) paint. Apply to the vase, allowing each coat to dry thoroughly before the next is added. When the final coat is dry, and wearing a protective face mask, lightly rub down the surface of the vase to reveal patches of the different coloured layers.

9 Paint the outlines of a small square near the top of the vase front. Apply a thin coat of water-based gold size to the square and leave it to become tacky (about 20 minutes). Apply a scrap of bronze metal leaf to the sized area with a soft brush, then glue an ornamental button in the square. Add decorative details to the sides of the vase, using bronze and silver gouache paints.

PETAL PICTURE FRAME

PLUMP, LUSTROUS PETALS GIVE THIS CAMEO FRAME A SUNNY AIR. ITS FLUTED EDGES ARE BUILT UP FROM PAPER PULP ON A CARDBOARD ARMATURE, WHICH DRIES TO A FIRM CONSISTENCY. THIS METHOD IS SUITABLE FOR MAKING AN ARRAY OF DIFFERENTLY SHAPED FRAMES, WHICH ARE IDEAL FOR DISPLAYING CAMEO-SIZED PICTURES. THE GILT CREAM FINISH RESEMBLES SILVER LEAF, BUT IS MUCH EASIER TO APPLY. SUSPENDED FROM WIDE, GROSGRAIN RIBBON, THE FRAME TAKES ON THE APPEARANCE OF A MEDALLION.

1 Trace and transfer the frame template at the back of the book to a piece of thin cardboard or paper and cut it out to make a template. Draw around the template on to a piece of heavy corrugated cardboard. Place on a cutting mat and cut out the frame, using a craft knife.

2 Cut a short length of thin copper wire and bend it over to make a loop. Push the ends of the wire into the top of one of the petals to make a hanger for the frame. Secure the hanger in place with undiluted PVA (white) glue.

3 Spread diluted PVA (white) glue over the front of the frame then, wearing rubber (latex) gloves and a face mask, build up the fluted surface with paper pulp. Use a modelling tool to help you to mould the pulp. ▶

MATERIALS AND EQUIPMENT YOU WILL NEED

TRACING PAPER • PENCIL • THIN CARDBOARD OR PAPER • SCISSORS • HEAVY CORRUGATED CARDBOARD • CRAFT KNIFE • CUTTING MAT •
THIN COPPER WIRE • WIRE CUTTERS • PVA (WHITE) GLUE • THIN RUBBER (LATEX) GLOVES • FACE MASK (RESPIRATOR) •
PAPER PULP (SEE BASIC TECHNIQUES) • MODELLING TOOL • OLD WIRE CAKE RACK • RECYCLED PAPER • PASTE • PAINTBRUSHES •
ACRYLIC GESSO • STEEL BLUE ACRYLIC PAINT • SILVER GILT CREAM • SOFT POLISHING CLOTH

4 Mould a ring around the opening of the frame, using small pellets of paper pulp. Leave to dry thoroughly on an old wire cake rack.

6 Prime the surface of the frame with two coats of acrylic gesso. Allow to dry, then add a coat of steel blue acrylic paint.

7 When the paint is dry, apply a coat of silver gilt cream to the frame, following the manufacturer's instructions.

5 When the frame is dry, tear small, thin strips of recycled paper and coat them with paste glue. Cover the entire frame with three layers of strips and leave it to dry thoroughly.

8 Gently polish the surface of the frame, using a soft cloth, to add depth and lustre to the silver finish.

FRAGRANT POMANDERS

ONCE BELIEVED TO PROTECT THE WEARER AGAINST INFECTION AND DISEASE, SWEET-SMELLING POMANDERS HAVE BEEN POPULAR FOR CENTURIES. ORIGINALLY BALLS OF AROMATIC HERBS, CARRIED TO COUNTER GERMS AND NASTY SMELLS, THEY EVOLVED INTO ROUND, PERFORATED CONTAINERS INTO WHICH THE HERBS WERE PLACED. THESE DELICATELY COLOURED PAPIER MACHE POMANDERS ARE MADE USING RUBBER BALLS AS MOULDS, AND FILLED WITH DRIED LAVENDER TO SCENT A ROOM, OR DRAWERS AND WARDROBES.

1 Smear a thin layer of petroleum jelly over the surface of each rubber ball so that it will be easy to remove the papier mâché when it is dry.

2 Tear small, narrow strips of newspaper and coat them with the glue paste. Cover each ball with six layers of strips, and stand each in an old egg cup to dry.

3 When the papier mâché is dry, draw a line around each ball to divide it into two equal halves. Secure each ball on a cutting mat with a blob of re-usable putty adhesive and cut carefully around the line, repositioning the ball as necessary. Gently separate the paper shells and leave them face-up to dry.

4 When the shells are dry, glue them back together with PVA (white) glue, aligning the cut edges precisely. Cover the joins with two layers of small, thin papier mâché strips and leave them to dry.

5 Place each dry pomander on a piece of scrap wood and pierce holes in the top with a bradawl (awl). Cut a thin section of cork into quarters. Make a small hole for the cork in the bottom of each pomander.

6 Prime the pomanders with a coat of white emulsion (latex) paint, then a coat of coloured paint, avoiding the holes. Using a paper funnel, fill each pomander with lavender and seal with the cork. Tie a ribbon bow around each pomander. Keep the ribbons in place with a blob of PVA (white) glue and pearl-headed pins.

MATERIALS AND EQUIPMENT YOU WILL NEED

PETROLEUM JELLY • SMALL SOLID RUBBER BALLS • NEWSPAPER • POWDERED GLUE PASTE • EGG CUPS • PENCIL •
RE-USABLE PUTTY ADHESIVE • CRAFT KNIFE • CUTTING MAT • PVA (WHITE) GLUE • SCRAP WOOD • BRADAWL (AWL) • ROUND CORK •
EMULSION (LATEX) PAINTS: WHITE AND A VARIETY OF COLOURS • PAINTBRUSHES • DRIED LAVENDER • DECORATIVE RIBBON • PEARL-HEADED PINS

INTRODUCTION

FEW PEOPLE, WHEN THEY SEE CARDBOARD IN USE AS AN EVERYDAY PACKING AND CARRYING MATERIAL, REALIZE HOW VERSATILE AND EXCITING A CRAFT MATERIAL IT CAN BE. IN THIS SECTION EACH PROJECT HAS BEEN CAREFULLY DESIGNED TO BE FULLY FUNCTIONAL, CREATING STUNNING BUT DURABLE PIECES FROM NEXT TO NOTHING. THIS SECTION WILL ENABLE YOU TO CREATE YOUR OWN CARDBOARD CONSTRUCTIONS BY FOLLOWING THE STEP-BY-STEP INSTRUCTIONS FOR EACH PROJECT. SIMPLE TECHNIQUES ARE GIVEN TO EXPLAIN THE DIFFERENT WAYS OF WORKING WITH THE CARDBOARD USED IN THE PROJECTS. THE GALLERY SHOWS A RANGE OF CARDBOARD STRUCTURES MADE BY ARTISTS AND SOLD IN RETAIL OUTLETS, AND AIMS TO INSPIRE YOU TO DEVELOP WORKS OF YOUR OWN DESIGN.

Left: Cardboard can be used to make a wide range of functional and decorative items.

HISTORY OF CARDBOARD

CARDBOARD HAS BEEN USED FOR OVER A HUNDRED YEARS PRIMARILY AS A PACKAGING MATERIAL. IT IS A VERY BASIC PRODUCT THAT WAS ORIGINALLY MADE FROM ROUGH WOOD PULP THAT CREATED QUITE A RAW FINISH. DESPITE ITS BLANDNESS, IT HAS BEEN EMPLOYED BY A NUMBER OF ARTISTS, DESIGNERS AND ARCHITECTS THROUGH THE DECADES. THE QUALITIES OF THE MATERIAL AND ITS AVAILABILITY AND CHEAPNESS HAVE MADE IT AN APPEALING MEDIUM TO MANY AND IT HAS BEEN USED FOR A DIVERSE RANGE OF PROJECTS.

Used mainly in the initial stages of sculpture, furniture and architectural design for mock-ups and model making, cardboard has also been used as the final product. One of the earliest noted designers to use cardboard was the Dutch furniture designer Gerrit Rietveld. In the 1920s he designed pieces that employed basic origami principles and created chairs made from single pieces of cardboard cut and folded in specific ways.

Using cardboard in a creative way became especially popular during the Second World War when resources were low. Cardboard was being used more and more as packaging for food and household goods, including ration and gas-mask boxes. Packaging was simple with very little printing on it and so it became a suitable material to use for crafts. Although it starts its life as a robust material, it becomes more fragile with time and

because of this and the fact that it was often considered a waste material, very few examples of cardboard crafts have survived. There are, however, examples of playing cards made from cardboard cigarette boxes and food packaging boxes, with the suits hand drawn on to them, made by prisoners of war.

The real growth in cardboard production started after the war when corrugated cardboard, made by combining outer layers

Above: A Christmas crib from Poland that is beautifully crafted out of cardboard.

known as liners and fluting papers in a liner-fluting-liner sandwich, became widely used. With this basic principle, a wide range of permutations could be created. By using different types of trees and varying the amounts of each ingredient used, many different cardboards could be made. As resources became available after the war, so the use of cardboard in crafts declined.

More recently, cardboard has become recognized as an acceptable material to create with. Designers in the 1960s started to explore the possibilities of cardboard but probably the most well known is Frank Gehry, an American architect who designed several pieces of cardboard furniture in the early 1980s. His "Easy Edge" chair, made from layers of cardboard laminated together, reinforced the reputation of his work for using materials despised and often not considered by fellow architects.

In the early 1980s a range of cardboard furniture was made for use in prisons. Although initially thought of as a safe and practical idea, with pieces that would not cause damage when thrown, the fire risk was thought to be too great and the furniture did not go into production.

Cardboard has, however, been used in upholstered furniture and is even available in coffin form that is now accepted by most crematoriums, making a very cheap and economical alternative to wood.

Recycling has become more and more of an issue in the last few years and the paper and cardboard industry has been recovering and re-using waste for years.

As well as being made from recycled materials – it is generally made from about 60% recycled pulp – cardboard can be transformed and recycled into craft projects when its original use has come to an end.

Right: This basket is woven from cigarette packets. It was probably made in the 1940s or 1950s, when other materials were in short supply.

Opposite: This patchwork-look laundry basket and waste paper basket are made from food packaging boxes using a traditional plaiting (braiding) technique, popular around the world, to weave flat materials together. Packing tape is used to bind around the edge of the waste paper basket and the top of the laundry basket, and a piece of carved wood is used as a handle. The laundry basket was made by Lois Walpole who is well known for her work using cardboard.

GALLERY

THE USE OF CARDBOARD IN A CREATIVE WAY HAS INCREASED ENORMOUSLY OVER RECENT YEARS. AT A TIME WHEN RECYCLING IS BECOMING MORE AND MORE IMPORTANT, MANY ARTISTS AND DESIGNERS ARE USING IT IN THEIR WORK. HERE IS A SELECTION OF SOME OF THE PEOPLE WHO ARE WORKING IN CARDBOARD AND SOME ITEMS MADE OUT OF CARDBOARD THAT CAN BE BOUGHT IN SHOPS (AT STORES) TODAY. THE DIVERSE RANGE OF STYLES ILLUSTRATES THE NUMBER OF WAYS IN WHICH THE MATERIAL CAN BE USED.

Right: COIL POTS
These coil pots are made from one long continuous strip of cardboard (food packaging boxes are used). The strip is rolled up into a coil and the outside edge is pulled up and out, to form a bowl shape. The cardboard is then carefully glued in place and covered with layers of papier mâché. Their lovely, slightly irregular quality adds to the pots' delicate look.
SARAH DREW

Left: CARTOON SHOW
This fantastic television is made predominantly from corrugated cardboard. Pieces of broken audio cassette and plastic debris have been used as additional decoration.
DAVID COX

Above: BOWL

This bowl is made from strips of unprinted packaging boxes using a twill plaiting (braiding) technique. The rim of the bowl is made from brown willow, which is flexible and strong. This is stitched on with tarred string, in keeping with the natural look of the piece. The underside of the bowl has been given a paint wash and the cardboard is coated with a polyurethane varnish to make it more durable.

POLLY POLLOCK

Left and below: FURNITURE

The Elevated Throne (left) and Chaise Longue (below) are made from rolling, stitching and weaving cardboard to create these splendid pieces of furniture. The designer uses packing cardboard and cardboard tubes as the basis for the pieces, and water-based glue and thick parcel tape to stitch them together. The cushion effect is made from parcel paper which is painted and then the whole piece is sealed with PVA (white) glue.

NIGEL WESTWOOD

Left: JAPANESE CARDBOARD ITEMS
These pieces make good use of the utilitarian look of plain cardboard. Muji produce a range of simple, well-designed accessories made from cardboard for the home. The drawers are made from single wall corrugated cardboard using a folding technique to create a very durable, practical storage idea. The round waste paper basket is made from a piece of curved corrugated cardboard held in place with plastic loops at the top and bottom. The fine flute corrugated gift bag is tied with plain cord in keeping with the overall style.
MUJI

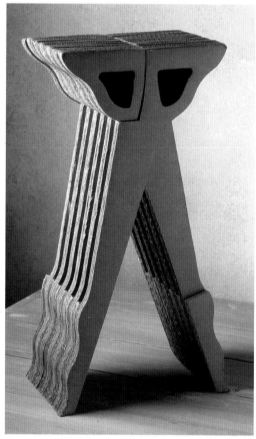

Right: STOOL
The inspiration behind this ingenious stool was the traditional Japanese head rest, but the basic principles have been given a modern interpretation. The cardboard has been used in such a way as to maximize its strength, and the stool folds up so that it can be stored easily. The individual pieces that make up the stool are die-cut by a cardboard box manufacturer and each layer is glued together to create a very stylish piece of furniture.
TOMOKO AZUMI

Left: TOY BASKET

Strips of cardboard have been woven together to make this toy or linen basket using a straight plaiting (braiding) or check weave technique. The cardboard is first painted in a colourful abstract pattern, using PVA (tempera) paints, before being cut into strips. Thin plastic tubing is used to bind around the top of the basket and a ledge is stuck inside to hold the drop-in lid in place.

POLLY POLLOCK

Above: HANDBAG

Made from strips of crisp packet boxes (food packaging boxes), this charming handbag makes use of the traditional bias plaiting (braiding) method of weaving. A plastic handle and toggle have been used to make it more practical. Although this particular example has been left in its natural state, it could be coated with a flexible varnish like polyurethane or acrylic for extra protection.

POLLY POLLOCK

Opposite:
WINDOW
DISPLAY
This cleverly
constructed
window installation
for the Conran Shop
is an ingenious way
to display products.
It was made on the
ground from layers
of single-faced
corrugated
cardboard (about
4.5km/2¾ miles
was used in total)
curved around the
products and glued
with hot glue. It was
then lifted up and
suspended from the
ceiling using thin
nylon thread pinned
through the
cardboard.
THOMAS
HEATHERWICK
(PHOTOGRAPH BY
MATTHEW MAY)

Right: ADDRESS
BOOKS
Carton Massif
design a range of
beautiful furniture
and accessories all
made from
cardboard. These
elegant address
books are made
with cardboard
constructed to
look like
panelling, then
painted in a range
of colours. They
are an excellent
example of how
plain cardboard
can be used to
create exquisite
pieces of work.
CARTON MASSIF

EQUIPMENT

MOST OF THE PIECES OF EQUIPMENT NEEDED FOR MAKING THE PROJECTS IN THIS BOOK ARE STANDARD HOUSEHOLD ITEMS. PROBABLY THE MOST IMPORTANT TOOL IS SOMETHING TO SCORE THE CARDBOARD WITH — THE BACK OF A WOODEN SPOON IS IDEAL. SOME OF THE PROJECTS REQUIRE MORE SPECIALIST (SPECIALITY) TOOLS BUT MOST OF THEM ARE OPTIONAL.

Bradawl (Awl) A bradawl (awl) is a useful tool for making small holes in cardboard (see Christmas tree decorations). It is suitable for using on most cardboards apart from single-faced corrugated boards which will tend to rip.

Clothes pegs (pins) are extremely useful for holding cardboard together while waiting for it to dry. They are also used to hold the woven basket while weaving the strips of cardboard together.

Craft knives are needed for most of the projects. A small craft knife with disposable blades is ideal so that the blade can be replaced when blunt. A heavier-weight knife is needed to cut through thick cardboard. Craft knives with small sharp points are also useful for cutting into small areas (see doll's house). Always keep the blade sharp to avoid ripping the cardboard when cutting.

Cutting mat Although quite expensive, it is worth investing in a good self-sealing cutting mat – the larger the better. The mat can be used time and again and will still have a smooth non-slip surface that makes cutting much easier.

Hammer A hammer is needed when joining metal eyelets together and making the basic wooden frame for the curtain border project.

Heavy-duty stapler A general household stapler is fine when joining lightweight cardboard, but when several thicknesses of corrugated cardboard are being secured together a heavy-duty stapler is needed.

Paintbrush A paintbrush is required for several of the projects. Use a soft-haired brush when painting corrugated cardboard so that the bristles can gently get into difficult corners.

Pair of compasses (Compass) Compasses are (A compass is) needed for drawing accurate circles and they have (it has) the added advantage that they mark (it marks) the centre of the circle, which is useful if the circle has to be divided up accurately. A sharp pencil is preferable to a pen.

Revolving hole punch is a useful tool for making neat holes in cardboard. It usually has six settings varying from about 2 mm ($1/16$ in) wide to 5 mm ($1/4$ in) wide and is easy to use.

Rulers Most of the projects require a ruler for measuring and also cutting. Wooden rulers are suitable for measuring accurately, but always use a metal ruler for cutting. Heavier-weight rulers with a rubber base are useful when cutting very thick cardboard as they do not slip.

Saws are needed for several of the projects in the book. A general-purpose saw is needed for cutting the wood for the curtain border and a smaller hacksaw is needed for cutting

the overflow tank coupler when making the card table.

Scissors in various sizes are handy when using single-faced board (packing cardboard) which can easily rip when cut with a craft knife. Small embroidery scissors are used when making the fringing for the curtain border as the blades are small enough not to cut right through the strips of cardboard. Cutting cardboard will blunt scissors quite quickly so have them sharpened regularly.

Wire cutters are needed to cut the wire for the chandelier. The wire is quite easy to cut and so lightweight wire cutters or general-purpose pliers will do the job well.

Wooden spoon A wooden spoon with a pointed end is a useful implement for scoring single and double wall cardboard because it flattens the flutes without ripping the surface of the cardboard. Any object with a blunt point will work well.

KEY

1 Bradawl (Awl)
2 Clothes pegs (pins)
3 Craft knives
4 Cutting mat
5 Hammer
6 Heavy-duty stapler
7 Paintbrush
8 Pair of compasses (Compass)
9 Rulers
10 Saws
11 Scissors
12 Wire cutters
13 Wooden spoon
14 Revolving hole punch

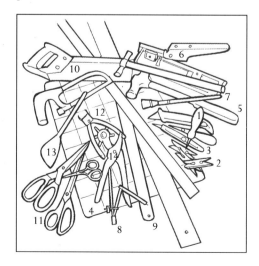

MATERIALS

HE PROJECTS IN THIS BOOK ARE MADE PRINCIPALLY OUT OF CARDBOARD, WITH A FEW USING PAINTS FOR DECORATION. IN ADDITION TO THE CARDBOARD, THE MOST IMPORTANT MATERIALS ARE THE DIFFERENT GLUES AND CLIPS TO HOLD THE CARDBOARD TOGETHER. IF MORE SPECIALIST (SPECIALTY) MATERIALS ARE REQUIRED, THESE ARE LISTED IN THE INDIVIDUAL PROJECTS.

CARDBOARDS

Corrugated cardboard is made from outer layers called liners. These are usually made from either unbleached kraft (German for strong) paper (made from a high proportion of pure wood pulp) or testliners (made from recycled waste with additives, such as starch to give strength, and dyed brown) and fluting papers, which are either water-based or semi-chemical made from hardwood pulp.

The thickness of cardboard is measured by its fluting. The fluting profile refers to the height and width of the fluting between the liners. They range from E type (height 1.2 mm/ $\frac{1}{20}$ in and width 3.25 mm/ $\frac{1}{7}$ in) to A type (height 4.7 mm/ $\frac{1}{5}$ in and width 8.5 mm/ $\frac{1}{3}$ in). The cardboards used in the projects in this book have been described in more general terms, either fine, medium or large fluting – the exact fluting size can be varied, apart from the card table and child's chair, which require the thickest cardboard available.

For the projects which require flat cardboard, think of the qualities needed for that item (whether it should be flexible, strong etc) when deciding what type to use.

Single wall corrugated cardboard is made from two layers of unbleached kraft paper with medium fluting laminated between them. It is generally used for dry food packaging and is strong and durable.

Single wall corrugated cardboard with a printed surface This is made into fruit boxes and again is strong and durable. (Both these types can be found in (at) markets and supermarkets and are therefore extremely economical to use for craft projects.)

Single wall corrugated cardboard with a smooth brown surface The fluting is medium which makes for a tough, robust cardboard with a neat finish.

Lower-grade single wall corrugated cardboard has similar qualities to the above but a slightly rougher look.

Double wall corrugated cardboard consists of an outer, inner and central liner, used to separate two layers of fluting paper. The fluting papers are usually different flute sizes from each other to increase the strength of the cardboard.

KEY

1 Single wall corrugated board
2 Single wall corrugated board with a printed surface
3 Single wall corrugated board with a smooth brown surface
4 Lower-grade single wall corrugated cardboard
5 Double wall corrugated cardboard
6 Artist's mounting board
7 Double thickness unlined chipboard
8 Bleached cardboard
9 Manila card (card stock)
10 Thin unlined chipboard
11 Recycled newspaper board
12 Unlined chipboard
13 Polyboard
14 Single-faced corrugated cardboard

15 + 17 Very fine single-faced corrugated cardboard with fine fluting
16 + 18 Medium fluted single-faced corrugated board

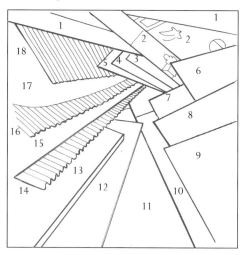

Artist's mounting board is a strong, inflexible board used to mount photographs and paintings. The board is usually white with a layer of coloured paper laminated to one side. It is available in a wide selection of colours and is smooth on the back with a slightly fibrous texture on the coloured side.

Bleached cardboard is very flexible and has a slightly glazed surface. It is ideal for projects which need to be strong but are curved or shaped. It has a very smooth finish which can be painted or covered in paper.

Manila card (card stock) has a lovely quality when it is left in its natural state, and makes an ideal material for greetings cards because it folds neatly. It is also available as oiled manila having been treated with linseed oil, which gives it a slightly mottled finish. This is generally used as stencil card (card stock) but makes a very appealing material for craft projects such as the lampshades.

Unlined chipboard is available in different weights. The thicker version is a very basic board with a slightly rough surface which is suitable for a variety of storage and box-making projects. The thicker the cardboard, the less flexible it will be.

Double thickness unlined chipboard is basically two sheets of chipboard stuck together to produce a tough, smooth-sided board. Available in its basic grey form, it can be easily painted and is suitable for straight-sided projects. It will need to be cut with a heavy-duty knife with a very sharp blade.

Thin unlined chipboard is a very basic board which is used for simple packaging. It is slightly flexible but bends and creases easily and is not particularly strong because it is made from a mixture of low-grade pulp.

Recycled newspaper board is specifically made for its decorative qualities and has similar qualities to the board above but is slightly more flexible. The flecks of newspaper are in keeping with the basic look of the board but add a more interesting finish.

Polyboard is made from two layers of very smooth bleached card laminated over a layer of polystyrene (styrofoam). It is quite strong and it cannot be folded and should be glued or pinned together.

Single-faced corrugated cardboard is usually made from a layer of chip paper or unbleached kraft paper with a wide fluted layer laminated to it. This is a general-purpose, very cheap corrugate which is used for packaging. It is used in several of the projects in this book and can be bought in very large quantities from (at) packaging suppliers or in small rolls from stationers and craft shops.

Very fine single-faced corrugated cardboard with fine fluting has very similar qualities to single-faced corrugated cardboard, but has a much smarter (more stylish), more finished look. It is very flexible and easy to cut and available in an array of bright colours as well as natural brown and grey.

Medium flute single-faced corrugated cardboard is available in several colours, as well as in metallic finishes, and is slightly less flexible than the single-faced boards because the flat cardboard used is slightly thicker.

GLUES AND PAINTS

Rubber solution glue is a spreadable glue which should be applied to both surfaces and left to dry before bonding. It has high adhesive qualities and excess glue can be removed easily by rubbing it off with your finger.

Water-based, high-tack, fast-drying glue is an excellent all-purpose glue that is ideal for sticking lighter-weight cardboards together. Because it dries quickly, it is ideal when making things which have to be held in place while drying.

Rubber solution (cement) and PVA (white) glue are easy to spread and give a strong bond, but take a while to dry thoroughly. They are therefore only suitable for projects which do not have to be held together while drying.

Spray adhesive is useful for sticking cardboard sheets together that may need repositioning. It is used for sticking two sheets together for the waste paper basket project. When the cardboard is curved to make the waste paper basket, the two layers may need to be repositioned slightly so that they bend together.

Wood glue is used on the curtain border base and is also a good glue to use for heavy-duty projects that need a strong bond.

Masking tape is a good tape to use on cardboard because it can be removed without ripping the card. Use a low-tack tape and test it on a piece of spare cardboard first.

Spray paint can be used on any cardboard and is an effective way of colouring it evenly. Available from (at) craft and DIY shops (do-it-yourself stores) in a wide selection of colours, as well as metallics, it should always be used in a well-ventilated space. Car spray paints can also be used. Alternatively, water-based paints give a good matt colour on cardboard.

Above, clockwise from bottom left: rubber solution (cement), wood glue, strong glue, PVA (white) glue, spray paint, spray adhesive and masking tape.

BASIC TECHNIQUES

CARDBOARD IS A VERY EASY MATERIAL TO HANDLE AND DOES NOT REQUIRE MANY SPECIALIST SKILLS. THE FOLLOWING ARE A FEW OF THE BASIC TECHNIQUES THAT ARE NEEDED FOR MAKING THE PROJECTS FOR THIS SECTION OF THE BOOK. READ THIS GUIDE TO BASIC TECHNIQUES BEFORE STARTING THE PROJECTS AND REFER BACK TO IT FOR ADDITIONAL INFORMATION AS NECESSARY.

SCORING FINE CARDBOARD

To bend cardboard neatly, it needs to be scored first. Always score the smooth side of corrugated cardboard or the flutes will break and look ugly. To score fine cardboard press the blade of a craft knife along the fold line, holding a metal ruler against the line and taking care not to cut into too much of the surface. Then gently fold the cardboard with the scored line inside the fold so that the outside of the fold is smooth.

SCORING ACROSS THE FLUTES ON THICK CARDBOARD

To get a neat fold on thick corrugated cardboard, use a wooden spoon with a blunt point on it or a blunt pastry wheel. Run the point of the spoon along the fold line, using a ruler as a guide. Try not to rip the surface of the cardboard; you should be just flattening the flutes.

SCORING ALONG THE FLUTES ON THICK CARDBOARD

If the score line runs along the flutes of the cardboard, just run the edge of your thumb firmly between the flutes to make an indent. Do not use your nail as this may rip the surface.

FOLDING THICK CARDBOARD

To fold thick corrugated cardboard along the scored line, hold a ruler to one side of the line firmly. Carefully push the cardboard up along the other side of the line. Hold the cardboard with the flat of your hand so that it does not bend in the wrong place.

MAKING HOLES

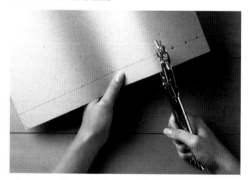

Use a revolving hole punch to make neat holes in the cardboard. Mark the position of the hole and, having chosen the required setting, squeeze the punch together firmly on the mark, twisting it slightly so that the hole will be cut properly.

MAKING CURVED SHAPES

To make curved shapes (as required for the arms of the Child's Chair project), simply mark where the curve is to be and, choosing a paint can, cup or plate of the right size, draw around a section of it on to the cardboard.

STRENGTHENING CARDBOARD

To strengthen corrugated cardboard further, sandwich several layers together with the flutes running vertically and horizontally to each other, so maximizing the strength of each layer. Use a strong glue and leave to dry completely before cutting.

PEELING OFF THE LINING PAPER

Some of the projects in this section require single wall corrugated cardboard to be bent, and to do this one of the liners needs to be removed. Sometimes this can be quite simply pulled off, but if the cardboard is tough the liner needs to be cut first.

1 With a sharp craft knife, cut slits along the flutes of the cardboard, making sure that you do not cut through to the other side.

2 Carefully peel away the strips of cardboard and discard them. Remove any small pieces of the liner that are still attached. The cardboard will now bend easily.

CURVING CARDBOARD

To curve cardboard, hold the edge of it with the palm of your hand and apply a little pressure until it bends slightly. Keep the pressure on until the cardboard will stay slightly bent when the pressure is removed.

JOINING CARDBOARD STRIPS TOGETHER

To join strips of cardboard together, cut away a small section of lining paper and fluting on the end of one strip, leaving just one layer of lining paper attached. Apply glue to this and stick the end of the other strip on top, butting up the ends.

GREETINGS CARDS AND GIFT TAGS

HOMEMADE GREETINGS CARDS ARE TO BE KEPT AND TREASURED AND MAKE A LOVELY GIFT. THESE STYLISH CARDS AND GIFT TAGS MAKE GOOD USE OF THE NATURAL LOOK OF FINE CORRUGATED CARDBOARD, WITH THIN MANILA CARDBOARD AND NATURAL RAFFIA ADDING THE FINISHING TOUCHES. CHOOSE ONE OF THESE MOTIFS OR DESIGN YOUR OWN FOR AN EVEN MORE PERSONAL APPROACH. YOU COULD MAKE ENVELOPES FROM LARGE SQUARES OF BROWN PARCEL PAPER WITH THE CORNERS FOLDED INTO THE MIDDLE AND SECURED WITH SEALING WAX. USE THEM FOR WRAPPING UP PRESENTS, TYING THEM WITH LENGTHS OF RAFFIA TO MATCH THE GIFT TAGS.

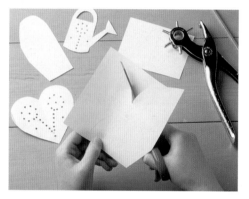

1 Trace the templates from the back of the book, enlarging to the required size, and transfer on to plain paper. Cut out the shapes and punch holes where indicated with the revolving hole punch using the smallest hole size setting.

3 Cut out the shapes from the corrugated cardboard with scissors. Punch holes where indicated, again using the hole punch on its smallest setting.

5 Cut out large rectangles of manila and natural coloured card (card stock), fold them exactly in half and stick the embroidered motifs in the centre. Cut out smaller squares and rectangles of card (card stock) and punch a small hole in each one for the gift tags. Stick more embroidered motifs on to them.

2 Place the cut-out paper shapes on to the smooth side of the corrugated cardboard and carefully draw around them with a pencil. Mark the positions of all the holes making sure that the template does not move.

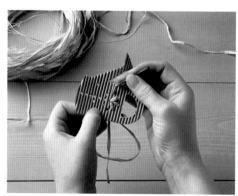

4 Cut a length of raffia and thread it through the darning needle. Stitch the shapes with the raffia using the photograph as a guide. Finish off the stitching with a small knot on the back of each shape.

6 For each gift tag, cut a length of raffia and fold in half to make a loop. Thread the loop through the hole, pass the ends through the loop and pull.

MATERIALS AND EQUIPMENT YOU WILL NEED

TRACING PAPER • PENCIL • PLAIN PAPER • SCISSORS • REVOLVING HOLE PUNCH • VERY FINE SINGLE-FACED CORRUGATED CARDBOARD •
NATURAL RAFFIA • LARGE DARNING NEEDLE • MANILA AND NATURAL COLOURED CARD (CARD STOCK) • HIGH-TACK GLUE

TABLE LAMP

CREATE AN UNUSUAL AND STYLISH TABLE LAMP BY BINDING TOGETHER RECTANGLES OF THICK, PLAIN GREY CHIPBOARD WITH SMALL KNOTS OF STRING. THE SHADE IS DESIGNED TO SIT OVER THE LAMP FITTING AND WILL CAST A WARM GLOW. MAKE SEVERAL SHADES IN DIFFERENT SIZES AND USE THEM OVER OUTDOOR NIGHT-LIGHTS FOR A SUMMER GARDEN PARTY TO LIGHT UP A PATH. PUNCH SMALL HOLES FROM THE CHIPBOARD PANELS SO THAT THE LIGHT WILL SHINE THROUGH. IF YOU ARE GOING TO USE THE SHADE OVER NIGHT-LIGHTS OR CANDLES, SPRAY THE BOARD WITH NON-FLAMMABLE SPRAY AND NEVER LEAVE IT UNATTENDED WHEN THE CANDLES ARE LIT.

1 Draw the shape for the lampshade on to a piece of chipboard: the base is 14.5 cm (5¾ in) wide, the height 25 cm (10 in) and the top 11 cm (4½ in) wide. Using a metal ruler, craft knife and cutting mat, cut out the rectangle. You will need four identical pieces.

2 With a pencil and ruler, mark a line 8 mm (⅜ in) from the edge along both long sides of each of the four pieces. Then mark a dot every 1 cm (½ in) along each line.

3 Using the hole punch, make a hole on every pencil mark along each line. Rub out all the pencil marks.

4 Hold two of the sides together. Using a short length of string, tie a double knot through the topmost holes, cutting the ends very short. Repeat at every alternate hole. Ease each knot so that it sits flat against one side of the shade rather than leaving the knot on the corner edges. Repeat until all four pieces of chipboard are held together.

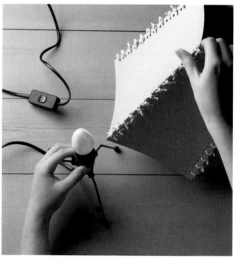

5 Assemble the simple table lamp. Place the lampshade over the lamp, guiding the flex (cord) gently between two of the sides so that it sits flat on a surface.

MATERIALS AND EQUIPMENT YOU WILL NEED

THICK UNLINED CHIPBOARD (YOU COULD USE THE BACK OF SKETCH BOOKS) • PENCIL • METAL RULER • CRAFT KNIFE • CUTTING MAT • REVOLVING HOLE PUNCH • RUBBER • STRING • SCISSORS • TWO-CORE FLEX • TWO-CORE FLEX (CORD) SWITCH • PLUG • CANDLE LIGHTBULB • PENDANT LAMPHOLDER SUITABLE FOR TWO-CORE FLEX (CORD) • 13 CM (5 IN) WIRE LAMPSHADE HOLDER

SHELF EDGING

EDGINGS ADD INTEREST TO PLAIN SHELVES AND CARDBOARD IS AN ECONOMICAL MATERIAL TO USE INSTEAD OF THE MORE TRADITIONAL LACE. CINNAMON STICKS GIVE OFF A LOVELY AROMA AS WELL AS BEING DECORATIVE AND WOULD FIT WELL ON A KITCHEN SHELF. FOR SHELVES IN A LINEN CUPBOARD, CHOOSE LITTLE BUNDLES OF LAVENDER INSTEAD. CARDBOARD EDGINGS LOOK GOOD ON FURNITURE TOO. TACK THEM ROUND THE TOP OF A TABLE OR GLUE THEM ALONG THE TOP OF CUPBOARD DOORS.

1 Draw a 12 cm (4¾ in) equilateral triangle on a scrap of plain card (card stock). Cut out and use as a template. Place on the flat side of the grey fine flute corrugated cardboard and draw around it. Move the template along so that it slightly overlaps the right-hand corner of the drawn triangle. Draw around the template and continue along the cardboard.

2 Cut out the shelf edging. Draw a line 4 cm (1½ in) from the top edge of each triangle, find the centre of each and put a pencil mark 7.5 mm (5⁄16 in) on either side of this line. Punch holes along the shelf edging at each pencil mark.

3 Trace the template from the back of the book. Cut out a star shape from plain card. Punch holes where indicated. Draw around the template on to the back of a piece of black medium flute corrugated cardboard and mark the holes. Cut 2 cm (¾ in) squares out of scraps of the corrugated cardboard, one for each triangle on your edging.

4 Make holes in the stars where marked. Punch holes in the small squares of cardboard about 1.5 cm (5⁄8 in) apart.

5 Take a length of raffia and thread it through the shelf edging from the back to the front. Thread one of the small squares on to this. Put a small blob of glue on to each end of the raffia if it is split and difficult to thread through the holes.

6 Thread the raffia through the holes in one of the stars and tie with a knot on the front. On alternate triangles place a cinnamon stick across the raffia and secure with a tight knot. Push the upholstery tacks through the shelf edging where the triangles meet and gently tack to the edge of the shelf.

MATERIALS AND EQUIPMENT YOU WILL NEED

PLAIN CARD (CARD STOCK) FOR THE TEMPLATE • PENCIL • SCISSORS • GREY FINE FLUTE SINGLE-FACED CORRUGATED CARDBOARD • CRAFT KNIFE •
CUTTING MAT • METAL RULER • REVOLVING HOLE PUNCH • TRACING PAPER • BLACK MEDIUM FLUTE SINGLE-FACED CORRUGATED CARDBOARD •
DOUBLE WALL CORRUGATED CARDBOARD • RAFFIA • GLUE • CINNAMON STICKS • BRASS UPHOLSTERY TACKS • HAMMER

CARDBOARD PLACE MATS

THESE STYLISH PLACE MATS ARE VERY EASY TO MAKE AND ADD A CONTEMPORARY LOOK TO THE DINNER TABLE. THE SMALLER GENTLY CURVING FLOWER SHAPE COULD BE USED TO MAKE COASTERS, WITH NAPKINS TIED IN CO-ORDINATING COLOURED CORDS.

MOUNTING CARD (CARD STOCK) IS AVAILABLE IN AN ARRAY OF BEAUTIFUL COLOURS, SO YOU CAN MATCH THE PLACE MATS TO YOUR CHINA. TO ADD EXTRA INTEREST, REVERSE THE COLOURS ON HALF OF

THEM SO THAT THEY CAN BE ARRANGED ALTERNATELY FOR A STRIKING LOOK. THE MATS CAN BE MADE IN ANY SIZE — MEASURE YOUR DINNER PLATES AND MAKE THE MATS LARGER SO THAT THEY WILL BE SEEN AROUND THE EDGE OF THE PLATE.

THE JOY OF CARDBOARD IS THAT IT IS VERY EASY TO WORK WITH AND EASILY RECYCLED, SO IF THE PLACE MATS GET DIRTY YOU CAN SIMPLY MAKE SOME MORE!

1 Using the diagram at the back of the book as a guide, make a template for the place mat. Draw around the template on to the mounting card (card stock).

3 Cut out both card shapes using a craft knife and a cutting mat. Ensure that the blade is very sharp and cut slowly and carefully so that the end result is very neat.

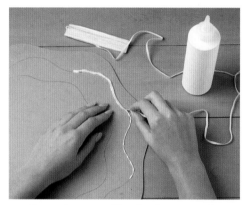

4 Draw the curved border line on to the base card (card stock) in pencil. Apply a fine line of glue, following the drawn line, then carefully stick the flat cord over the glue line. Cut and butt up the cord ends where they meet.

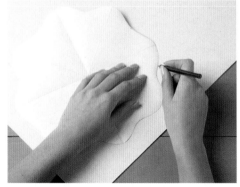

2 Make a pattern piece in the same way for the smaller inside shape and draw it on to the other colour of card (card stock).

5 Glue the inside shape in place within the curved border.

MATERIALS AND EQUIPMENT YOU WILL NEED

TRACING PAPER • PENCIL • MEDIUM-WEIGHT MANILA CARD (CARD STOCK) IN TWO COLOURS • CRAFT KNIFE • CUTTING MAT • HIGH-TACK GLUE • FLAT CORD

TRUG

THIS UNUSUAL TRUG IS A GOOD WAY TO RECYCLE OLD FRUIT BOXES. TRY TO FIND LARGE FRUIT BOXES — APPLE BOXES ARE IDEAL. SMALL FRUIT AND VEGETABLE BOXES TEND TO BE MADE FROM VERY THICK CARDBOARD WHICH WILL NOT BEND. SAVE THE LONGEST LENGTHS OF CARDBOARD FOR THE FINAL STRIPS ACROSS THE BOTTOM OF THE BASKET. A HEAVY-DUTY STAPLER IS NEEDED TO STAPLE THE SEVERAL LAYERS OF CARDBOARD TOGETHER.

THE BASKET CAN BE USED AS A TRADITIONAL GARDEN TRUG FOR CARRYING CUT FLOWERS AND TOOLS OR IT COULD BE MADE WITHOUT THE HANDLE AND USED AS A FRUIT BOWL.

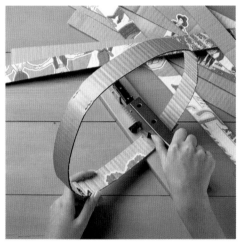

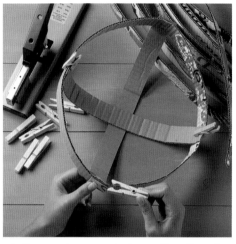

1 Cut long strips from the fruit boxes 4 cm (1½ in) wide, using a metal ruler, craft knife and cutting mat. Take two of the strips and join them together by overlapping the ends slightly and stapling them in place.

2 The strips of cardboard need to be bent slightly to make the trug. To do this, hold a strip with your left hand, gripping it between your thumb and the edge of your forefinger. Take the end of the strip with your right hand and pull it through your left hand, curving the cardboard. Repeat with all the cardboard strips.

3 Peg a strip across the loop of cardboard. Take a joined strip of cardboard and peg in position across the loop, bisecting the first strip at right angles. Staple together.

MATERIALS AND EQUIPMENT YOU WILL NEED

SINGLE WALL CARDBOARD FRUIT BOXES • METAL RULER • CRAFT KNIFE • CUTTING MAT •
HEAVY-DUTY STAPLER AND STAPLES • CLOTHES PEGS (CLOTHESPINS) • PAINTBRUSH • MATT POLYURETHANE VARNISH

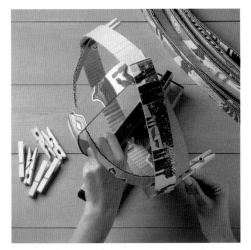

4 Staple a strip from one end of the loop to the other, overlapping each end over the strip already stapled on to it. Run it along the bottom of the loop. Always peg the strips in position to check that they are in the right place before stapling them. Cut off any excess cardboard at the end.

6 Keeping the longest strips for the bottom, peg and staple the last strip in place, overlapping the last strip on either side of the basket. Press the stapler firmly, as the staples will need to go through several layers of cardboard.

8 Join two more of the strips by stapling them together as before. This will be the rim of the basket. Peg it in place all the way round the top of the basket and staple in position approximately every 10 cm (4 in), ensuring that the staples go through all of the layers.

5 Continue to peg and then staple the strips across the initial loop, overlapping the edges slightly. Staple strips on alternate sides of the loop and keep checking that they are even on each side, otherwise they will not meet properly in the middle. Use the first stapled strip and the pegged strip as guides.

7 Take two strips and curve one of them the other way so that the plain side curves upwards. Hold these together and peg on to the basket to make a handle. When they are in the right position, staple them firmly in place, using several staples on each side.

9 When all the strips are in place, rest the basket on some scrap paper and paint with varnish. Paint along the strips and dab the varnish outside and inside the basket. Apply extra layers of varnish if you need a tougher finish, but ensure that each layer of varnish is completely dry before applying another. The varnish may discolour the cardboard slightly, so test it out on a spare piece first.

STORAGE BOXES

THESE LARGE STORAGE BOXES ARE IDEAL FOR STORING CLOTHES AND BEDDING. THEY CAN BE MADE TO ANY SIZE SIMPLY BY SCALING THE TEMPLATE UP OR DOWN, TO MAKE BOXES FOR SEWING ACCESSORIES, KITCHEN THINGS OR TO USE AS GIFT BOXES. MAKE SEVERAL BOXES AND LINE THEM UP WITH ALTERNATE CONCAVE AND CONVEX FRONTS TO CREATE A LOVELY WAVY EFFECT ALONG A SHELF. THE PAINTED MANILA PAPER AND ROPE KNOT HANDLE ADD TO THEIR UTILITARIAN LOOK BUT THE SHAPED ENDS ADD AN INTERESTING TWIST. TIE ON BROWN LUGGAGE LABELS WITH THE CONTENTS OF EACH BOX LISTED ON THEM FOR AN IDEAL STORAGE SOLUTION.

1 Using the diagrams in the back of the book as a guide, draw the six pieces of the box on to cardboard. Cut out one lid, one base, two side and two lid side pieces, using a craft knife and metal ruler for the straight edges.

2 On the side and lid side pieces, score along the short dotted lines as indicated, using a sharp instrument such as a bradawl. Fold the cardboard so that the score will be on the outside of the fold, to make the corners. Holding each side piece at the corners, bend it to curve and shape the cardboard, bending one side and one lid side piece to form a concave shape and the remaining side and lid side to form a convex shape (see Basic Techniques).

3 Dilute some cream paint to make a wash and paint lines freehand on to the manila paper using a piece of sponge cut into a 2.5 cm (1 in block). Leave the paint to dry thoroughly.

►

MATERIALS AND EQUIPMENT YOU WILL NEED

MEDIUM-WEIGHT BLEACHED CARDBOARD • PENCIL • CRAFT KNIFE • METAL RULER • CUTTING MAT • BRADAWL • CREAM WATER-BASED PAINT • MANILA PAPER • PIECE OF SPONGE • SCISSORS • WALLPAPER PASTE • GLUE • CLOTHES PEGS (CLOTHESPINS) • CREAM ROPE

4 Cut the manila paper to the same size as the cardboard side pieces, allowing an extra 3 cm (1¼ in) along the long edges. Stick the paper on to the cardboard using wallpaper paste. Fold and stick the border of manila paper along one edge of each of the four pieces. Snip into the other border at regular intervals with scissors.

6 Carefully tip the box on its side and glue the snipped edges all around the edges of the base. Leave it until completely dry.

8 Cut a piece of manila paper the same size as the lid template and glue in place on top of the box lid. Leave to dry.

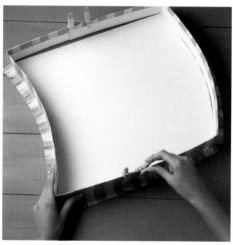

5 Place the base flat and bend the side pieces around it, matching the centre markings. Glue the overlapping edges together and hold together with clothes pegs (pins) until completely dry and secure.

7 Place the lid flat and bend the lid side pieces around it, matching the centre markings. Glue the overlapping edges together and hold together with clothes pegs (pins) until completely dry and secure. Carefully tip the lid on its side and glue the snipped edges all around the edges of the lid in the same way as before.

9 Cut a hole in the centre of the lid, through the cardboard and paper layers. Make a knot near the end of the rope, thread the rope through the hole, then tie another knot, to make a knotted handle. Cut off any excess rope and fray the ends to make tassels.

STATIONERY FOLDER AND BOX

THIS STATIONERY FOLDER AND BOX CAN BE MADE TO FIT ANY SIZE OF PAPER AND ENVELOPES AND IS A GOOD PROJECT TO MAKE TO ORGANIZE YOUR WRITING DESK. TO GIVE IT A UTILITARIAN FEEL, THE CARDBOARD IS KEPT NATURAL AND THE PLAIN CANVAS IS FINISHED WITH ROUGH HAND STITCHING. IN KEEPING WITH THE STATIONERY THEME, THE FOLDER IS HELD TOGETHER WITH PAPER FASTENERS. THE FOLDER IS FINISHED WITH TWO LOOPS OF STITCHED CANVAS PINNED ON TO BOTH HALVES OF THE FRONT WITH A TWIGGY PENCIL ACTING AS A FASTENER.

THE CORRUGATED CARDBOARD USED INSIDE THE FOLDER IS AN EFFECTIVE PEN HOLDER BECAUSE PENCILS AND PENS FIT IN BETWEEN THE RIDGES IN THE CARDBOARD.

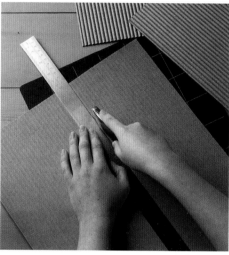

1 To make the folder, measure and cut out a rectangle of the single wall corrugated cardboard measuring 30 x 40 cm (12 x 16 in) using the metal ruler, craft knife and cutting mat. Measure and cut out two pieces of the cardboard measuring 15 x 40 cm (6 x 16 in).

2 Take a sheet of the medium flute single-faced corrugated cardboard and measure three rectangles with the same dimensions as in step 1, drawing on to the flat side of the cardboard. Cut them out.

3 Measure two rectangles 40 x 10 cm (16 x 4 in) on to the canvas. Cut out with sharp scissors.

MATERIALS AND EQUIPMENT YOU WILL NEED

SINGLE WALL CORRUGATED CARDBOARD • PENCIL • METAL RULER • CRAFT KNIFE • CUTTING MAT • MEDIUM FLUTE SINGLE-FACED CORRUGATED CARDBOARD •
NATURAL CANVAS • SCISSORS • DRESSMAKER'S PINS • EMBROIDERY THREAD (FLOSS) IN CONTRASTING COLOUR • TAPESTRY NEEDLE • PAPER FASTENERS •
TWIGGY PENCIL • HIGH-TACK GLUE • WOODEN SPOON

4 Turn over about 1 cm (½ in) all the way round the canvas, folding the corners over first. Take a long length of embroidery thread (floss), thread it through the needle and tie a knot in one end. Roughly stitch around the canvas from back to front. Do not worry about the stitches being too neat. Make sure that the needle goes through all the layers of fabric at the corners. Finish with a knot.

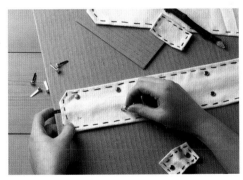

5 Make five pencil marks in the fabric at equal spaces and about 1 cm (½ in) from both long edges. Make small slits with the scissors. Place the two smaller pieces of single wall cardboard at either side of the large rectangle and lay the canvas over the joins (seams). Push the paper fasteners through the slits in the fabric and through the cardboard, opening the clips out on the back. Continue until all the paper fasteners are in place on both pieces of canvas at either side of the large rectangle. Make two small strips of stitched canvas large enough to hold the twiggy pencil and attach them to the front of the folder, one on each front piece.

6 Cut a strip of canvas measuring 22 x 7.5 cm (8½ x 3 in), then cut five right-angled triangles with two sides of 12 cm (4¾ in) and a smaller strip long enough to hold your envelopes. Turn over all the edges and stitch with embroidery thread (floss) as before. Turn the corners of the triangles over first, as in step 4.

7 For the pen holder, cut slits in the long 22 cm (8½ in) strip of canvas about 2 cm (¾ in) apart. Check that your pens will slot through each loop. Position the canvas strip across the middle of one of the smaller pieces of medium flute single-faced corrugated cardboard. Fasten with paper fasteners. Cut slits in the corners of the triangles and fasten to the larger piece of medium flute cardboard, as shown.

8 Open out the folder and apply glue to the inside. Stick the three medium flute corrugated cardboard pieces on top of the single wall cardboard pieces and press down firmly to ensure adhesion. Put the pens, paper and envelopes into the folder. Close the folder and push the twiggy pencil through the two loops on the front to keep it closed. Pull the pencil out of one of the loops to open it.

9 To make the stationary box, draw a rectangle on to another piece of the single wall corrugated cardboard 42 x 36 cm (16½ x 14 in). Draw lines 10 cm (4 in) from the edge on all four sides. Cut the whole rectangle out. Cut out two pieces measuring 8 x 22 cm (3¼ x 8½ in) for the lid flaps.

▶

10 Take the large rectangle, and draw flaps about 2 cm (¾ in) wide on both ends of what will be the longest sides of the box. Draw a line cutting the corners off. Cut out the corner sections of the large rectangle on a cutting mat, using the metal ruler.

12 Cut out two strips of canvas measuring 22 x 5 cm (8½ x 2 in) and two strips of 22 x 7.5 cm (8½ x 3 in). As before, fold over the edges by about 12 mm (½ in) and stitch in place with embroidery thread. Cut four slits along both edges (1.25 cm/⁹⁄₁₆ in) on both of the shorter strips and attach the box and lid pieces with paper fasteners. Attach the longer strips on to the lid flaps. Tie them together to close the box.

11 Use your thumb to score over the pencil lines along the length of the corrugated cardboard and use a wooden spoon against the direction of the ridges (see Basic Techniques). Bend the cardboard along the fold lines and make two small slits at each corner. Push a paper fastener through the slit and both pieces of cardboard to join the corners.

WASTEPAPER BASKET

THIS SIMPLE WASTEPAPER BASKET HAS A VERY CONTEMPORARY SHAPE WITH ITS SLIGHTLY CURVED RIM AND METAL STUDS. THE LARGE EYELET MAKES A USEFUL HANDLE. THE FLECKED CARDBOARD IS MADE FROM RECYCLED NEWSPAPER, WHICH CARRIES THROUGH THE THEME OF WASTE PAPER, GIVING A WITTY CROSS REFERENCE. TO JOIN THE TWO SIDES TOGETHER, YOU WILL NEED A LARGE EYELET (GROMMET) PUNCH TO INSERT THE EYELET. THESE ARE AVAILABLE FROM (AT) BOATING AND LEATHER GOODS SUPPLIERS.

1 Using the diagram at the back of the book as a guide, draw the shape on to the recycled cardboard. If this is very thin, stick two layers together. Cut out the shape. Decide where the eyelet (grommet) should go and draw around the inside. Cut out this circle, being careful not to go over the pencil line.

3 On the inside of one straight edge of the basket, draw a line 1 cm ($\frac{1}{2}$ in) from the edge. Do the same on the outside of the other edge. Put pencil marks every 5 cm (2 in) apart down both lines. Make holes at every mark large enough for the metal studs to fit through snugly. Glue the two edges together so that the pencil lines do not show and the holes match up.

5 Draw a circle on another piece of recycled cardboard with a radius of 10.5 cm ($4\frac{1}{4}$ in). Draw another circle inside this with a radius of 9 cm ($3\frac{1}{2}$ in), using the same centre. Cut out the larger circle. Score a line along the inner circle with a craft knife, being careful not to cut into the cardboard.

2 Place the bottom of the eyelet (grommet) punch on a solid surface and lay the larger section of the eyelet on top. Put the cardboard over this with the eyelet through the hole. Place the ring of the eyelet around the hole, then put the punch on top and hammer several times.

4 Push one half of a metal stud through one of the holes, insert the other half from the other side of the bin (basket) and hammer in place on a solid surface. Continue along the line of holes until all the studs are securely in place.

6 Cut triangles from the outside edge of the circle to the inner circle about 1.5 cm ($\frac{5}{8}$ in) apart. Do not cut into the inner circle. Continue all the way round. Fold the flaps down and apply glue to the outside of the flaps. Push the circle into the basket until it is level and sits comfortably inside. Leave to dry.

MATERIALS AND EQUIPMENT YOU WILL NEED

TRACING PAPER • PENCIL • RECYCLED NEWSPAPER CARDBOARD • SPRAY ADHESIVE • CRAFT KNIFE • CUTTING MAT • METAL RULER • 35 MM ($1\frac{1}{2}$ IN) DIAMETER METAL EYELET (GROMMET) • LARGE EYELET (GROMMET) PUNCH • HAMMER • REVOLVING HOLE PUNCH • METAL STUDS • GLUE • PAIR OF COMPASSES (COMPASS) • SCISSORS

LAMPBASE

THIS SIMPLE AND ELEGANT LAMPBASE IS MADE FROM CORRUGATED PACKING CARDBOARD CUT INTO DIFFERENT-SIZED STRIPS AND GLUED AROUND A CENTRAL CORE. BUY THE LIGHT FITTINGS FROM (AT) AN ELECTRICAL SHOP (STORE) AND SIMPLY THREAD THE FLEX (CORD) THROUGH THE HOLE RUNNING DOWN THE CENTRE OF THE LAMPBASE. IF THE LAMPBASE IS UNSTEADY, YOU CAN STICK IT ON TO A CIRCLE OF WOOD TO MAKE IT SECURE. IF THE CARDBOARD FLUTES BECOME SQUASHED DURING ROLLING, CAREFULLY RE-FORM THEM WITH YOUR FINGERS.

1 Make the base by cutting a rectangle of corrugated cardboard measuring 120 x 40 cm (47 x 15¾ in). Apply glue over the smooth side of the cardboard and roll it up, leaving a central hole to insert the flex (cord). Try to keep the roll tight to make the lampbase more stable. Hold the cardboard in place until the glue is dry.

2 Cut more strips of corrugated cardboard, varying the sizes, and glue these around the main roll. Use a long length to glue around the bottom to create a solid base. Hold the glued cardboard in place until it is stuck firmly.

3 Cut narrower strips of cardboard and glue these around the larger ones. Try them in different positions before gluing, until you are happy with the arrangement.

4 Thread the flex (cord) with the lampholder attached through the central hole until the lampholder sits on the top of the lampbase.

5 Using a craft knife, carefully cut a groove from the centre to the edge of the base of the lampbase large enough for the flex (cord) to sit comfortably in. Lay the flex (cord) in the groove and tape in place. Alternatively, stick a circle of fabric or thin cardboard on the base.

MATERIALS AND EQUIPMENT YOU WILL NEED

SINGLE-FACED CORRUGATED PACKING CARDBOARD • METAL RULER • CRAFT KNIFE • CUTTING MAT • HIGH-TACK, FAST-DRYING GLUE • THREE-CORE GOLD FLEX (CORD) • LAMPHOLDER WITH 7.5 CM (3 IN) THREADED ROD AND BRASS SWITCH • MASKING TAPE • PLUG • LIGHT-BULB

DOLL'S HOUSE

THIS QUIRKY DOLL'S HOUSE IS MADE BY SLOTTING TOGETHER THICK GREY CHIPBOARD. ITS ANGLES AND ASYMMETRY GIVE IT A RATHER RAMSHACKLE LOOK, AND THE CARDBOARD PILLARS AND SCROLLS REMOVE IT FROM THE TRADITIONAL DOLL'S HOUSE DESIGN. THE HOUSE COULD BE PAINTED WITH WATER-BASED PAINTS AND DECORATED INSIDE WITH WRAPPING PAPER OR SCRAPS OF FABRIC. ENCOURAGE CHILDREN TO MAKE THEIR OWN CARDBOARD FURNITURE FOR THEIR TOYS. THE TWO FRONT PIECES COULD BE MADE SLIGHTLY LONGER AND LEFT WITHOUT HINGES SO THAT THEY CAN JUST BE PROPPED UP AGAINST THE HOUSE AND REMOVED COMPLETELY FOR PLAYING.

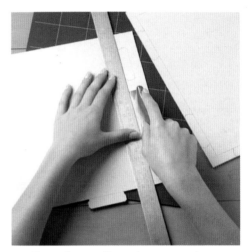

1 Using the diagrams from the back of the book as a guide, make templates for the front and the back of the doll's house. Transfer on to the chipboard. Mark the position of the window on the front piece and cut out, then cut the piece in half. Mark the positions of the slits in the back piece and carefully cut them out using a sharp craft knife, cutting mat and metal ruler.

2 Draw the two side pieces for the house on to chipboard. Cut them out, cutting carefully round the tabs. Cut out the windows and the slits where marked.

3 Draw the two floor pieces on to the chipboard and carefully cut them out. You may need to change the blade frequently to ensure that the craft knife is always sharp. ▶

MATERIALS AND EQUIPMENT YOU WILL NEED

TRACING PAPER • PENCIL • THICK UNLINED GREY CHIPBOARD • CRAFT KNIFE • CUTTING MAT • METAL RULER • HIGH-TACK GLUE •
SINGLE-FACED CORRUGATED PACKING CARDBOARD • SCISSORS • STRONG GLUE • GLUE GUN (OPTIONAL) • METAL HINGES

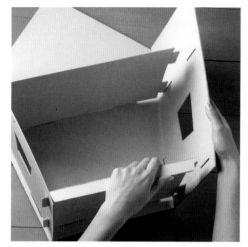

4 Score along the flap at the front of the floor piece and gently fold it over. Lay the back piece on the surface and slot the two floor pieces into this. Slot the side pieces into the back and floor pieces, easing them in gently by carefully bending the chipboard.

5 For the roof, cut out a 64 x 32 cm (25½ x 13 in) rectangle from the chipboard. Mark a line down the middle of the length. Score along the line lightly. Cut two extra pieces measuring 29 x 28 cm (11½ x 11 in).

6 Glue the two pieces of chipboard on to each half of the roof piece a few millimetres from the central score line. Carefully bend the roof so that it folds along the score line. Apply glue along the top of the two side walls and the back of the house, then stick the roof in place, butting up the panels inside the roof to the glued edges. For extra strength, glue a triangle of cardboard inside the roof.

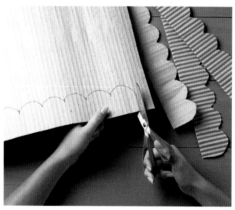

7 Using the diagram in the back of the book as a guide, draw the tile pieces on to the back of the corrugated cardboard. Cut out with scissors. Starting from the bottom, glue the tiles on to the roof, overlapping them slightly, until the whole roof is covered. Cut a strip of cardboard along the corrugated ridges and glue to the ridge of the roof.

8 Cut out rectangles of corrugated cardboard for the pillars, 6 x 32 cm (2½ x 13 in) and 6 x 30 cm (2½ x 12 in). Bend them over slightly and glue them on to each front piece. Make scrolls out of strips of cardboard, securing them with glue. Cut out the awnings using the templates at the back of the book and stick along the roof edge of the fronts. Cut strips of corrugated cardboard to edge the windows and door, and glue them in position.

9 Hold each front piece against the house in the required position and make two marks inside on the front panel and side wall for the hinges. Glue the hinges in place, using strong glue and a glue gun if necessary. Glue a strip of corrugated cardboard along the edges of the front of the roof. Cut out curtain shapes and brick shapes and glue in place.

CURTAIN BORDER

CURTAIN BORDERS, OR PELMETS, ARE PRACTICAL AS WELL AS DEC-ORATIVE IN THAT THEY DISGUISE CURTAIN HEADINGS AND POLES AND ARE AN EFFECTIVE WAY OF FINISHING WINDOW TREATMENTS.

THIS CARDBOARD CURTAIN BORDER USES WOOD AS ITS BASE TO MAKE IT MORE DURABLE. THE FINE FLUTE CORRUGATED CARDBOARD HAS BEEN DECORATED WITH STARS, BEADING AND FRINGING MADE OF CORRUGATED PACKING CARDBOARD. RAFFIA TASSELS COMPLETE THE EFFECT. THE CURTAIN BORDER CAN BE MADE TO FIT ANY SIZE OF WINDOW, HOWEVER BEAR IN MIND THAT IT SHOULD NOT DOMINATE THE WINDOW BUT ADD THE FINISHING TOUCH AND FIT IN WITH THE OVERALL SCHEME OF THE ROOM. IT CAN BE USED WITHOUT CURTAINS AS A PURELY DECORATIVE FEATURE, AS HERE.

1 Cut two pieces of wood 15 cm (6 in) long and one piece 90 cm (36 in) long. Sand all the edges smooth.

2 Apply wood glue to one end of each of the short pieces and hold them at right angles at either end of the longer piece. Hold in position until the glue has partially dried. Tack in place using the tacks and hammer.

3 Cut a piece of plywood 17.5 x 90 cm (7 x 36 in) for the top of the border. Spread glue along one edge of the curtain border frame and position the plywood on top. Tack in position. Wipe away any excess glue with a soft cloth. ▶

MATERIALS AND EQUIPMENT YOU WILL NEED

1.2 M (48 IN) OF 2.5 x 10 CM (1 x 4 IN) WOOD • SAW • TAPE MEASURE • SANDPAPER • WOOD GLUE • TACKS • HAMMER • PLYWOOD • SOFT CLOTH •
TRACING PAPER • PENCIL • GREY FINE FLUTE SINGLE-FACED CORRUGATED CARDBOARD • MASKING TAPE • METAL RULER • CRAFT KNIFE •
CUTTING MAT • LARGE FLUTE SINGLE-FACED CORRUGATED PACKING CARDBOARD • SMALL SCISSORS • RAFFIA • HIGH-TACK GLUE • DRESSMAKER'S PINS •
L-SHAPED BRACKETS • SCREWDRIVER • SCREWS

4 Using the diagram at the back of the book, make a template for the curtain border. Place the fine corrugated cardboard on the work surface smooth side up. You may need to join two pieces together – butt them up exactly and run a piece of tape along the edges to be joined. Draw a rectangle 34 x 110 cm (13½ x 43¼ in). Draw a line 10 cm (4 in) from each side edge. Draw a horizontal line 25 cm (10 in) from the bottom of the cardboard. Place the template along the top edge of the large rectangle and draw the shaped edge.

6 Cut a long strip of corrugated packing cardboard about 6 cm (2½ in) wide. Make rough snips all the way along the strip a few millimetres apart. Do not worry if some of the strips come off. Cut enough to edge the whole curtain border.

8 Enlarge the template of the star to size. Cut out three stars measuring 12 cm (4¾ in) from the corrugated packing cardboard. Mark the centre of each star, then score lines from the centre to each point. Turn over and score from the centre to the nearest points on the corrugated side. Gently fold along the score lines to make them three-dimensional.

5 Cut out the shaped piece and cut away the two 10 cm (4 in) corner pieces. Using a craft knife and metal ruler, gently score along the pencil lines, making sure that you do not cut into the cardboard. Carefully fold the cardboard over. Apply glue over the wooden frame and glue the cardboard in place.

7 Cut two pieces of spare cardboard about 12 cm (4¾ in) square. Hold the end of a handful of raffia at the bottom and bind it around both pieces about four times, ending at the same place where you started. Thread a couple of strands of raffia through the two pieces of cardboard and pull up to the top. Tie with a secure knot. Slip the blade of a pair of scissors between the two pieces of cardboard and cut the tassel off. Wrap a few strands of raffia around the tassel about 3 cm (1¼ in) from the top. Make another tassel in the same way.

9 From the grey cardboard cut a diamond slightly larger than the big star and stick it in the middle of the curtain border with the corrugated lines horizontal. Edge with strips of packing cardboard cut along the corrugated ridges and glued in position. Glue the stars on either side, then glue the fringed edging in place, pinning it until it has dried. Tape the tassels in place. Secure the curtain border to the wall with the L-shaped brackets.

CHILD'S CHAIR

THIS CHILD'S CHAIR IS MADE FROM DOUBLE WALL CORRUGATED CARDBOARD, WHICH IS AVAILABLE IN LARGE SHEETS FROM PACKAGING AND BOX MANUFACTURERS. IT COULD BE MADE EVEN TOUGHER BY USING TRIPLE WALL CARDBOARD, ALTHOUGH THIS CAN BE DIFFICULT TO GET HOLD OF. THE CONSTRUCTION OF THE SEAT, BY FOLDING THE CARDBOARD INTO TRIANGLES, MAKES A STURDY BASE AND THE SHAPED BACK CREATES A MINIATURE THRONE. PAINTED COTTON MOULDS, WHICH ARE SOLD BY JEWELLERY SUPPLIERS, ARE STUCK ON TO THE POINTS OF THE CROWN SHAPE, BUT YOU COULD USE TABLE TENNIS BALLS INSTEAD.

1 Cut a 96 x 72 cm (38 x 28½in) piece of cardboard for the back and sides. Draw a line 34 cm (13½ in) from each side edge with the corrugated ridges running vertically, leaving a 28 cm (11 in) wide centre panel.

2 Following the diagram at the back of the book, draw a line 41 cm (16 in) from the bottom edge across the two 34 cm (13½ in) widths. Draw another line 6 cm (2½ in) above that and another one 7 cm (2¾ in) above that.

3 Make a paper template of a crown shape, then draw a crown shape on the back section of the chair (following the diagram at the back of the book). Line up the bottom of the template with the lines on either side of the central panel, tape in place and draw around with a pencil. Cut along the top line on either side of the chair and around the crown shape.

4 Draw a faint line 10 cm (4 in) long and 12 mm (½ in) from the innermost line on either side of the chair back 25 cm (10 in) from the bottom edge. Draw a horizontal line 10 cm (4 in) long, 10 cm (4 in) from the end of the first line. Mark the centre of these lines and with a set square (triangle), put a mark at right angles 9.5 cm (3¾ in) from this. Join the marks together to form a triangle. Repeat this on either side of the chair. ▶

MATERIALS AND EQUIPMENT YOU WILL NEED

DOUBLE WALL CORRUGATED CARDBOARD • HEAVY-DUTY CRAFT KNIFE • METAL RULER • PENCIL • CUTTING MAT • TRACING PAPER • MASKING TAPE • SET SQUARE (TRIANGLE) • SMALL PAINT CAN OR PLATE • WOODEN SPOON • GLUE GUN • STRONG GLUE • THREE COTTON MOULDS • PAINT • PAINTBRUSH

5 Cut out the triangles using the craft knife and metal ruler. Take a small paint can or plate and use it to draw a curve on the arm of the chair. Draw a line from the edge of the curve vertically to the edge of the cardboard on the outermost panel. Cut around the curve and along the line.

6 To make the seat, draw a rectangle measuring 28 x 70 cm (11 x 27½ in) in the centre of a piece of cardboard, with the longest length cutting across the corrugated ridges. Draw two lines 10 cm (4 in) apart from each other at both ends of the rectangle. Measure and put a pencil mark 5.5 cm (2¼ in) from the corners at one end of the rectangle. Mark 4 cm (1½ in) out from the second line along and 7 cm (2¾ in) out from the next line along. Draw lines joining the marks up.

7 Measure and mark 5.5 cm (2¼ in) from the other end of the rectangle. Join the end of the first line up with these marks. Repeat on both sides of the rectangle.

8 Put marks 10 cm (4 in) from the outside lines of the centre rectangle and draw a line from these marks 10 cm (4 in) vertically. Join the bottom of the two lines together with a pencil line. Cut out the middle section.

9 Take the back piece of the chair again. Using a wooden spoon or anything with a blunt point on it, score along the two lines that form the arms. Press down firmly, but ensure that the surface is just flattened slightly and not broken. Score the arm lines and fold over.

10 Score along the lines on the seat by running the edge of your thumb along the lines between the grooves of the corrugated cardboard. Bend the cardboard along the score lines.

11 Bend the back of the chair along the score lines and carefully slot one side of the seat into the cut-out triangles. Gently ease the other side of the seat into the triangles on the other side. The side piece may need to be bent very gently to slot it in, but be careful not to bend it too much. Glue along the edge of the arms with strong glue and fold it over and stick it on to the side of the chair. Paint the cotton moulds and glue them on to the points of the crown shape.

OAK LEAF FRAME

THIS ORNATE BAROQUE "GILT" PICTURE FRAME, DECORATED WITH OAK LEAVES, IS BASED ON A TRADITIONAL FRAME. FOLDING THE LEAVES SLIGHTLY AND ARRANGING THEM IRREGULARLY GIVES THE FRAME MORE DEPTH.

THIS PROJECT HIGHLIGHTS THE VERSATILITY OF CARDBOARD, TURNING IT FROM A PLAIN, BASIC MATERIAL INTO SOMETHING MUCH MORE ORNATE WHICH, WHEN SPRAYED GOLD, CAN EVEN EMULATE TRADITIONAL GILDING.

1 Cut a rectangle measuring 40 x 48 cm (16 x 19 in) from the medium flute corrugated cardboard. Draw a smaller rectangle inside this 14 cm (5½ in) from the edge. Cut out the centre opening on a cutting mat.

2 On the smooth side of the fine flute corrugated cardboard, draw a line 2 cm (¾ in) from the edge and then parallel lines 3 cm (1¼ in), 2 cm (¾ in), 6 cm (2½ in), 1.5 cm (⅝ in), 1.5 cm (⅝ in) and 5 mm (¼ in) apart from each other. Cut along this last line (strip measures 16.5 cm (6¾ in) wide). Cut two lengths 48 cm (19 in) long.

3 Cut the corners off the 2 cm (¾ in) strip. Using a craft knife and metal ruler, gently score along the parallel lines, being careful not to cut the cardboard. Cut the opposite corners at a 45-degree angle, from the end of the second line to the edge of the cardboard.

4 Fold the cardboard along the score lines. Draw a line along each side of the frame 12 cm (4¾ in) from the edge. Glue the strip with the corners cut off along the edge of the long side of the frame. Fold the cardboard over, lining up the edge with the pencil line, and glue in place. ▶

MATERIALS AND EQUIPMENT YOU WILL NEED

MEDIUM FLUTE SINGLE WALL CORRUGATED CARDBOARD • METAL RULER • PENCIL • CRAFT KNIFE • CUTTING MAT •
FINE FLUTE SINGLE-FACED CORRUGATED CARDBOARD • HIGH-TACK GLUE • LARGE FLUTE SINGLE-FACED CORRUGATED PACKING CARDBOARD •
CARD (CARD STOCK) FOR TEMPLATES • TRACING PAPER • SCISSORS • GOLD SPRAY PAINT

5 Cut two more strips of scored cardboard 40 cm (15¾ in) long for the top and bottom of the frame. Cut off the corners and stick these two strips and the remaining long piece in place. It does not matter if the corners do not meet exactly. Leave to dry.

6 Cut a strip of large flute corrugated packing cardboard 2 cm (¾ in) wide and stick it along the inner strip of the frame as shown. Mitre the corners.

7 Trace the leaf-shaped template from the back of the book and enlarge to size. Cut out small and large oak leaf shapes from the fine flute and large flute cardboard. Score a line along each leaf on the smooth or corrugated side so that they can be bent a little.

8 Trace the second template from the back of the book and enlarge to size. Cut out four shapes from large flute cardboard. Fold them over, smooth side out, and glue the ends together. Cut strips of cardboard about 12 mm (½ in) wide and 50 cm (20 in) long. Loop them over three times and glue together at the bottom. Glue on to the first shape. Repeat on the other three and glue one to the middle of each side of the frame.

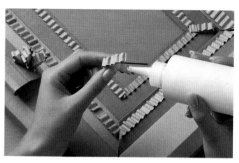

9 Cut strips of large flute cardboard about 12 mm (½ in) wide and edge the frame opening, leaving a gap a few millimetres from the edge. Glue a small loop of cardboard to each corner.

10 Make four more loops of large flute cardboard strips and secure with glue. Stick one to each corner. Arrange the leaves in the desired design, overlapping them slightly. When you are happy with the design, glue them all in place.

11 When the glue is dry, put the frame on some scrap paper in a well-ventilated space and spray with gold paint. Spray the underside of the leaves, covering them as evenly as you can with the paint.

SUNBURST CLOCK

THIS SUNBURST CLOCK WITH ITS GENTLE RADIATING CURVES IS MADE BY GENTLY SCORING AND FOLDING THIN CHIPBOARD. A SIMPLE BATTERY-OPERATED CLOCK MECHANISM CAN BE BOUGHT FROM CRAFT SUPPLIERS AND IS EASY TO SLOT THROUGH THE CHIP-BOARD CLOCK FACE, OR OLD CLOCK PARTS WITH ORNATE HANDS CAN BE USED INSTEAD. GILT CREAM GIVES A MATT GOLD FINISH THAT IS DIFFERENT FROM THE FINISH OF METALLIC PAINT. APPLYING THIS OVER DEEP RED PAINT GIVES THE GOLD A DEEPER, ANTIQUE LOOK.

1 Trace the templates from the back of the book and enlarge to your required size. Draw the main clock shape on to the chipboard. Cut out the inner shape and the two hands with a craft knife and metal ruler. Do the same on the main clock shape, but cut the curved part out freehand with the craft knife.

3 Turn the chipboard over, draw lines on the back, and score, as before. Turn the inner piece over and score along the lines on that as well.

5 Using a soft cloth, gently wipe the gilt cream all over the clock slightly unevenly so that some of the red paint just shows through. Leave to dry.

2 Score along all the pencil lines gently on the front of the clock face with the craft knife, being careful not to cut the chipboard. Do the same on the inner piece. Score along the lines on the hands.

4 Gently fold along all the score lines ensuring that the chipboard does not crease. Concertina (Accordion) the fold lines together to make the folds. Do the same with the centre piece. Paint all the pieces with the red paint and leave to dry.

6 Cut holes into the middle of the back and front pieces of the clock and push through the clock mechanism. Screw on the metal screw. Glue the cardboard hands on to the plastic ones and push on to the clock.

MATERIALS AND EQUIPMENT YOU WILL NEED

TRACING PAPER • PENCIL • PAPER FOR TEMPLATE • THIN UNLINED CHIPBOARD • CRAFT KNIFE • METAL RULER • CUTTING MAT •
DEEP RED WATER-BASED PAINT • PAINTBRUSH • SOFT CLOTH • GILT CREAM • CLOCK PARTS

CHANDELIER

THIS ELEGANT CHANDELIER WILL LIGHT UP ANY DINNER PARTY. MADE IN THE STYLE OF A TRADITIONAL CRYSTAL CHANDELIER, WITH STRINGS OF BEADS AND CRYSTAL-SHAPED DROPLETS, IT IS AN EXTREMELY CHEAP ALTERNATIVE. USING A CARDBOARD TUBE AS ITS CENTRAL CORE, THE ARMS ARE MADE FROM GALVANIZED WIRE, THEN COVERED IN CORRUGATED PACKING CARDBOARD. SMALL METAL PÂTISSERIE TINS ARE USED AS THE CANDLE HOLDERS FOR CANDLES OR NIGHTLIGHTS. MAKE SURE THAT THESE ARE NOT TOO HEAVY OR THE ARMS WILL DIP TOO MUCH AND THE CHANDELIER WILL LOSE ITS DELICATE SHAPE. NEVER LEAVE THE LIGHTED CANDLES UNATTENDED.

1 Measure a 28 cm (11 in) length of thick cardboard tube and cut with a saw. You may need to sand the cut edge.

2 Draw a line round the tube 3 cm (1¼ in) from the end. Mark six pencil marks on the line, measuring them with a tape measure to ensure that they are about the same distance apart. Using the bradawl (awl), make holes at these points. Make three holes about 2 cm (¾ in) from the other end, with equal spaces between them.

3 Cut six lengths of wire 110 cm (44 in) long using wire cutters. Take one piece of wire and hold it against the bottom of the glass candle holder. Carefully bend the wire so that it coils around the candle holder two to three times. Then bend the wire down into a curve. Use the first coil of wire as a guide for the remaining five wires, so that they are all the same shape.

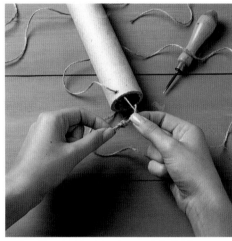

4 Cut three lengths of string measuring 60 cm (24 in) long. Thread them through the holes at the top of the tube, securing them with a large knot inside the tube. Put tape on the end of the string if it will not go through the holes easily. Tie the three pieces of string together near the ends with a knot.

▶

MATERIALS AND EQUIPMENT YOU WILL NEED

TAPE MEASURE • PENCIL • THICK CARDBOARD TUBE • SAW • FINE SANDPAPER • BRADAWL (AWL) • 2 MM (⅟₁₆ IN) GALVANIZED WIRE • WIRE CUTTERS •
GLASS CANDLE HOLDER • STRING • MASKING TAPE • LARGE FLUTE SINGLE-FACED CORRUGATED PACKING CARDBOARD • HIGH-TACK GLUE •
TRACING PAPER • MEDIUM FLUTE SINGLE-FACED CORRUGATED CARDBOARD • CRAFT KNIFE • CUTTING MAT • SCISSORS •
METAL RULER • SIX PÂTISSERIE TINS (TART PANS)

5 Push the straight end of one of the wire arms through a hole in the bottom of the tube and feed it through to the top. Bend the end of the wire over the top of the tube – about 2 cm (¾ in). Do the same with the five remaining wire arms.

7 Cut strips of large flute corrugated packing cardboard 2.5 cm (1 in) wide and long enough to cover the coils of wire. Apply glue to the flat side. Glue around the coiled ends of the wire arm, and hold in place until stuck firmly.

9 Trace the bead templates from the back of the book. Draw about 150 small shapes (75 round ones, 75 elongated ones) and six droplet shapes on the medium flute corrugated cardboard. Cut out with a craft knife on a cutting mat.

6 Cut lengths of large flute corrugated packing cardboard 1.5 cm (⅝ in) wide and long enough to run down the tube and along the arm of the chandelier, plus about 10 cm (4 in) extra. Coil the end of the strip over at the end and glue the strip down the tube and along the wire arm. Glue another strip along the underside of the arm. Hold in place until the glue has dried. Do the same on the remaining five arms.

8 Roll up strips of large flute packing cardboard tightly and then let go to make loose coils. Make 12 coils and stick six on the bottom of the tube between the long strips and six on the underside of the arms.

10 Cut 12 lengths of string and thread the cardboard beads on to them – 12 on each string. You will need 12 strings of beads. Glue on to the chandelier from the top of the tube to the arms, draping them slightly. Thread string through the droplets, add a bead, then tie and glue them on to the underside of the coils of wire at the ends of the arms. Finish by gluing strips of cardboard around the top and bottom of the tube. Hang the chandelier up with the string at the top of the tube, which can be altered to any length. Place pâtisserie tins (tart pans) in the wire coils.

TRAY

GLUING TOGETHER LAYERS OF SINGLE WALL CORRUGATED CARD-BOARD MAKES A STURDY TRAY, ALTHOUGH ONE THAT IS MORE FOR DECORATION THAN EVERYDAY USE. THE HANDLES, MADE BY PUSHING PAPER FASTENERS THROUGH THE CARDBOARD AND THEN BENDING THEM INSIDE THE ROLLED HANDLE, ARE SURPRISINGLY STRONG. USE CARDBOARD THAT HAS A VERY FLAT, SMOOTH LAYER ON AT LEAST ONE SIDE, RATHER THAN CARDBOARD THAT SHOWS FLUTE LINES, FOR A SMARTER LOOK. THE TRAY COULD BE VARNISHED TO MAKE IT MORE ROBUST OR IT COULD BE PAINTED OR DECORATED WITH COLLAGE OR DECOUPAGE AND THEN VARNISHED.

1 On the cardboard draw out ten rectangles 38 x 50 cm (15 x 20 in). Cut them out on the cutting mat using the metal ruler and craft knife. Draw the pencil lines on the wrong side of the cardboard (not the side that will show).

2 Draw a line 5 cm (2 in) from the edge on six pieces of the cardboard, and cut out the centre rectangle on each one. Put the spare pieces aside to use for the handles.

3 Take one of the large pieces of cardboard and again measure 5 cm (2 in) from the edge all the way round. Draw an equilateral triangle measuring 3 cm (1¼ in) on a piece of spare card (card stock). Cut it out. Starting at the centre and working towards the corners, place the triangle template along the inner side of one of the pencil lines and draw around it, again on the wrong side of the cardboard.

4 Continue along all four sides, finishing with a square at each corner. Cut out around the triangles, cutting from the pencil line to the point of the triangles.

▶

MATERIALS AND EQUIPMENT YOU WILL NEED

SINGLE WALL CORRUGATED CARDBOARD • PENCIL • METAL RULER • CRAFT KNIFE • CUTTING MAT •
TRACING PAPER • TWO LARGE METAL PAPER FASTENERS • HIGH-TACK GLUE

5 On two of the remaining complete pieces of cardboard, draw lines 7.5 cm (3 in) from the edges all the way round. Cut out the inner rectangles and discard.

7 Following the diagram at the back of the book, make a template for the handle. Cut out a cardboard triangle and cut holes as indicated. Peel off one side of the cardboard.

9 Push the roll down on to the cardboard stems. Spread glue on the underside of the loose flap of cardboard and press in place. Hold firmly until the glue is dry.

6 On the back of one of the first pieces of cardboard, measure two points 10 cm (4 in) apart on either side of the centre of each short side. Make small slits with a craft knife. Insert a paper fastener into each slit from the wrong side. Cut pieces of cardboard measuring 5 x 3 cm (2 in x 1¼ in) and peel the back off (see Basic Techniques). Wrap them round the base of the paper fasteners and glue in position.

8 Roll up the triangle of cardboard quite tightly and hold it firmly in position. Push the roll on to the paper fasteners. It should slot on to the fasteners quite easily. If it does not, then push firmly so that the fasteners push through the cardboard.

10 Lay the remaining complete piece of cardboard right side up on your work surface. Glue the back of each piece. Glue on the two pieces with rectangles cut out, then the piece with the triangular edge. Finally glue the six rectangular frames on top of each other, finishing with the handles. Wipe away any excess glue with your finger.

WALL SCONCE

THIS ELEGANT WALL SCONCE LOOKS LIKE AN OLYMPIC TORCH WITH ITS CORRUGATED CONE AND CARDBOARD FLAMES. MAKE A PAIR OF THEM AND DISPLAY ONE ON EITHER SIDE OF A PAINTING OR ILLUMINATE YOUR HALLWAY.

A SMALL METAL PÂTISSERIE TIN IS USED AS THE CANDLE HOLDER. AS A SAFETY PRECAUTION, THE SCONCE MUST BE SPRAYED WITH A NON-FLAMMABLE SPRAY BEFORE USE. USE TALL CANDLES AND NEVER LEAVE THEM UNATTENDED WHEN THEY ARE LIT.

1 Trace the oval template from the back of the book and enlarge to size. Cut out one oval from single wall cardboard measuring 18 cm (7 in) at the longest length, and one smaller oval measuring 10 cm (4 in) at its longest length. For each oval, cut out three slightly larger pieces of cardboard. Stick one of the ovals on to one piece of cardboard and cut round it. Repeat with the two remaining pieces. Do the same with the other oval. (Each oval now has four layers of cardboard.)

2 Measure and cut out a piece of cardboard 25 x 11 cm (10 x 4½ in), with the shortest edge running along the grooves. Peel the back off either by gently pulling it away or by cutting it in strips if it is very tough (see Basic Techniques). Cut two smaller strips of corrugated packing cardboard measuring 12 x 2 cm (4¾ x ¾ in) wide.

3 Spread glue over the corrugated side of the rectangle of cardboard and roll it up tightly. Hold it in place until the glue has dried. Put glue on the flat side of the two smaller strips and glue them on to the ends of the roll. Glue the small oval of cardboard in the middle of the large one. ▶

MATERIALS AND EQUIPMENT YOU WILL NEED

TRACING PAPER • PENCIL • SINGLE WALL CORRUGATED CARDBOARD • CRAFT KNIFE • CUTTING MAT • METAL RULER • HIGH-TACK GLUE • SINGLE-FACED CORRUGATED PACKING CARDBOARD • PAIR OF COMPASSES (COMPASS) • SMALL METAL PÂTISSERIE TIN (TART PAN) • NON-FLAMMABLE SPRAY • PLATE HOOK DISK

4 Put glue on one end of the roll of cardboard and stick it on to the middle of the small oval. Apply plenty of glue because the adhesion needs to be fairly strong. Using a pair of compasses (compass), draw a circle on to a piece of single wall cardboard with a radius of 2.5 cm (1 in). Cut it out, stick it on to another piece of cardboard and cut out so that the circle is two layers thick. Glue on to the end of the roll.

5 On the smooth side of a large piece of packing cardboard, draw a right-angled triangle 54 cm (21½ in) wide and 29 cm (11½ in) long. Cut it out with a very sharp craft knife. Packing cardboard tends to tear if the blade is not sharp.

6 Starting from the longest length, roll up the triangle, applying blobs of glue every so often and finishing by gluing the end in place. Be careful not to squash the cardboard as you roll it. Gently reshape any grooves that are slightly flat.

7 Stick the rolled cone on to the circle on the end of the roll (see step 4). Cut out a circle with a radius of 2 cm (¾ in), one with a radius of 2.5 cm (1 in) and another one with a radius of 4 cm (1½ in). Using the method from step 1, make the two smaller circles two layers of cardboard thick and the largest circle four layers thick. Glue them all centrally on top of each other in graduating sizes and stick on to the cone.

8 Trace the flame-shaped templates from the back of the book, enlarging to size, and cut out five of the larger shaped flames and five of the smaller shapes from packing cardboard. Draw the shapes on the flat side and cut out with a craft knife, ensuring that it is very sharp. Glue the large flame shapes around the pâtisserie tin (tart pan).

9 Continue to stick the flame shapes on to the dish, sticking the smaller shapes between the large shapes. Glue the dish on to the sconce and gently bend the flames so that they are slightly curved away from where the candle will sit. Cut a strip of packing cardboard 15 x 1 cm (6 in x ½ in) and glue it around the base of the pâtisserie tin (tart pan) and flames. Spray the whole sconce with a non-flammable spray. Glue a plate hook disk on to the back for hanging.

WALL BRACKET

ADD A TOUCH OF FOLLY TO A ROOM WITH THIS CARDBOARD WALL BRACKET. THE WHITE-PAINTED DESIGN EMULATES OLD PLASTERWORK AND THE TRADITIONAL ACANTHUS LEAVES GIVE IT A CLASSICAL LOOK. THE WALL BRACKET COULD BE LEFT IN ITS NATURAL CARDBOARD FINISH FOR A CONTEMPORARY LOOK, OR PAINTED TO MATCH THE COLOUR OF THE WALL WHERE IT WILL HANG. USE IT TO DISPLAY A VASE (CHECK THAT IT IS STRONG ENOUGH) OR TO HOLD POSTCARDS OR PHOTOGRAPHS. IT WILL LOOK ESPECIALLY GOOD IN A ROOM WHERE THE ORIGINAL PLASTERWORK FEATURES HAVE BEEN RETAINED.

1 Measure and cut out two rectangles of double wall cardboard 20 x 16 cm (8 x 6¼ in). Glue them together. Cut out two rectangles measuring 18 x 20 cm (7 x 8 in) and glue them together.

2 From the same cardboard, cut out two rectangles measuring 14 x 17 cm (5½ x 6¾ in) and two more 15 x 17 cm (6 x 6¾ in). Glue them together.

3 Take the two larger pieces of double wall cardboard from step 1. Apply glue to the longer edge of the smaller piece and place it flat on the work surface. Ensuring that it is the right way round, press the other piece at right angles against the glued end and hold it in place firmly until it is dry. Do the same with the two smaller pieces of double wall cardboard, then glue these inside the larger bracket.

4 From the corrugated packing cardboard, cut out a rectangle measuring 100 x 30 cm (40 x 12 in). Draw a line on the corrugated side 7.5 cm (3 in) from both long edges using a ruler. Carefully score along the line with a craft knife, taking care not to cut into the cardboard.

▶

MATERIALS AND EQUIPMENT YOU WILL NEED

DOUBLE WALL MEDIUM FLUTE CORRUGATED CARDBOARD • CRAFT KNIFE • CUTTING MAT • GLUE • SINGLE-FACED CORRUGATED PACKING CARDBOARD • PENCIL • METAL RULER • TRACING PAPER • SCISSORS • WATER-BASED WHITE PAINT • PAINTBRUSH • PLATE HOOK DISK

5 Fold the packing cardboard over along the score lines with the corrugated sides together. Roll it up loosely from one end, with the join (seam) on the inside, to form a large roll. Turn the cardboard over and roll from the other end to form a scroll shape. Glue both rolls in place.

6 When the glue is dry and the scroll stuck firmly, apply glue along the top and back of the scroll and fix it (put) in position on the bracket. Leave to dry.

7 Cut strips of packing cardboard about 1 cm (½ in) wide and long enough to fit right round the scroll. Glue the corrugated sides, stick them on to the scroll about 2 cm (¾ in) from the edge. Cut a smaller strip about 4 cm (1½ in) wide and stick it over the join (seam) on the lower part of the scroll, then stick a strip of 1 cm (½ in) wide cardboard, corrugated side up, down the middle of that.

8 Cut long strips of packing cardboard wide enough to cover the edges of the bracket and glue in place. Stick the strips around the edge of the large outer bracket and along the edge of the smaller inner bracket. Hold them in place to ensure a good adhesion.

9 Trace the template from the back of the book and enlarge it, then cut out the acanthus leaves in four different sizes. Draw round the shapes on to the flat side of the packing cardboard and cut them out with scissors. Cut a strip of cardboard, about 17 cm (6¾ in) long and 2 cm (¾ in) wide at one end, tapering to 1 cm (½ in) wide at the other.

10 Glue the leaves in place on to the scroll, smallest at the top, overlapping them slightly so that they curl upwards. Glue the tapered strip down the middle. When the glue is dry, paint the bracket with white paint, dabbing the brush inside the scroll and behind the leaves so that no plain cardboard is visible. Glue a plate hook disk on to the back.

CARD TABLE

THE INGENIOUS CONSTRUCTION OF THIS TABLE MEANS THAT IT IS NOT ONLY A VERY STRONG, STURDY PIECE OF FURNITURE, BUT DUAL PURPOSE AS WELL. SWIVEL THE TOP ROUND AND OPEN IT OUT TO USE IT AS A CARD TABLE OR KEEP IT FOLDED AS A SIDE TABLE. THE TABLE ILLUSTRATES THE DURABILITY OF CARDBOARD AND SHOWS THAT IT REALLY CAN BE USED FOR SO MANY THINGS WHEN THE CONSTRUCTION IS CAREFULLY THOUGHT OUT. WHEN PUTTING THE TABLE TOGETHER, WORK ON A VERY FLAT, SOLID SURFACE TO ENSURE THAT THE LEGS AND RAILS ARE ALL LEVEL SO THAT THE TABLE WILL NOT WOBBLE.

1 Following diagram A at the back of the book, draw and cut out four leg pieces from cardboard. Using the wooden spoon and wooden ruler, score along the fold lines. Press down firmly, being careful not to rip the cardboard.

2 Carefully fold the cardboard along the lines, gently easing it into place. Lift and fold the central line away from the surface and fold the lines on either side the other way so that the cardboard concertinas (acordions) slightly.

3 Fold the cardboard right over so that the two flat edges meet. Apply wood glue to one side and press them together firmly. Put elastic (rubber) bands around the whole leg to keep the glued flaps together.

MATERIALS AND EQUIPMENT YOU WILL NEED

TRACING PAPER • PENCIL • DOUBLE WALL CORRUGATED CARDBOARD • METAL RULER • HEAVY-DUTY CRAFT KNIFE • CUTTING MAT • WOODEN SPOON • WOODEN RULER •
WOOD GLUE • ELASTIC (RUBBER) BANDS • CLOTHES PEGS (PINS) • PLASTIC OVERFLOW TANK COUPLER (2 CM/¾ IN) • HACKSAW • SCISSORS • FELT • PVA (WHITE) GLUE

4 Peg (pin) the glued flaps together with a clothes peg (clothespin) to hold them in place . Leave to dry completely. Repeat with the remaining three legs. Remove the pegs (clothespins) and elastic (rubber) bands.

5 Using diagrams B and C as a guide, cut out four side rails – two long and two short. Score along the fold lines with the wooden spoon on all four pieces.

6 Carefully fold the cardboard along the long scored lines until the side flaps meet. Apply plenty of wood glue to one side and sandwich the rail together.

7 Put elastic (rubber) bands around the rail until it is completely dry. Repeat with the remaining three rail pieces. Remove the elastic (rubber) bands when the glue is dry.

8 Following diagram D, cut out a piece of cardboard for the cross rail. As before, score along the fold lines and fold the longest lines over. Stick in place with wood glue and secure with elastic (rubber) bands until dry. Remove the elastic (rubber) bands and fold the end flaps over.

9 Take a side rail and slot it into the top of one of the legs of the table. Bend the longest flap over at each end of the rail so that it forms a triangle with the other smaller flap. When you are sure that the rail piece fits well into the leg, glue it in place.

10 Slot the other side rail pieces into the legs, again making sure that they fit well before gluing in place. Make sure that all the rails are the right way up. The single fold should be at the top.

▶

11 Take the cross rail and slot it between the two long rails as shown in diagram G. It should be a snug fit. Glue in position and then leave to dry completely.

12 Cut out a rectangle of cardboard 130 x 100 cm (51 x 39½ in) and two pieces 100 x 75 cm (39½ x 29½ in) for the table top (see diagrams E and F). Measure and draw a line 10 cm (4 in) from the edge all the way round on each piece. Mitre the corners so that when they are folded over the corners will fit neatly together. Score along the pencil lines with the wooden spoon. Fold the flaps inwards, and cut out a rectangle of cardboard to fit inside the central area. Repeat for each piece of the table top, but for the larger rectangle cut it in half. Stick the rectangles in place then glue down the flaps. Weigh down the corners with weights or pans of water until the glue is dry.

13 Next, mark the position of the swivel joint (the overflow coupler) on one of the smaller pieces of the table top. Measure 21 cm (8¼ in) from one end of the inset rectangle and 7.5 cm (3 in) from the longest edge. Saw the overflow coupler in half and draw around the widest part. Cut out a hole in the inset layer of cardboard. Cut a smaller hole (wide enough for the thread of the coupler to fit through) in the other layer of cardboard. Insert the coupler.

14 Place the large piece on the work surface, mitred side up, and apply glue liberally all over it. Stick the two smaller pieces on top, lining up the corners. Put weights on top while it dries.

15 Cut out a piece of felt and stick it on to the solid side of the cardboard table top with PVA (white) glue. Press it down well and smooth out any air bubbles with the palm of your hand. When the glue is dry, fold the table top in half and bolt the top on to the base using the coupler. To open the table out, turn it so that it lies flat on the base.

16 Cut a hole in the crossrail to take the coupler in diagram E. Lay the table top on the surface crossrail with the coupler sticking up. Push the coupler through the hole in the cross rail, put the washer on top and screw the nut on tightly.

CHEST OF DRAWERS

THIS CHEST OF DRAWERS IS MADE FROM CHILDREN'S SHOE BOXES PAINTED IN LOVELY BRIGHT COLOURS, SO IT WILL APPEAL TO CHILDREN OF ANY AGE. IT CAN BE MADE BIGGER USING LARGER SHOE BOXES AND IS IDEAL FOR STORING STATIONERY, SEWING TOOLS AND BITS AND BOBS (ODDS AND ENDS) AS WELL AS CHILDREN'S THINGS. FOR A FINAL DECORATIVE TOUCH, PAINTED WOODEN HANDLES OR TASSELS LOOK GREAT AND KNOTS OF COLOURFUL CORD COULD ALSO BE USED TO EMBELLISH THE BOXES.

1 Measure the height and width of one box and multiply both measurements by three, then measure the length of one box, and add 1 cm ($\frac{1}{2}$ in) to each of these three measurements. Cut eight pieces of polyboard: two for the top and base, which are the length by the width plus the thickness of four pieces of polyboard; two for the horizontal struts, which are the length by the width plus the thickness of two pieces of polyboard; and four for the vertical struts, which are the length by the height plus the thickness of two widths of polyboard. Cut slits wide enough to take the thickness of one piece of polyboard a third and two thirds of the way along two of the horizontal struts and two of the vertical struts.

2 Slot the pieces of polyboard together at right angles as shown. Put to one side.

3 Lay one of the pieces of polyboard you cut for the top and base on the work surface. This will be the base. Glue the two remaining vertical struts at right angles at either end of the base. Pin them in place to secure. When the glue has dried, glue the top pieces, pinning them in place. Leave to dry. ▶

MATERIALS AND EQUIPMENT YOU WILL NEED

NINE SHOE BOXES • METAL RULER • POLYBOARD • PENCIL • CRAFT KNIFE • CUTTING MAT • WOOD GLUE • DRESSMAKER'S PINS • WATER-BASED PAINTS IN THREE COLOURS • PAINTBRUSH • NINE WOODEN KNOBS AND SCREWS • BRADAWL (AWL) • SCREWDRIVER • SINGLE WALL CORRUGATED PACKING CARDBOARD

4 Lay the open box shape on the work surface. Apply glue to all the ends of the polyboard grid and place it inside the box. Pin from the outside through the polyboard so that it is securely fixed together. Cut a piece of polyboard the width and height of the whole box and glue and pin it to the back of the frame.

5 Paint the shoe boxes with one of the water-based paints. Paint the lid as well. The inside of the boxes could be painted with a co-ordinating paint or lined with patterned wrapping paper if desired. You may need to give them two coats of paint for an even coverage. Paint the chest in another colour and leave to dry.

6 Paint the wooden handles with the same colour of paint as the chest. When the paint on the boxes and the handles is dry, make a hole with a bradawl in the front of each box. Fix a handle to each box front.

7 Cut a long piece of corrugated packing cardboard the width of the chest and long enough to make a scroll shape for the feet. Roll it up from both ends until the rolls are the required size and equal to each other. Glue in place.

8 Cut another strip of corrugated packing cardboard the same width and long enough to cover the top of the chest in a wavy shape. Paint the long strip and the rolls with the third paint colour.

9 Stick the long strip up the side of the chest, turning the edge under the bottom of the chest, and glue in three waves across the top. Glue down the other side and leave to dry. Pin in place down the sides.

10 Apply glue to the top of each roll and centre the chest on top. Leave to dry.

SATCHEL

THIS SATCHEL HARDLY LOOKS LIKE CARDBOARD AT ALL. IT MAKES CLEVER USE OF THE TYPE OF WAX USED TO WATERPROOF CLOTHING, WHICH NOT ONLY MAKES THE BAG MORE PRACTICAL BUT ADDS A LOVELY MOTTLED PATINA TO THE MATERIAL. THE SATCHEL IS BOUND WITH PAPER STRING IN KEEPING WITH THE CARDBOARD THEME AND THE BINDING MAKES FOR A VERY STURDY, ROBUST RESULT. AS A CONTRAST TO THE PLAIN CARDBOARD, THE BAG CAN BE LINED WITH WALLPAPER, AS IT HAS BEEN HERE, OR WITH PATTERNED FABRIC TO GIVE A NICE FINISH INSIDE. ALTHOUGH IT IS MADE IN THE STYLE OF A TRADITIONAL SCHOOL SATCHEL, IT IS SMART ENOUGH FOR AN OFFICE, AND YOU COULD ADD A LONGER PLAITED STRING HANDLE TO CREATE A SHOULDER BAG.

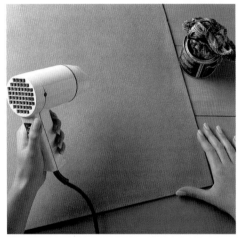

1 Spray adhesive on to the back of the wallpaper and stick it on to one side of the corrugated cardboard. Start from one edge and gently wipe over the wallpaper to achieve a smooth finish free of air bubbles.

2 Using a soft cloth, apply wax all over the other side of the card, ensuring that there is an even coverage. Using a hairdryer, melt the wax so it soaks in and is less greasy.

3 Using the diagram at the back of the book, cut out piece A which is the back and front flap. Score the lines with the blunt point of a wooden spoon (see Basic Techniques). Do not use a craft knife as this will cut into the wallpaper. Cut small holes for the eyelets and insert eyelets. Cut out the oval holes for the fastenings on the front flap. Punch holes all around the outside, 1.5cm (⅝ in) apart.

▶

MATERIALS AND EQUIPMENT YOU WILL NEED

WALLPAPER • SPRAY ADHESIVE • SMALL FLUTE SINGLE WALL CORRUGATED CARDBOARD • SOFT CLOTH • WAX FOR WATERPROOF CLOTHING • HAIRDRYER • TRACING PAPER • PENCIL • CRAFT KNIFE • METAL RULER • CUTTING MAT • WOODEN SPOON • EYELETS AND EYELET PUNCH • REVOLVING HOLE PUNCH • PAPER STRING • PLASTIC PIPING • METAL FASTENERS AND WASHERS

4 Cut out the outside front (B), two side pieces for the pocket (D), two side pieces for the satchel pocket (C) and the pocket front (E) from the wallpapered cardboard. Also cut out the inside pocket divider (F), which should be papered on both sides. Punch holes 1.5 cm (⅝ in) apart along three sides, leaving the top edge free.

6 Score along all the fold lines on the two side pieces (C) and bend along all the lines. Stitch one of them around the back satchel piece (A) and continue threading the string through all the holes on the flap. Lay the inside pocket divider (F) on top of this and lay the second side piece (D) on top. Stitch through all the layers.

8 Cut out a handle (G) and fold along the lines as indicated. Punch holes 1.5 cm (⅝ in) apart along the longest sides. Thread a double thickness of string through both of the eyelet holes and tie with a knot. Wrap the cardboard handle around the string and stitch together. (It is a good idea to use a piece of plastic piping to reinforce the handle.)

5 On the unprepared side of the side piece for the pocket (D), score along the fold lines, then make the folds. Centre the pocket (E) on the satchel front (B) and mark the position. Put the pocket (E) to one side. Position the pocket side (D) along the marked line, then punch matching holes in the two layers of cardboard and stitch on to the front of the satchel by threading the string through the holes, starting and ending with a knot on the papered side. Fold over 2 cm (¾ in) along the straight edge of the pocket front (E) and attach to the pocket side (D).

7 Hold the front of the satchel (B) in place against the side strip (C). Stitch in place with the string, finishing by threading the string back through the previous hole and tying a knot inside.

9 Hold the front flap flat against the satchel. Using a pencil, mark the positions for the backs of the fastenings on the pocket front. Carefully push the backs of the metal fasteners through the cardboard. Bolt the other parts of the fasteners in the position marked. Use washers to stop them cutting through the cardboard.

CHRISTMAS TREE DECORATIONS

THESE DELICATE DECORATIONS STARTED LIFE AS THE CARDBOARD BACKING ON ENVELOPES, WHICH MAKES THEM VERY ECONOMICAL AND AN ELEGANT WAY TO RECYCLE! THEY ARE CONSTRUCTED FROM TWO PIECES OF ORNATELY SHAPED CARDBOARD SLOTTED TOGETHER AND DECORATED WITH BEAUTIFUL BEADS. YOU COULD MAKE THEM IN DIFFERENT SIZES AND HANG THEM ON THE CHRISTMAS TREE, OR DISPLAY THEM IN A WINDOW BY HANGING THEM FROM RIBBONS OF DIFFERENT LENGTHS.

1 Trace the templates from the back of the book. Draw around them on to the card (card stock), drawing two pieces for each decoration. Cut out each shape using small scissors (such as embroidery scissors) or a craft knife.

3 Using a bradawl (awl), make a small hole close to the bottom edge of one piece for the central bead drop, a hole at the top of the corresponding piece for the hanging loop, and holes close to the edges underneath the top curling shapes to hang more beads.

5 Using long-nosed pliers, bend each wire close to the top of the beads and hook through a hole in the card. Wrap the wire ends around the pin a few times to secure, and trim the ends.

2 Mark the slotting slits down the centre of both pieces and cut them out with a craft knife, metal ruler and cutting mat. Do not overcut the slits or the shapes will not hold together tightly.

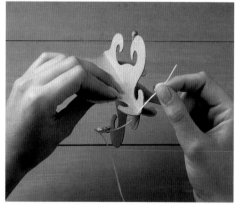

4 Thread the beads on to flat-headed pins to make the droplets, one for the base centre and one for each of the four top curls.

6 Slot the two beaded card (card stock) pieces together until they match at top and bottom edges, to make a three-dimensional shape. Thread a piece of cord through the top hole and tie the ends to make a hanging loop. Trim the excess cord.

MATERIALS AND EQUIPMENT YOU WILL NEED

TRACING PAPER • PENCIL • MEDIUM-WEIGHT MANILA CARD (CARD STOCK) • PENCIL • SMALL SCISSORS (OPTIONAL) • CRAFT KNIFE • METAL RULER •
CUTTING MAT • BRADAWL (AWL) • BEADS • FLAT-HEADED PINS • LONG-NOSED PLIERS • THIN CORD

WOVEN BASKET

THIS BASKET IS AN INGENIOUS WAY OF USING FOOD PACKAGING BOXES. IT USES A TRADITIONAL WEAVING TECHNIQUE WHICH CREATES A ROBUST BASKET THAT IS HARDLY RECOGNIZABLE AS CARDBOARD AT ALL. IT HAS BEEN GIVEN A MODERN LOOK BY PAINTING IT IN BRIGHT COLOURS WITH A SIMPLE PATTERN THAT IS EASY TO DO. THE CONSTRUCTION MAKES IT STRONG ENOUGH TO USE AS A

SHOPPING BASKET AND IT WOULD LOOK GREAT FULL OF FRUIT AND VEG FROM THE MARKET.

THE EYELET (GROMMETS) AND ROPE CAN BE BOUGHT FROM (AT) BOATING SHOPS (STORES) AND THE REVOLVING HOLE PUNCH IS A VERY HANDY TOOL, AVAILABLE FROM (AT) HARDWARE STORES, WHICH IS WELL WORTH INVESTING IN IF YOU PLAN TO MAKE WOVEN-CARDBOARD BASKETS.

1 Open out the cardboard boxes into large sheets and paint with a bold random pattern. Leave to dry. On the unpainted side, rule into 4 cm (1½ in) wide strips – rule across the corrugations, not along them – in the following lengths: three x 110 cm (43 in), nine x 80 cm (32 in), eight x 120 cm (47 in) and two extra x 120 cm (47 in) (for spares).

2 Using a pair of scissors, cut up the strips of cardboard.

3 Take the three 110 cm (43 in) strips and make a mark across the middle of all three strips. Take one 80 cm (32 in) strip and make a mark along the middle of the strip at a central point. With the paint side down, lay out the three long strips, lining up the marks. Lift up the middle strip, and lay one of the 80 cm (32 in) strips across and on top of the remaining two 110 cm (43 in) strips, using the marks to line up the strips. This is the first woven strip and should travel over, under, then over the other three.

MATERIALS AND EQUIPMENT YOU WILL NEED

TWO OR THREE CARDBOARD BOXES • PVA (TEMPERA) PAINT IN SEVERAL COLOURS • PAINTBRUSH • METAL RULER • PENCIL •
SCISSORS • 20–30 HINGED CLOTHES PEGS (CLOTHESPINS) • STRONG THREAD • SHARP NEEDLE WITH LARGE EYE • BODKIN • STRONG, QUICK-DRYING GLUE •
HOLE-MAKING TOOL • FOUR 1 CM (½ IN) BRASS EYELETS (GROMMETS) AND "PUNCH AND DIE" KIT • BRIGHTLY COLOURED POLYPROPYLENE STRING •
MATT POLYURETHANE VARNISH • PAINTBRUSH • 1.5–2 M (60–80 IN) OF 1 CM (½ IN) DIAMETER ROPE • MASKING TAPE

4 Beginning on one side of the single strip, fold the two outer strips tightly up over the central strip. Lay a second strip on top of the middle of the three 110 cm (43 in) strips, as close as possible to the first woven strip. Line up the ends of the strips.

6 Continue until there are five 80 cm (32 in) strips woven through the three 110 cm (43 in) strips. Peg (pin) the two corners, turn the work around then weave the remaining four 80 cm (32 in) strips on the other side of the central 80 cm (23 in) strip. Peg the corners. Check that every strip has travelled "over one, under one" to give a chequered effect.

8 Make sure the weaving strip closely follows the line of the edge of the base – there should be no gaps between the base and the sides. Aim to get sharp corners, as this will influence the shape of the finished basket.

5 Fold the two outer strips back down so that they lie as smoothly as possible over the second woven strip. Fold the central 110 cm (43 in) strip tightly up over the two woven strips. Lay a third strip on top of the two outer 110 cm (43 in) strips, as close as possible to the first two woven strips.

7 Bend up the strips around the edge of the woven base – these will now be called the side stakes. Take one of the 120 cm (47 in) strips and, starting just to one side of the centre of a long edge, place the end of the strip between two of the side strips, maintaining the "over one, under one" weave pattern up the sides. Check that this pattern will continue when deciding where to place the first 120 cm (47 in) weaving strip. Begin working around the base, folding the side strips from the inside tightly down over the weaving strip, and those from the outside tightly to the inside. Peg (pin) the strips that fold to the outside.

9 At the end of this (and each following) row, overlap the ends of the weaving strip, so that it runs in a double layer across three or four of the side strips. Begin the second row as the first, but on the opposite long edge. Remember to check that the "over one, under one" weave pattern is continued. ▶

10 Work six rows, beginning each row on alternate sides. Measure a length of thread that goes easily twice around the basket. With the side stakes upright and using a bodkin, stitch around the top row of weaving to secure it. Using scissors, trim off the excess side strips slightly below the top edge of the final row.

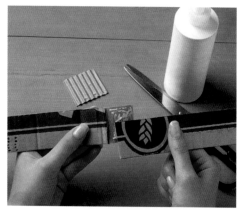

11 Take one of the remaining 120 cm (47 in) strips (a border strip), glue the back and stick it to the inside of the top row of the basket. Use clothes pegs (clothespins) to hold the strip in place, and to create sharp creases at the corner points. Overlap the ends (see Basic Techniques). Glue the back of the other border strip and stick it to the outside of the top row, again using pegs to hold it in place until the glue is completely dry, and making sure the corners are sharp.

12 Using a hole punch, make two clean holes for the brass eyelets in each long side of the basket. These should be three "squares" in from the outer edge, in the row below the border strip (there will be three "squares" between the holes). Mark the positions of the holes first to check they are in the correct place.

13 Insert and secure the brass eyelets using the punch and die, following the instructions on the packet.

14 Measure a length of coloured string that goes easily three and a half times around the basket. Work blanket stitch around the border strips, spacing the stitches 4 cm (1½ in) apart to correspond to the width of the cardboard strips. If necessary, enlarge the stitching holes with a bodkin. Keep the stitching tight and even. Varnish the basket inside and out to protect it.

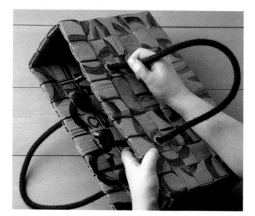

15 Cut the rope in half, taping the ends to stop them fraying. Make a knot at one end. Thread the rope through the first eyelet hole from inside to outside, leaving the knot on the inside of the basket. Thread the other end of the rope through the second eyelet hole from outside to inside, then make a knot in the other end of the rope. Repeat for the second handle, making sure the handles are the same length.

INTRODUCTION

Bookbinding is an ancient practice that has developed into a modern art and a practical craft. Bookbinding can enhance and transform a seemingly dull cover, and act as a source of inspiration for creating personalized albums and record books.

The following section provides all the information you need in order to embark on this fascinating and rewarding craft. The first few pages explore the development of bookbinding from the purely functional to an art form in its own right, and the gallery pages show an inspirational selection of stunning examples of bookbinding designs and styles of the latter part of the 20th century. Thereafter, clear, illustrated instructions describe the basic techniques you will need to make a range of distinctive books and albums, and guide you through 14 projects of varying complexity.

The combination of detailed advice and beautiful images cannot fail to inspire you to create your own fabulous books and albums to treasure forever.

Left: Bookbinding only requires the use of basic materials and tools, making it simple to create a wide range of books and albums.

HISTORY OF BOOKBINDING

THE WORD "BOOK" DERIVES FROM "BOC", AN OLD ENGLISH WORD MEANING "WRITTEN SHEET". ANCIENT PEOPLES HAD BEEN WRITING THINGS DOWN IN VARIOUS WAYS FOR THOUSANDS OF YEARS, BUT IT WAS THE ANCIENT ROMANS WHO INVENTED THE FIRST BOUND BOOK, OR CODEX, AS THEY CALLED IT — WAX-COVERED WOODEN TABLETS BOUND TOGETHER AT THE SIDES WITH THONGS.

During the 2nd century BC, the peoples of Africa, Europe and Asia began using animal hide to make the pages for books. Parchment was developed by the people of Asia Minor using a process that involved soaking goat and sheep hides in water, covering them in lime, and then scraping away the remains of hair and tissue. Finally, the clean hides were stretched over wooden frames and left to dry and bleach in the sun. Bleaching was also achieved using the application of chalk or lime. About 12 sheepskins were needed to make a single book of 150 pages.

The Chinese were the first to practise paper making, which they developed during the early years of the 2nd century AD. They soaked hemp, mulberry, bamboo, tree bark or rags in water, and then pounded the mixture to form a pulp. A wire mesh tray was dipped into the vat to gather up the pulp and the water was allowed to drain off. The pulp was then pressed and dried. By the 5th century AD, Chinese writers were using paper, which they folded accordion-style to form books.

In time, papermaking spread from China; indeed, during the Arab conquest, captive Chinese taught the art to the Arabs, with the result that between the 7th and 12th centuries AD cities such as Damascus and Baghdad became great centres of book production. The Islamic

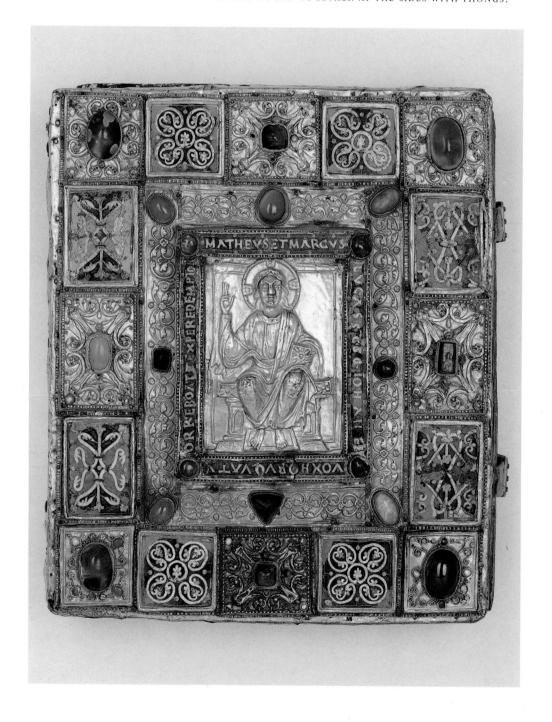

Right: A 10th-century book cover of the Sion Gospels. This stunning example of early German bookbinding is made of wood, and has a gold embossed overlay studded with precious jewels.

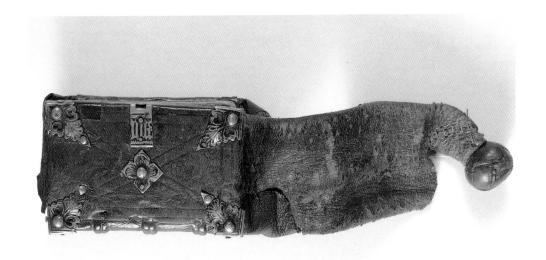

was first used in the 5th century AD and is still used to this day. In a technique known as "blind tooling", the tool is heated and then pressed into the leather to leave an impression. Another decorative technique, "gold tooling", involves pressing the tool into gold leaf and "glaire" (a mixture of

Left: A Girdle book. This book was used in Europe in the Middle Ages; the owner would tuck the knot at the side into his girdle or belt so that he would not lose the book when he wasn't reading it.

Below: An enamelled pocket book. This book was also designed to be tied to the owner's belt, this time by means of the metal loops on the top.

Arab Empire enjoyed a high literacy rate, with one in five Arabs being able to read.

It took until the 12th century AD for the art of paper making to spread to the West and even then it was distrusted by many; in some parts of medieval Europe, anything written on paper had no legal standing. During the Middle Ages, bookbinders were patronized by royalty, wealthy private patrons and the Church. Monks were particularly prolific bookbinders, most of their books being produced for use in the monasteries. The parchment pages of these books, which bore beautiful illuminated text, were stitched together and laced into wooden boards to keep the parchment flat. The books were generally leather bound, but sometimes so-called "treasure bindings" were worked in gold and silver and elaborately decorated with jewels. Emperors of the Byzantine era even paraded in public processions their most sumptuously decorated books as ostentatious displays of their wealth.

Leather bindings were often decorated using tools made from engraved brass dyes held in wooden handles. This technique

Above: An embroidered prayer book and bag incorporating gold and silver thread.

Right: Sir Julius Caesar's Travelling Bookcase, circa 1620.

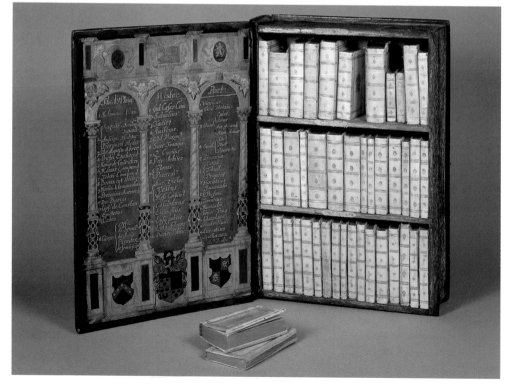

vinegar and egg (which helps the gold to stick), before pressing it on to the leather.

Book spines were not decorated prior to the 16th century, since books were stored either flat or on a shelf with the fore edge facing outwards. It was not until the 17th century that titles and authors' names were tooled on to the spine.

The advent of the printing press meant that smaller, lighter and cheaper books could be produced. The pocket book, developed in Italy in 1507, was so popular that it soon spread across Europe. By the 16th century most books were printed on paper, and bookbinding had developed both structurally and decoratively. Panel and roll stamped decoration replaced the more time-consuming tooling techniques.

The Industrial Revolution forced a split in the bookbinding trade. On the one hand, there were mechanized workshops, which were able to produce low-cost books bound in cloth, paper or leather to meet the growing demands of an increasingly literate population; on the other, there were small craft workshops which continued to produce unique bindings in the traditional manner. The latter were generally small establishments, run by a qualified binder assisted by a couple of apprentices and a journeyman (a qualified binder unable to afford his own premises).

Throughout the history of bookbinding, a huge range of materials has been used to make and decorate book covers, including leather, papier-mâché, embroidered canvas, tortoiseshell, ivory and elaborate gold and silver work. For the contemporary bookbinder, the choice is greater still: diverse synthetic materials are available, spanning a broad range of textures, colours and properties.

The hand-binding techniques used today are much the same as those used by 16th-century hand binders. However, in recent times, the traditional concepts of book cover design have given way to freedom of artistic expression, and today bookbinders' creations may be regarded as works of art in themselves.

Above: A 19th-century Persian book with a painted and lacquered binding.

Left: A selection of Art Deco bindings. These brightly coloured books are now valuable collector's items.

GALLERY

THE NOTION THAT A BOOK'S BINDING SHOULD REFLECT THE ESSENCE OF ITS CONTENTS IS A RECENT ONE, AND ONE THAT INSPIRES CONTEMPORARY BINDERS TO CHALLENGE BOOKBINDING CONVENTIONS. THESE BOOKBINDERS INCORPORATE ALL KINDS OF MODERN MATERIALS AND TEXTURES IN THEIR DESIGNS TO CREATE WORKS OF ART THAT ARE ALMOST ARCHITECTURAL OR SCULPTURAL.

Right: VIKRAM AND THE VAMPIRE or TALES OF HINDU DEVILRY
The covering leather of this book is black goatskin over an underlayer of white kid glove leather decorated with leather dyes sprayed through stencils and various mesh screens. Inlays are of snakeskin, metallic-surfaced leather and acrylic cabochons.
TREVOR JONES, 1993

Below: MOMENTS OF FORCES
These books use French folded graph paper for the interior, with machine-sewn plastic ribbed sleeves for the cover and hand-drawn inside-the-body images and wireframe computer drawings. Both the covers and the sewing at the spine are reinforced with sheets of printmaking paper offcuts.
SUSAN JOHANKNECHT, 1997

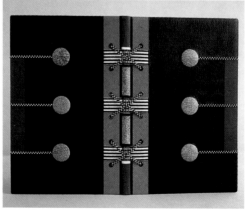

Left: SONGS FROM SHAKESPEARE'S PLAYS
The sewing structure features prominently here. Black goatskin on the sides contrasts with strongly coloured onlays. The top edge was first gilt and then sewn with red linen thread to three black-and-white striped tapes through a concertina-fold continuous guard.
TREVOR JONES, 1995

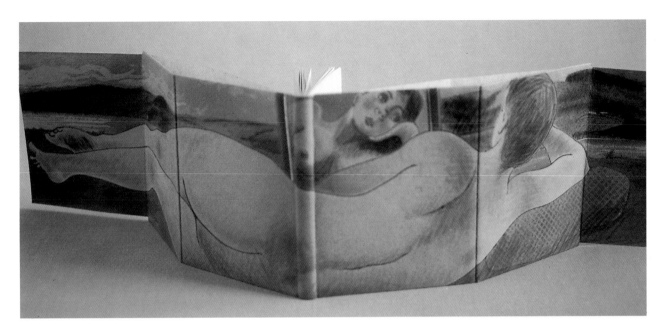

Left: POMES PENYEACH by James Joyce, 1927
This single-section book was sewn through the original three sewing holes on to a stub, then endpapers of handmade paper, dyed to match the text paper, were added. The covering leather is archival natural calfskin decorated with spirit dyes, using stencils and resists.
TREVOR JONES, 1991

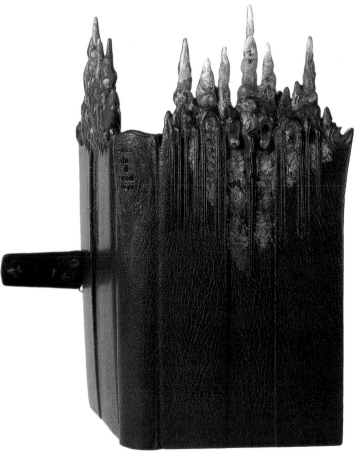

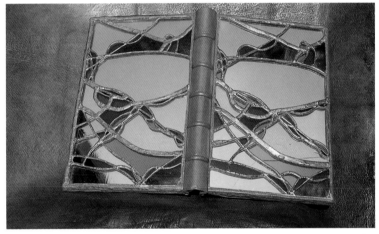

Left: THE SILMARILLION by J.R.R. Tolkien, 1977
Standing on four glass bead-headed pins, the peaks of this book are integral with the covers, simply being extended above the book. The covers are built from millboard (pasteboard), balsawood, thin wooden dowels and epoxy-putty modelling supported by brass rods.
PHILIP SMITH, 1983

Above: STAINED GLASS BOOK
This piece is made from stained glass which has been laminated on to pieces of mirror. This has then been laminated on to board for rigidity. It is held together by a stout spine made from goatskin, which is also used around the edges, and measures 47 x 33 cm (18½ x 13 in).
GAVIN ROOKLEDGE, 1995

Right: A SELECTION OF
BLANK BOOKS
This series of books was
made to explore the
potential of sewing on to
rods. Each section and
wooden cover board was
sewn on to its own rod
before the whole book was
assembled using vellum
strips across the spine.
The combinations shown
are made from ebony,
brass, pine, mahogany
and copper.
PETER JONES, 1996

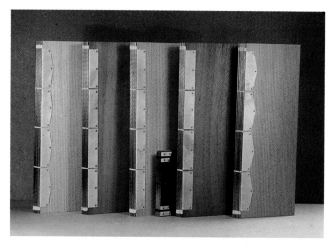

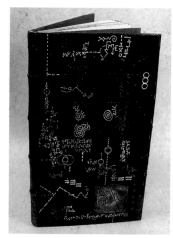

Left: METAMATHICA
Ten sections of D'Arches
cover-weight paper were
re-sized with gelatine and
then with pigments,
stainless steel dust and
acrylic resin to make this
book. Japanese paper was
sized, printed and worked
in the manner of leather
for the spine. The final
drawing in white was
achieved with airbrush
acrylic paint.
TIMOTHY C. ELY, 1990

Left: EMISSIONS
A transparent book with
all parts observable
through the back. Screen-
printed on to archival
polyester, each copy
contains encapsulated
transparencies, hair wax,
wire and body prints.
There are a total of
20 pages sewn into a
vellum spine.
SUSAN JOHANKNECHT, 1992

Above: MOBY DICK
by Herman Melville, 1851
This book is bound in
black, dark green and dark
blue scarph-joined
goatskins with various sea-
coloured onlays. Most of
the surface of the book is
built from emulsified maril
(a mixture of fine shavings
of the grain side of
coloured leathers mixed
with PVA (white) glue),
and modelled with shaped
bone folders and card
templates.
PHILIP SMITH, 1990

Above: SPANISH
LANDSCAPES
This is a full leather
binding. The book was
sewn on linen tapes laced
into boards, then given
red silk headbands and a
hollow back with one false
band, which was covered
in bright yellow. Natural
goatskin was painted with
leather dye using an
airbrush, brushes and
cotton wool. The boards
were covered and small
onlays of yellow and
purple applied. The title
was lettered in blind on
the lower front board.
SUSAN ALLIX, 1994

Above: THE GARDEN
AND OTHER POEMS
by Andrew Marvell
Full leather flexible
binding is used with a
double cover. The cover is
in archival calf leather
dyed with blind tooling
and then cut into leaf
shapes. The fly leaves are
made of calf leather with
blind tooling imitating the
texture of a tree.
EVANGELIA BIZA, 1993

Below: BIRD NESTING
by John Clare, 1987
This book is sewn on three
hidden tapes and four
visible green-dyed canvas
tapes with restraining
thongs threaded through
eyelets in the sides. The
exposed sewing thread is
protected by false raised
bands of yellow archival
goatskin with white
acrylic-painted edges.
TREVOR JONES, 1990

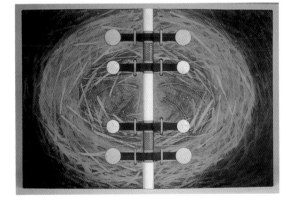

Right: HANDS II
(New Testament and
Psalms in sculpture)
These life-size hands are
made from carved
balsawood reinforced with
epoxy putty and covered
with brown goatskin. The
book boards blend into the
palms of the hands and
fingerprints in ink on light
brown acrylic decorate the
book edges.
PHILIP SMITH, 1986

EQUIPMENT

PERHAPS BECAUSE OF ITS ANCIENT ORIGINS, BOOKBINDING DOES NOT REQUIRE A GREAT VARIETY OF TOOLS. MUCH OF THE EQUIPMENT YOU WILL NEED TO COMPLETE THE PROJECTS IN THIS SECTION IS BASIC AND, SHOULD YOU NOT ALREADY OWN IT, READILY AVAILABLE FROM HARDWARE STORES. POWER TOOLS ARE NOT REQUIRED, NOR ARE SPECIALIST SKILLS. THE MORE SPECIALIST TOOLS, SUCH AS DECKLE-EDGED SCISSORS AND A BONE FOLDER, CAN BE OBTAINED FROM BOOKBINDING SUPPLIERS.

Bone folder Inexpensive and very useful implement for creasing paper and smoothing out the air bubbles on pasted boards, available from specialist bookbinding shops. Broad ice cream (popsicle) sticks make a satisfactory substitute.

Bradawl (awl) Used, with a hammer, to make single, fine holes in paper or thin card (cardboard).

Brushes Various sizes are used for spreading glue. After using water-soluble glue, clean and dry the brushes carefully so that you will be able to use them again and again.

Craft knives Useful for accurate cutting of paper and thin card (cardboard); some have removable and replaceable blades. Handle the blades with extreme caution, and dispose of them safely after use. Always cut on a cutting mat.

Cutting mat One should always be used to protect your work surface when cutting paper or boards. A self-healing kind is preferable. You will be able to exert more pressure if you kneel and work on the floor.

Deckle-edged scissors Used to cut fancy edges on paper and thin card (cardboard). They are available in a range of patterns from specialist supply shops.

Revolving hole punch This tool has a selection of punches that punch holes of a corresponding size in fabric and cardboard, as well as leather.

Metal ruler Important for accurate measuring and to provide a good edge against which paper or board can be cut with a craft or utility knife. Choose a long ruler if possible.

Pencils Used to mark measurements on paper or board. A sharp pencil (or knitting needle) can also be used to punch a hole in polyboard. Rotate the pencil until the desired hole size is achieved, then trim the edges of the hole against the pencil tip using a craft knife.

Pinking shears These cut a zigzag edge, and can be used in the same way as deckle-edged scissors to create interesting page edge effects.

Pliers-type paper hole punch This inexpensive tool is useful for punching holes of a regular size in paper and thin card (cardboard). It has a single punch, which allows you to place the holes precisely as you choose.

Punches Used, with a hammer, to make holes in plastic or fabrics. Available in various sizes

Rotary cutters Useful for cutting paper. They are low-friction cutting tools, so exert less drag on the paper than a craft knife does.

Tack hammers Used to tap in panel pins, or to tap a bradawl (awl) to make a hole, or to tap a chisel to make a slot. (A heavier hammer is generally not necessary for bookbinding projects.)

Utility knives For cutting denser material such as cardboard and millboard. Use one to trim the uneven pages of a newly completed book against a metal ruler. A non-retractable utility knife is probably the safest type to use. Always cut on a cutting mat.

Weights All types are useful for pressing pasted boards or finished books, to prevent warping while the glue dries. Use cooking weights, fitness training weights or telephone directories, and try to exert an even pressure on the boards. When pressing a finished book, remember to protect the spine.

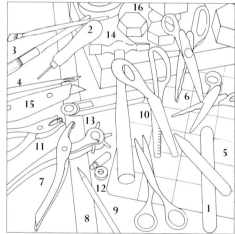

Key

1 Bone folder
2 Bradawl (awl)
3 Brushes
4 Craft knife
5 Cutting mat
6 Deckle-edged scissors
7 Leather punch
8 Metal ruler

9 Pencil
10 Pinking shears
11 Pliers-type punch
12 Punch
13 Rotary cutter
14 Tack hammer
15 Utility knife
16 Weights

MATERIALS

THE STRUCTURE OF ANY BOOK — THE COVER, PAGES AND BIND-TING — WILL DETERMINE THE BASIC MATERIALS REQUIRED. FOR THIS REASON THERE ARE SEVERAL STANDARD MATERIALS YOU WILL NEED FOR MOST PROJECTS IN THIS SECTION: GLUE OR PASTE, PAPER, AND SOME FORM OF BOARD. BOOKBINDERS' SUPPLIERS PROVIDE MATERIALS SUCH AS ENDPAPERS, BOOK CLOTHS, GLASSINE PAPER AND GLUE. FOR SOME OF THE MORE UNUSUAL PROJECTS YOU WILL NEED TO OBTAIN SPECIFIC MATERIALS FROM SPECIALIST SHOPS.

Beeswax Used to lubricate linen thread. Pull the thread through the wax to make it glide more easily during stitching.

Book cloth This paper-backed book-covering cloth is available from specialist bookbinders' suppliers. You can make your own book cloth by gluing thin paper to your choice of fabric.

Cake boards Readily available in supermarkets, cake decorating shops and department stores. They make unusual but practical book boards.

Cardboard All types are useful for bookbinding. Corrugated cardboard is a very flexible material, which is available in a range of colours, including metallic colours, from paper suppliers.

Double-sided heavy-duty carpet tape Can often be used instead of glue.

Embroidery threads (flosses) Available in many colours. Use two or three strands together, or combine different coloured threads to achieve unusual effects.

Endpapers Specially designed sheets of paper, which are pasted to the inside of the cover, leaving an additional flyleaf. Wrapping paper and other decorative papers can also be used, but first apply paste to a small scrap to check whether the paper is colourfast, and that it does not stretch too much when wet.

Fabric Various types can be made into book cloths.

Glassine paper Available from specialist shops, this thin, transparent acid-free paper is traditionally used between the pages of photograph albums.

Glue sticks Source of acid-free adhesive for light-weight materials.

Handmade papers Available in a wide range of colours, effects and designs, some with flower and grass inclusions.

Linen tape Available from haberdashers (notions) or specialist supply shops. It is used to reinforce the spine of books.

Linen thread Used to stitch pages. Run the thread through beeswax before stitching, to make it glide more easily.

Millboard (pasteboard) Extremely tough and dense board, which is available in different grades of thickness. Millboard is ideal for making portfolios, but hardboard is a good alternative.

Moss paper As its name suggests, this is a furry, moss-like paper that makes interesting book covers or endpapers. It is available from model and hobby shops.

Mull Used to reinforce the inside of a book's spine. Open-weave cotton bandage makes an effective substitute.

Neutral PVA (white) glue Also known as conservation paste, this is available from specialist shops. It is acid free and suitable for archive-quality work.

Paper doilies Inexpensive lacy paper decorations available from supermarkets and kitchenware shops.

Polyboard (foam board) Smooth light-weight card (cardboard). It cannot be fold-ed, but makes a strong book cover.

Polypropylene Type of flexible plastic used for making book covers. It is available in a wide range of colours.

Self-adhesive cloth tape Book cloth with a self-adhesive backing. Doubled back on itself, it makes a neat, strong tab.

Two-part epoxy glue Also known as epoxy resin glue, this dries very quickly, so prepare only a small quantity at a time. It takes about 24 hours to set but, once set, it makes an excellent bond.

Wallpaper paste Can be mixed with PVA (white) glue to produce a strong, slippery glue that allows for repositioning before the paste becomes too tacky.

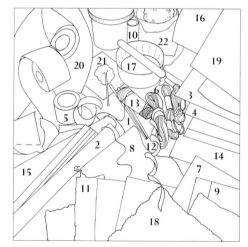

KEY

1 Beeswax	**11** Handmade papers
2 Book cloth	**12** Linen tape
3 Cake boards	**13** Linen thread
4 Cardboard	**14** Millboard (pasteboard)
5 Double-sided heavy-duty carpet tape	**15** Moss Paper
	16 Mull
6 Embroidery threads (flosses)	**17** Neutral PVA (white) glue
7 Endpapers	**18** Paper doily
8 Fabrics	**19** Polypropylene
9 Glassine paper	**20** Self-adhesive cloth tape
10 Glue Sticks	**21** Two-part epoxy glue
	22 Wallpaper paste

BASIC TECHNIQUES

MOST BOOKBINDING MATERIALS ARE EASY TO HANDLE, BUT BEFORE YOU ATTEMPT SOME OF THE MORE COMPLICATED PROJECTS THERE ARE A FEW TECHNIQUES THAT YOU SHOULD FAMIL-IARIZE YOURSELF WITH. READ THIS SECTION BEFORE STARTING THEM.

CUTTING TECHNIQUES

Different materials require different cutting techniques and equipment. It is worth learning the appropriate techniques for reasons of speed and safety.

Cutting board

When cutting a dense material, such as millboard (pasteboard), it is best to cut with a non-retractable craft knife against a metal ruler. Always cut on a protective surface, such as a cutting mat. You will be able to exert more pressure if you kneel and work on the floor.

Cutting polyboard (foam board)

Polyboard has a layer of polystyrene (styrofoam) sandwiched between two layers of laminated card (cardboard). It can be partially cut through to form a hinge. This makes it an easy option for making a book cover.

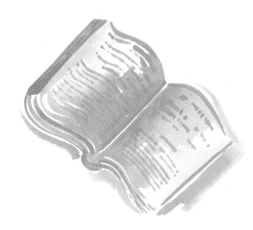

Partially cutting polyboard

1 Using a sharp craft knife and ruler, cut two parallel lines, taking care to cut through the first layer of card (cardboard) and foam but not through the bottom layer.

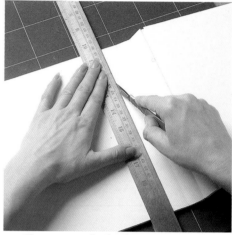

3 If you want the back to hinge from the spine cut another two parallel lines on the opposite side.

2 Score corresponding lines on the inside of the card and bend into a book shape so that the cut becomes the spine. This can be reinforced with mull or open-weave bandage.

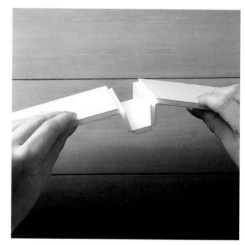

4 Score the backs of these lines and fold as shown.

MAKING HOLES

Making a hole gauge

Cut a strip of scrap paper or card (cardboard) the exact length of the pages of your book. Measure and mark the position of the holes you need on each page. Align the hole gauge with the spine of the first page, or set of pages, and, using it as your guide, mark the position of the holes on the page. Use it to mark all the pages or sets of pages of the book. Use a bradawl (awl) or bodkin to make the holes.

Making holes in paper and thin card (cardboard)

For paper and thin card, a pliers-type hole punch is best. It has a single punch so you can place the holes as you choose.

Making holes in polyboard (foam board)

1 A sharp, pointed implement, such as a pencil or knitting needle, is best for making holes in polyboard.

2 When the point emerges on the other side of the board, swivel it around until you achieve the desired hole size. Trim the edges against the tip of the pencil or knitting needle using a craft knife.

Making holes in heavier card (cardboard) and leather

Use a rotary hole punch with an adjustable head to make holes in thicker card (cardboard) or leather. When working with very dense card, you will have to swivel the board as you press, or try from both sides. It is possible to drill holes, but first test drill in a scrap piece of card.

MAKING ALBUMS

Make allowances for the bulk of the contents of albums by either adding an extra strip of card (cardboard) to the margin, or allowing an extra 2.5 cm (1 in) on the page width and fold this in. Protect photographs with glassine paper cut slightly smaller than the page and inserted into the folded edge.

MAKING PASTE

PVA (white) glue is a good all-purpose glue, but it grips so efficiently it does not allow for easy repositioning. If you mix it with wallpaper paste in a ratio of 1:1, it will be more slippery and will allow you to reposition the surfaces. It is worth experimenting first, especially if you are using expensive materials.

STICKING DOWN BOOK COVERS

1 Use a brush to ensure an even coating. Lay your work on a fresh sheet of scrap paper each time you glue and make sure you spread the glue right to the edge.

2 Line up the paper or book cloth carefully before positioning it. Once in position, smooth with a bone folder, taking care to remove any air pockets.

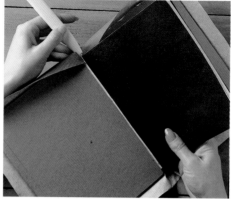

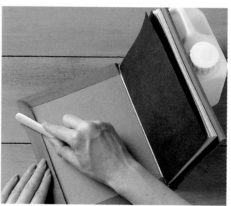

3 For the spine, carefully cut two parallel slits in the cover to correspond with the edges of the spine. Don't cut right up to the book; allow 2mm (¹⁄₁₆ in) for turning. Using a bone folder or similar, tuck in the book cloth overlap at the top and bottom of the spine.

4 Before turning in the sides, cut diagonally across the corners, about 2 mm (¹⁄₁₆ in) (or the thickness of the board) from the corners of the board. Pinch the corners with your fingernail or a bone folder before you start to turn the edges in. Turn the top and bottom edges first, then the side edges, and smooth over with a bone folder.

LINING A BOOK COVER

Cut the lining paper to size. Lay the cover, right side down, on a fresh sheet of scrap paper. Apply paste to the inside of the cover, and lay the lining paper on top. Smooth out any creases or air bubbles using a bone folder. Sticky-backed felt can be used as an alternative to paper; in this case, you do not need glue, but take care when you remove the backing, and try to avoid making creases.

MAKING A BOOK CLOTH

Readymade book cloth is available from bookbinders' suppliers, but it is a simple matter to make your own by lining your choice of fabric with a thin sheet of paper. Simply cut the paper larger than the fabric, spread PVA (white) glue on to the paper and wait until it becomes tacky. Then place the fabric, right side up, on to the glued paper and smooth out any air bubbles using a bone folder. Turn over, smooth the paper and allow to dry.

WEIGHTING OR PRESSING

Weighting pasted boards

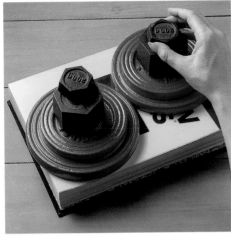

Pasted boards should be weighted until the glue has dried, to prevent them from warping. First, place a telephone directory on the board to weight it evenly. Then place weights, bricks or other heavy objects on the top.

Weighting a finished book

When pressing a finished book, be sure to protect the spine. Sandwich the book between two sheets of cardboard or two telephone directories, allowing the spine to protrude so that the weights do not press on to it.

TRIMMING PAGES

Often when you have made the body of the book, the pages are a little uneven. Trim the edges against a metal cutting ruler, keeping your hand steady and maintaining firm pressure on a utility knife. You may need to make several strokes in order to cut through the bulk of pages.

DECKLE EDGING

All sorts of fancy scissors are available, with patterned cutting edges to give petal effect borders. These patterns work best when paper in subtle and contrasting colours is used, but it is worth experimenting for yourself.
Corner cutters are also available.

STITCHING

Traditional bookbinding is a painstaking craft involving several stitching techniques. However, a few simple yet effective stitching methods are all you need to make interesting books. The easiest of these methods, a simple stabbing technique, involves a single stitch passing through folds of paper and a cover, before being tied. A slightly more sophisticated method involves stitching together several groups of pages, as in the Garden Notebook, shown here. In this example, three sets of pages have been stitched alongside each other.

This simple technique can be extended for decorative use. Here, three folded sets of pages have each been stitched three times to achieve an elegant effect.

JAPANESE BINDING

This is both a decorative and functional form of binding. It is an easy way to bind single sheets of paper, as it is the stitching that holds the pages of the book together: gluing is not necessary.

1 After making corresponding holes in the pages with a hammer and bradawl (awl) or punch, line up the pages and hold them securely. Wax the thread before you begin stitching as this makes it easier to pull through the holes.

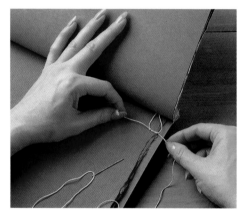

2 Start the binding by tying a knot in the thread on the inside, near the spine at the bottom of the book.

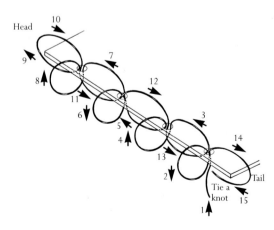

3 Pass the needle on the underside through the first hole, then around the spine and back through the same hole, forming a loop over the back of the spine. Then take the needle down to the next hole, and again around the spine, repeating this pattern until you have reached the last hole. Now take the thread over the top of the book, back through the top hole, then thread in and out of the holes and around the bottom, as shown in the diagram. Conceal the knot on the inside of the cover.

USING RIBBON OR STRING

Other materials, such as thin ribbon or string, can be used for stitching, as long as the holes are big enough. In the Japanese Stork Album, braided string is threaded through the holes using a twisted bit of wire as a guide.

ALL-IN-ONE STITCHING

This method is used for the Classic Notebook and the Triangular Book. It is a moderately difficult technique and the instructions need to be followed carefully.

1 Make a hole gauge on a margin of scrap paper cut to size. Use this to ensure all the holes correspond with each other. Make the holes using a bradawl (awl) or bodkin.

2 Open out a sheet of folded paper and on one side draw parallel lines 2.5 cm (1 in) and 5 cm (2 in) from the fold. Fold the paper along these lines to make a "W". The short stub that is left on one side is called the "wasted edge". Trim this to a width of 4 cm (1½ in). Glue the endpaper to the edge of the "W" fold nearest the wasted edge. Make two the same.

3 Using a long length of linen thread, start stitching through the "W" fold of the last page and endpaper, going in and out of the holes. When you reach the bottom hole, add the next section by stitching through the corresponding hole and continue in running stitch to the top of the book.

4 Once the first section has been attached to the "W" folded endpaper, pull the thread tightly in the direction of the thread, taking care not to tear the holes, and make a double knot.

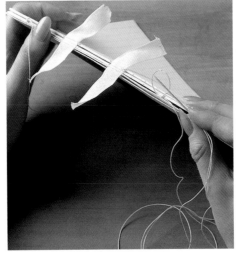

5 Continue to add in the other sections in the same way, binding back under the previous section at the top and bottom through the loop, as shown. Slide two strips of seam binding or linen tape under the stitches across the spine.

6 When all the sections and both endpapers have been bound, knock the spine of the book firmly on the work surface to align the pages.

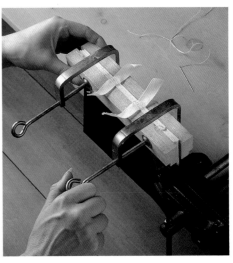

7 Put the body of the book into a vice and clamp two strips of wood in position, one on each side of the spine.

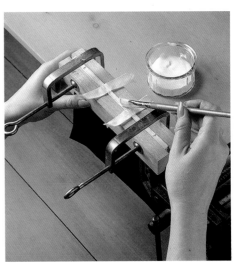

8 Apply neat PVA (white) glue along the spine of the book and place a strip of mull over the top. Apply more glue over the mull.

CD RECORD BOOK

IF YOU WANT TO PERSONALIZE A BOOK BUT DON'T WANT TO GO TO THE BOTHER OF MAKING IT YOURSELF, AN EASIER OPTION IS TO CUSTOMIZE A READYMADE ONE. HERE AN ORDINARY SPIRAL-BOUND BOOK GETS A FUNKY, FUTURISTIC LOOK WITH SILVER SPRAY AND THE ADDITION OF A CD AND SMALL CONVEX MIRROR ON THE FRONT. CDs ARE OFTEN GIVEN AWAY FREE WITH MAGAZINES, AND MAKE AN INEXPENSIVE DECORATION. SELF-ADHESIVE MIRRORS ARE AVAILABLE FROM CAR ACCESSORY SHOPS. USE THIS BOOK TO KEEP NOTES OF YOUR FAVOURITE MUSIC, OR TO KEEP TRACK OF CDs YOU HAVE BORROWED FROM OR LENT TO FRIENDS.

1 Spray the front cover of the book with silver paint. Don't forget to include the side edges. Once dry, turn over and spray the back cover.

2 Attach the mirror to the centre of the CD, so that it covers the central hole.

3 Using two-part epoxy glue, glue the CD to the front cover of the book and allow the glue to dry.

MATERIALS AND EQUIPMENT YOU WILL NEED
SPIRAL-BOUND BOOK • SILVER SPRAY PAINT • SMALL CIRCULAR CONVEX SELF-ADHESIVE MIRROR • SPARE CD • TWO-PART EPOXY GLUE

SLATE SKETCHBOOK

THIS EASY-TO-MAKE SKETCHBOOK UTILIZES TWO SLATE DRAW-ING BOARDS FOR ITS COVERS, ALLOWING YOU TO PRACTISE YOUR ARTWORK BEFORE COMMITTING YOURSELF TO PAPER. THE INSIDE PAGES ARE MADE FROM INDIAN KHADI PAPER. KHADI PAPER HAS A ROUGH TEXTURE SUITABLE FOR PASTEL AND CHARCOAL WORK, BUT YOU CAN USE WHATEVER PAPER YOU LIKE. THE ELASTIC BINDING ALLOWS FOR EXPANSION, SHOULD YOU WANT TO GLUE BULKY MATE-RIAL INSIDE. EXTRA PAGES CAN EASILY BE ADDED, IF NECESSARY.

1 Drill two corresponding holes in each slate board, about 6 cm (2½ in) apart.

2 Crease the edges of the paper and tear with a metal ruler to get a deckle-edge effect. Glue two tabs cut from narrow cloth tape on each page, about 4 cm (1½ in) apart, so that the centres of the tabs are 6 cm (2½ in) apart. Fold the tabs so that they stick to both sides of the page. Make a hole in each tab with a hole punch (see Basic Techniques).

3 Thread the elastic through the holes in the back cover board, page tabs and front cover board and tie in a bow at the front.

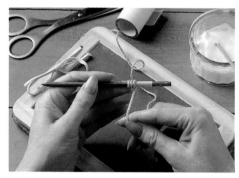

4 Wrap double-sided carpet tape around the top of the slate pencil. Wrap a length of string around the tape, starting at the lower end, and tie in a knot at the top. Glue the knot in place. Tie the free end of the string to the top hole on the back cover board.

5 Lay a piece of wide cloth tape face-down on the frame of the front board, so that it extends over the side. With the sticky sides together, stick a thinner strip over it, to form the pencil loop. Bring the wide tape over the frame and stick down.

6 Reinforce the loop by gently hammering in panel pins that have been snipped to size. Take care not to split the slate.

MATERIALS AND EQUIPMENT YOU WILL NEED

DRILL • DRILL BIT • 2 SLATE BOARDS • HANDMADE PAPER • METAL RULER • SELF-ADHESIVE CLOTH TAPE, NARROW AND WIDE • SCISSORS • PVA (WHITE) GLUE • HOLE PUNCH • ELASTIC • DOUBLE-SIDED CARPET TAPE • SLATE PENCIL • HEMP STRING • SMALL PANEL PINS • HAMMER

SUEDE DESK PAD

THIS FUNCTIONAL AND STYLISH DESK ACCESSORY IS MADE FROM A RICH RED SUEDE, ALTHOUGH FLAT LEATHER WOULD BE JUST AS EFFECTIVE. IT IS SIMPLY STITCHED AROUND THE EDGE IN A CONTRASTING COLOUR, AND THE SHOELACE AND FEATHER FASTENING GIVES IT AN APPEALING "ANTIQUE" LOOK. THIS PROJECT REQUIRES ONLY BASIC SEWING SKILLS FOR THE OVER-STITCHING AND THE PAGE BINDING. LEATHER AND SUEDE SCRAPS CAN BE BOUGHT FROM LEATHER GOODS MANUFACTURERS OR BOOKBINDERS' SUPPLIERS.

1 Cut a rectangle of suede or leather and fold in half to check that it is square and even. Mark a 12 mm (½ in) border around the edge, on the wrong side, and punch evenly spaced small holes along this border.

2 Mark out the spine and the position of three parallel rows of three large stitches, using a ruler and pencil.

3 In order to punch the marked holes for the stitches, you will need to bunch up the hide into the jaws of the punch. If you are unable to reach the marked positions, use a bradawl (awl) to punch the holes.

4 Thread a bodkin with a double length of string. Using the pre-punched holes, overstitch all round the edge of the cover.

5 Divide the paper into three sets. Fold each set in half to mark the spine and mark the stitching holes using a hole gauge (see Basic Techniques). Use a bradawl to punch the holes.

6 Lay the first set of pages down inside the cover. Stitch the pages to the spine of the cover. Do not cut the string once you have stitched this set in place; instead, start stitching the next set. When the three sets of paper are stitched in place, tie a knot in the two ends of the string and tuck the knot out of sight inside the spine. The three lines of stitches on the spine should be parallel and straight. Slip the shoelace under the central set of stitches, as shown. Find a suitable feather with which to finish off.

MATERIALS AND EQUIPMENT YOU WILL NEED

RULER • PENCIL • SUITABLE PIECE OF SUEDE OR LEATHER • SCISSORS • LEATHER HOLE PUNCH • BRADAWL (AWL) • BODKIN •
STRING IN A CONTRASTING COLOUR • GOOD-QUALITY PLAIN WRITING PAPER • SCRAP PAPER • LONG SHOELACE, COLOUR TO MATCH THE STRING • FEATHER

PRECIOUS PAMPHLET

ADD A PERSONAL TOUCH TO A SPECIAL FAMILY OCCASION WITH THIS UNIQUE PAMPHLET MADE FROM BEAUTIFUL HANDMADE PAPER, A WORTHY KEEPSAKE OF ANY HAPPY EVENT. USE A METALLIC PEN TO WRITE THE NAME OR NAMES ON THE FRONT COVER AND INSIDE. HERE, PRESSED FLOWERS HAVE BEEN USED TO DECORATE THE FRONT, COMPLEMENTING THOSE INCORPORATED IN THE PAPER. THIS IS THE SIMPLEST TYPE OF BOOK TO MAKE, BEING HELD TOGETHER BY ONE STITCH, WHICH IS THEN TIED IN A BOW ON THE SPINE.

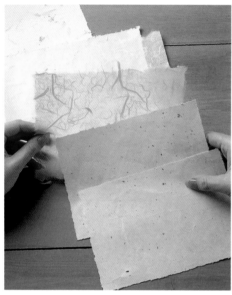  

1 Tear the edges of each piece of paper by first creasing it then pulling a metal ruler along the crease to give a natural-looking deckle edge. Vary the sizes of the inner sheets of paper. Collate the pages in order of size, the largest at the back, smallest at the front. Fold in half together to form a booklet.

2 Using a bradawl (awl), make two evenly spaced holes along the spine. Thread the bodkin with a length of raffia and, starting on the outside, make a stitch through the holes, emerging on the outside again. Tie the raffia in a bow on the spine.

3 Glue a small square of paper, the edges torn as before, on the front cover. This is for the name of the baby or wedding couple. Arrange the pressed flowers on the front cover as desired, then glue in place with glue diluted with water.

MATERIALS AND EQUIPMENT YOU WILL NEED

ASSORTED HANDMADE PAPERS, SOME WITH FLOWERS • METAL RULER • BRADAWL (AWL) • BODKIN • RAFFIA •
PVA (WHITE) GLUE • PRESSED FLOWERS

ARTIST'S POCKET BOOK

THIS UNIQUE "POCKET BOOK WITH A POCKET" WOULD MAKE AN IDEAL GIFT FOR A NATURE-LOVING ARTIST. THE WATERCOLOUR PAPER IS FOLDED TO ALLOW FOR A SINGLE, PANORAMIC PAINTING OR SEVERAL SMALLER PAINTINGS, AND A MINIATURE PAINTBOX TUCKS INTO THE POCKET. HERE, THE COVER IS NATURAL LINEN BUT VELVET, WITH COLOURED PAPER PAGES, WOULD GIVE A MORE EXOTIC FEEL.

1 Cut two rectangles each of polyboard (foam board) and of wadding (batting), 11 x 15 cm (4¼ x 6 in). The four rectangles should all be identical.

2 From linen, cut out two identical larger rectangles for the cover. Cut out a smaller square for the pocket to hold the paintbox, plus extra for trimmings. Using the selvedge edge as the top of the pocket, fold in the sides and bottom, shaping it as shown.

3 Pin the pocket to the centre of one linen rectangle. Using running stitch and contrasting embroidery thread (floss), sew the pocket in place, gathering it very slightly to allow for the bulk of the paintbox. Leave the top open. Attach a long piece of tape to the centre of the other linen rectangle, using three cross stitches in a different colour of thread.

4 Stick double-sided tape around the edge on one side of a polyboard (foam board) rectangle. Sandwich a wadding (batting) rectangle between the linen rectangle (linen tape facing down) and the polyboard rectangle (double-sided tape facing up). Stretch the linen over each edge of the rectangle and attach it to the double-sided tape. Trim the corners to reduce bulk. Repeat for the front cover.

5 Cut or tear (for a deckle-like edge) a long strip of watercolour paper. Using a pencil, mark out identical intervals, slightly less than the width of the cover. It is important to be accurate at this stage, or the pages will lie askew. Using a bone folder and metal ruler, score every alternate marking, then turn the paper over, and again score alternate markings.

6 Fold the paper accordion-style, using the scored markings. Using double-sided tape or glue, attach one end of the folded paper to each cover. Press firmly to ensure the paper has fully adhered.

MATERIALS AND EQUIPMENT YOU WILL NEED

CRAFT KNIFE • METAL RULER • CUTTING MAT • POLYBOARD (FOAM BOARD) • WADDING (BATTING) • NATURAL LINEN • SCISSORS •
MINIATURE PAINTBOX • DRESSMAKER'S PINS • EMBROIDERY THREAD (FLOSS), IN 2 BRIGHT COLOURS • EMBROIDERY NEEDLE • LINEN TAPE •
DOUBLE-SIDED CARPET TAPE • EXTRA-LARGE SHEET OF WATERCOLOUR PAPER • PENCIL • BONE FOLDER • PVA (WHITE) GLUE (OPTIONAL)

CLOUD PILLOW BOOK

THIS SOFT, BILLOWING CLOUD BOOK WILL TUCK NICELY UNDER YOUR PILLOW, WAITING FOR YOU TO FILL ITS PAGES WITH THE REMNANTS OF YOUR DREAMS. USE SILVER INK TO COMPLEMENT THE BLUE PAGES AND TO MATCH THE SILVER BINDING. BOOKS DON'T HAVE TO HAVE FOUR RIGHT-ANGLED CORNERS — THINK OF INTERESTING SHAPES TO SUIT VARIOUS THEMES AND DESIGN YOUR OWN BOOKS.

1 Make a cloud template and draw two cloud shapes on to polyboard (foam board) or card (cardboard). Cut out the clouds using a craft knife.

3 Lay a wadding cloud on top of a polyboard cloud, then stretch the corresponding fleecy cloud over and fix over the edge using double-sided carpet tape. Trim off any bulky areas of fleece.

5 Use the template to cut 20 cloud pages from cloud-effect paper. Punch six holes on the straight edge of each page with a hole punch and strengthen each hole with a ring reinforcer.

2 Using the cloud template cut out two wadding (batting) and two felt clouds. Cut two more clouds from fleecy fabric, allowing an excess of 1.5 cm (⅝ in) all around. Cut the fleecy cloud for the back cover in reverse, so that the fleece is on the outside.

4 Lay a sticky-backed felt cloud over the unfinished side of each cloud, then carefully remove the backing and smooth out any creases.

6 Place the pages between the covers. Using silver elastic and a bodkin, stitch through the padding (but not the polyboard) and the holes, making diagonal stitches. Work back up the spine, crossing over the first row of stitches with stitches in the opposite direction.

MATERIALS AND EQUIPMENT YOU WILL NEED

PENCIL • PAPER • POLYBOARD (FOAM BOARD) OR CARD (CARDBOARD) • CRAFT KNIFE • CUTTING MAT • SCISSORS • WADDING (BATTING) •
WHITE STICKY-BACKED FELT • CREAM FLEECY FABRIC • DOUBLE-SIDED CARPET TAPE • CLOUD-EFFECT BLUE PAPER, A4 SIZE (8½ X 11 IN)•
HOLE PUNCH • WHITE SELF-ADHESIVE RING REINFORCERS • SILVER CORD ELASTIC • BODKIN

GARDEN NOTEBOOK

THIS USEFUL BOOK WOULD MAKE A WONDERFUL PRESENT FOR A SOMEONE WHO ENJOYS GARDENING. THE MOSS PAPER ON THE COVER MAKES A CLEVER FRAME FOR THE PICTURE OF A GARDEN, CUT FROM A GREETINGS CARD, WHILE THE FLOWERS AND TINY GARDEN IMPLEMENTS ARE FROM A DOLL'S HOUSE SHOP. THE THEME OF THIS BOOK COULD BE ADAPTED FOR A HOME IMPROVEMENT ENTHUSIAST, SUBSTITUTING A SUITABLE PICTURE FRAMED BY DOLL'S HOUSE BRICK-EFFECT WALLPAPER, AND ADDING A SET OF MINIATURE TOOLS.

1 Cut a piece of polyboard (foam board) 42 cm x 20 cm (16½ in x 8 in), and a piece of moss paper slightly larger. Mark two lines in the centre, 2.5 cm (1 in) apart, for the spine. Mark a square on the right-hand side of the polyboard for the picture and cut it out to make a window.

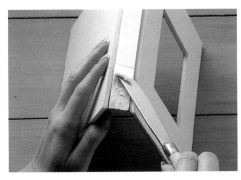

2 Partially cut through the polyboard on the spine. Remove the top layer of board and the foam with a knife.

3 Glue the moss paper to the front cover. Bend the board into a book shape then glue the moss paper to the spine and the back cover.

4 Glue the excess moss paper on to the inside, or stick down with double-sided carpet tape. Cut across the corners diagonally to reduce the bulk.

5 Make diagonal cuts in the moss paper from corner to corner of the window. Cut off most of this paper, fold the edges to the inside and stick down with glue or tape. Glue the picture, face down, behind the window.

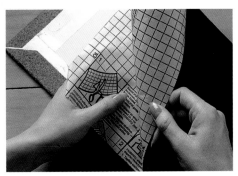

6 Cut a piece of sticky-backed felt to fit the inside of the board. Carefully remove the backing and stick the felt down, taking care not to crease it. ▶

MATERIALS AND EQUIPMENT YOU WILL NEED

CUTTING MAT • METAL RULER • CRAFT KNIFE • PENCIL • POLYBOARD (FOAM BOARD) • FLAT KNIFE • MOSS PAPER • PVA (WHITE) GLUE • DOUBLE-SIDED CARPET TAPE (OPTIONAL) • PICTURE OF A GARDEN • GREEN STICKY-BACKED FELT • BRADAWL (AWL) • DOLL'S HOUSE FLOWERS • MINIATURE GARDEN IMPLEMENTS • GREEN EMBROIDERY THREAD (FLOSS) • EMBROIDERY NEEDLE • THIMBLE • GOOD-QUALITY PLAIN WRITING PAPER • BONE FOLDER

7 Using a bradawl (awl), poke holes in the polyboard at the bottom of the window. Push the flower stalks in, applying a blob of glue to each stem beforehand.

9 Cut 21 sheets of plain writing paper and, using a bone folder, fold them in half. Lay them one inside the other in three sets of seven.

11 Each time you bring the needle out on to the spine, try and make the stitch straight and the same length as (and parallel to) the previous stitch.

8 Using embroidery thread (floss), stitch the miniature garden tools around the frame. Use a thimble to help you push the needle through the board.

10 Use the bradawl to make two holes in the fold of each set of pages, at an even distance from the top and bottom. Stitch each set of pages, starting from the inside and emerging on the spine.

12 Each time you return the needle to the inside, tie the ends of the thread in a neat bow.

CHRISTMAS ALBUM

PLAID CAKE BOARDS (AVAILABLE IN CATERING SHOPS DURING THE FESTIVE SEASON) ARE JOINED TOGETHER BY METAL SCREW POSTS (AVAILABLE IN CRAFT SHOPS) TO FORM THE COVER OF THIS FESTIVE ALBUM. SCOTTIE DOGS, CUT FROM STICKY-BACKED FELT, COMPLEMENT THE THEME AND MAKE A CHARMING FRONT COVER. USE THIS BOOK WHEN PLANNING YOUR CHRISTMAS FOR GUEST LISTS, SEATING PLANS, SPECIAL RECIPES AND GIFT IDEAS, AND AFTER THE FESTIVITIES IT IS THE PERFECT PLACE FOR CHRISTMAS MEMORABILIA.

1 Place the cake boards side by side and find the best position to join them (aim for an even distribution of pattern). Stick a 2 cm (¾ in) strip of double-sided carpet tape down both the edges to be joined.

3 Line the inside with green sticky-backed felt. Make holes in the top and bottom of the back board, close to the edge of the cardboard, using the hole punch. Push a screw post into each hole.

5 Poke two holes with a pencil through the corrugated cardboard (avoiding the cake board) on the front cover side of the spine. Thread black tape through the holes and tie in a bow for decoration.

2 Cut a strip of corrugated cardboard about 11 x 25 cm (4 x 10 in). Stick this over the tape, joining the boards but allowing a small gap between them.

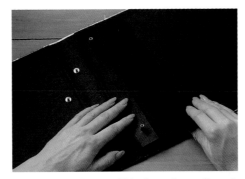

4 Cut 30 sheets of black card (cardboard) 24 cm (9½ in) square. Cut 30 card strips 4 x 24 cm (1½ x 9½ in). Make a hole gauge (see Basic Techniques) and punch out the holes in the card pages and strips. Slip them alternately on to the posts.

6 Make a template of a Scottie dog, and use this to cut out a black and a white felt dog. Cross a short length of narrow plaid ribbon at the neck of each dog and glue in position. ▶

MATERIALS AND EQUIPMENT YOU WILL NEED

2 PLAID FOIL CAKE BOARDS, 25 CM (10 IN) SQUARE • DOUBLE-SIDED CARPET TAPE • SCISSORS • METALLIC RED CORRUGATED CARDBOARD •
STICKY-BACKED FELT: GREEN, BLACK AND WHITE • REVOLVING HOLE PUNCH • 2 SCREW POSTS • BLACK CARD (CARDBOARD) • PENCIL • TRACING PAPER •
BLACK COTTON TAPE • NARROW PLAID RIBBON • PVA (WHITE) GLUE • SELF-ADHESIVE BLACK CLOTH TAPE • BRADAWL (AWL) • 4 SPLIT PINS

7 Remove the backing from each dog. Stick the dogs on to the lower right corner of the front cover, so that the white one slightly overlaps the black one.

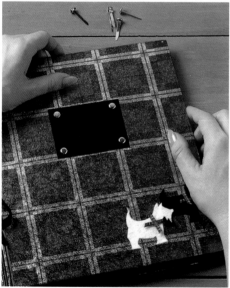

8 Cut a rectangle of self-adhesive black cloth tape to make a title plaque. At each corner, push a hole through the cloth, board and green felt using a bradawl (awl). Insert a split pin through each hole and open it up on the inside.

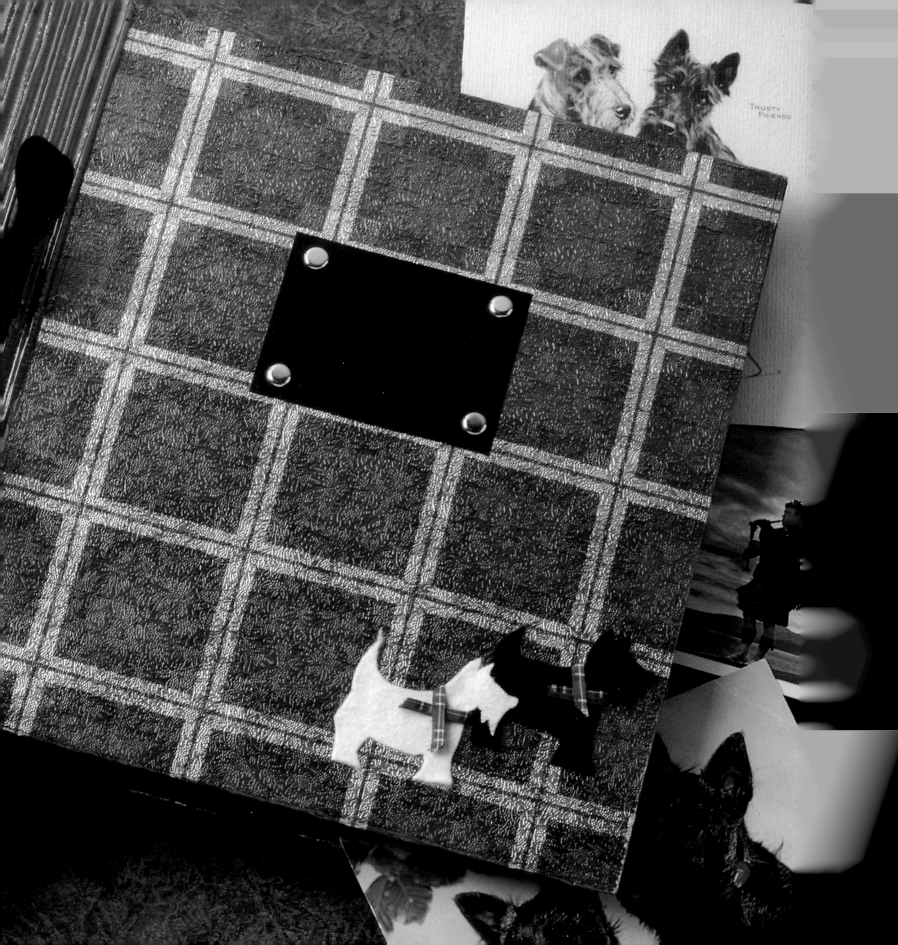

PORTFOLIO

THE ADVANTAGE OF MAKING YOUR OWN PORTFOLIO IS THAT YOU CAN MAKE IT ANY SIZE, AND YOU CAN COVER IT IN A FABRIC OF YOUR CHOICE. THE NATURAL-LOOK COVER FABRIC USED HERE IS PRINTED WITH FEATHERS AND BIRDS' EGGS, AND COMPLEMENTS THE PLAIN CALICO USED ON THE INSIDE. IRON-ON FUSIBLE (BONDING) WEB IS AN EASY OPTION FOR ATTACHING THE FABRIC, BUT FOR A MORE DURABLE METHOD YOU CAN MAKE YOUR OWN BOOK CLOTH BY GLUING A THIN PAPER BACKING TO FABRIC AND LEAVING IT TO DRY.

1 Using a utility knife, cut out all the pieces in the diagram from millboard (pasteboard). Trim off any rough edges and sand smooth.

2 Cut a piece of cover fabric (or book cloth and lining fabric) for each board. Then cut a piece of fusible (bonding) web for each piece of fabric. (If you are using book cloth, you will not need fusible web.)

3 Sandwich a piece of fusible (bonding) web between each board and its cover fabric, and iron to bond the fabric to the board. (Use glue if you are using book cloth.)

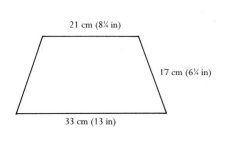

21 cm (8¼ in)
17 cm (6¼ in)
33 cm (13 in)
x 2

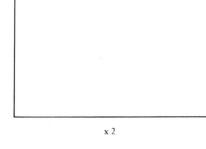

45 cm (18 in)
33 cm (13 in)
x 2

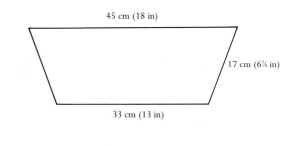

45 cm (18 in)
17 cm (6¼ in)
33 cm (13 in)
x 1

MATERIALS AND EQUIPMENT YOU WILL NEED

UTILITY KNIFE• MILLBOARD (PASTEBOARD) • CUTTING MAT • PENCIL • RULER • SANDPAPER • FABRIC FOR COVER, OR BOOK CLOTH •
FUSIBLE (BONDING) WEB • CALICO FOR LINING • PEN • SCISSORS • IRON • 12 MM (½ IN) STRAIGHT-EDGE CHISEL • HAMMER • CRAFT KNIFE •
NARROW LINEN TAPE, 2 LENGTHS EACH 50 CM (20 IN) • BRADAWL (AWL) • PVA (WHITE) GLUE • SELF-ADHESIVE CLOTH TAPE • BONE FOLDER

4 Midway along the inside edge of both short flaps on the cover side, about 2.5 cm (1 in) in from the edge, hammer a chisel in at an angle, to make a slot.

5 Working on the reverse side and using a craft knife, carefully remove a thin channel of board below the slot, to make a recess the width of the linen tape.

6 Use a bradawl (awl) to push the linen tape through the slot from the cover.

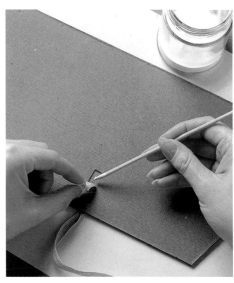

7 Glue the end of the linen tape into the recess on the reverse side and leave to dry.

8 Using fusible web as before, iron lining fabric on to each piece of board. (Use glue if using book cloth.) The lining will hide the tape in the recess on the short flaps.

9 Using self-adhesive cloth tape, tape the side and top edges of the front cover board, and reinforce the bottom corners of both cover boards. Allowing a 2.5 cm (1 in) gap between the edges of the boards, join the bottom edges with a strip of tape on both sides (the tape acts as a hinge). ▶

10 Tape the side and top edges of the two short flaps and one long flap. You may find it easier to stick the tape to one side all along the edge, then fold it over the edge and secure it on the other side.

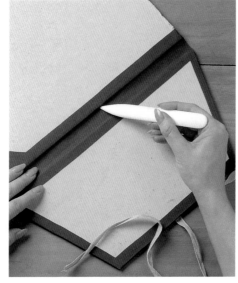

12 Run a bone folder along the taped joins (seams) to give definition and to ensure that the tape is firmly stuck. Smooth out any creases in the tape.

11 Tape the bottom edges of the short flaps to the side edges of the back cover, using a strip of tape on both sides and leaving a 2.5 cm (1 in) gap between the edges of the boards as before.

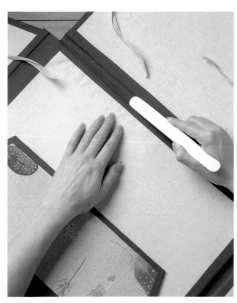

13 Tape the bottom edge of the long flap to the top edge of the back cover as before. Finally, run over all of the taped joins with a bone folder, to ensure good bondage.

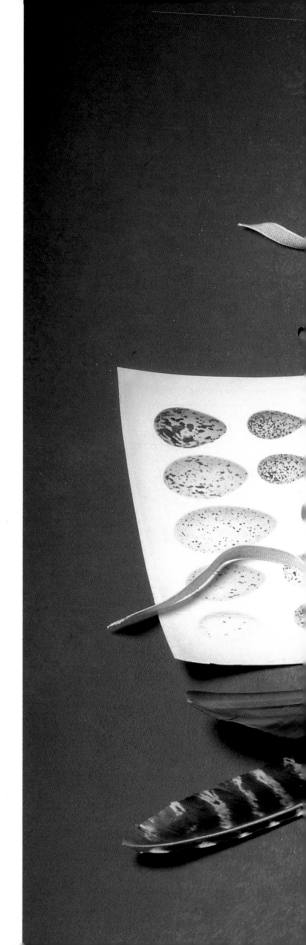

SCENTED CHRISTENING BOOK

DELICATELY SCENTED DRAWER LINING PAPER COMES IN PRETTY PATTERNS AND IS DELIGHTFUL FOR A SPECIAL OCCASION BOOK. ASK THE CHRISTENING GUESTS TO WRITE IN IT THEIR SPECIAL MESSAGES FOR YOUR CHILD. USE PAPERS IN SOFT TONES AND CHOOSE SILK RIBBON TO COMPLEMENT YOUR COLOUR SCHEME. DECKLE-EDGE THE PAGES AND ARRANGE THEM IN ORDER OF SIZE TO ACHIEVE A PLEASING PETAL EFFECT. FOR THE FINISHING TOUCH, FRAME A PHOTO OF YOUR BABY OR A VICTORIAN SCRAP PICTURE ON THE COVER.

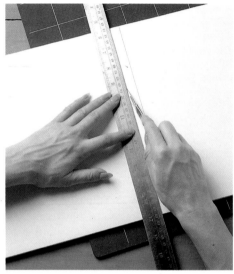

1 Cut a piece of polyboard (foam board) 65 x 29 cm (25½ x 11½ in). Mark two parallel lines across the centre, 1.5 cm (⅝ in) apart. Partially cut through the polyboard (see Basic Techniques) along the lines, to form the spine.

2 Bend the polyboard into a book shape. Paste drawer lining paper on to the board (see Basic Techniques), making sure that you fit the paper right into the cut lines.

3 Line the inside of the cover using the same paper. Leave to dry under a couple of telephone directories to prevent warping. Mark the position of two holes on the back board, about 7.5 cm (3 in) apart and 2.5 cm (1 in) from the spine. Use a sharp pencil to punch the holes.

MATERIALS AND EQUIPMENT YOU WILL NEED

POLYBOARD (FOAM BOARD) • CUTTING MAT • CRAFT KNIFE • METAL RULER • PASTE (SEE BASIC TECHNIQUES) • BONE FOLDER • SCENTED DRAWER LINING PAPER • TELEPHONE DIRECTORIES • SHARP PENCIL • WADDING (BATTING) • PAPER OR FABRIC LACE • SQUARE OR RECTANGULAR DOILY • DOUBLE-SIDED CARPET TAPE • GLUE STICK • BABY PHOTOGRAPH OR VICTORIAN SCRAP PICTURE • SCISSORS • NARROW SILK RIBBON • ASSORTED DECKLE-EDGED SCISSORS • ASSORTED PASTEL-COLOURED PAPER • SCRAP PAPER • HOLE PUNCH

4 With the tip of the pencil protruding through the hole on the inside, trim the rough edges of the hole using a craft knife.

6 Use double-sided carpet tape to stick first the wadding, then the paper and finally the lace to the centre of the front cover.

8 Cut two pieces of ribbon about 5 cm (2 in) longer than the entire cover, and two about 5 cm (2 in) longer than the spine. Run the glue stick along the ribbons before sticking them down along the cover on the outside, about 2 cm (¾ in) from the edge. The ribbons should cross at the corners and end on the inside.

5 Cut same-size rectangles of paper, wadding (batting) and lace. Cut the decorative border off a doily. Choose patterns and textures to suit the cover drawer lining paper.

7 Using a glue stick, fix the doily border around the edge of the lace to make a frame. Glue a photograph or Victorian scrap picture on to the lace, in the centre of the frame.

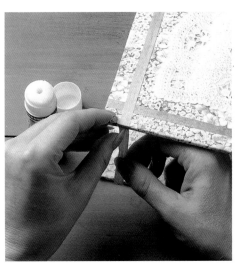

9 Cut two pieces of ribbon just shorter than the spine. Glue them inside the front and back covers so that they hide the ends of the ribbons, which extend over from the front.

▶

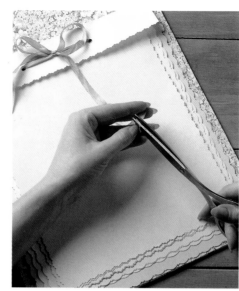

10 Using various deckle-edged scissors, cut sheets of paper, each one slightly smaller than the last. Make one sheet 4 cm (1½ in) longer than the others.

12 Working from the back, thread the ribbon through the holes in the cover. Next, thread the long sheet on, just through the holes in the page (lift the flap out of the way). Thread all the pages on, in decreasing size order, and, lastly, thread the ribbon through the holes in the flap from the long back page. Tie the ribbon in a bow and trim the ends at an angle.

11 Make a hole gauge (see Basic Techniques) and punch two evenly spaced holes near a narrow edge of each sheet. Using a bone folder, score and fold the extra-long sheet 4 cm (1½ in) from one narrow edge. Using the hole gauge as a guide, punch two holes through both layers of paper.

TRIANGULAR BOOK

THIS BOOK PRESENTS A REWARDING CHALLENGE FOR THE MORE EXPERIENCED BOOKBINDER. ITS STYLISH AND CONTEMPORARY LOOK AND SHAPE SUGGEST THAT IT BE USED WHERE CONVENTIONS NEED TO BE BROKEN DOWN. NOVELTY SHAPES FOR BOOKS ARE NOT A MODERN PHENOMENON — IN THE BIBLIOTHÈQUE NATIONALE IN PARIS THERE IS A BEAUTIFUL HEART-SHAPED, ILLUMINATED MEDIEVAL MANUSCRIPT, WHICH CONTAINS LOVE SONGS. WHEN YOU SET ABOUT DESIGNING A SHAPE, CHOOSE ONE TO SUIT THE BOOK'S PURPOSE.

1 Cut 18 sheets of good-quality writing paper into diamond shapes, with all the edges measuring 21.5 cm (8½ in). Fold them in half to make two equilateral triangles. Group into six sets of three.

2 Make a "W" fold (see All-in-One Stitching, Basic Techniques) in a diamond-shaped sheet of textured paper and glue to one of the folded sheets of writing paper. Remove all but a 4 cm (1½ in) margin along the spine edge of the purple paper and the underside. This is the "wasted edge". Make another the same. Stitch the sets of pages together, following the instructions in steps 3–6 of All-in-One Stitching, Basic Techniques.

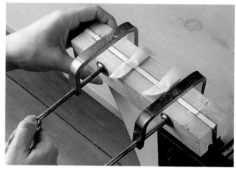

3 Clamp the spine between two strips of wood. Apply PVA (white) glue along the spine, lay a strip of mull or bandage along the spine and apply more glue over the top.

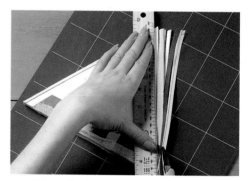

4 Place the book on a cutting mat and, pressing firmly, trim the uneven edges of the pages against a metal ruler, using a utility knife. You may need to make repeated cuts to get through the pages.

MATERIALS AND EQUIPMENT YOU WILL NEED

METAL RULER • SCISSORS • WHITE OR CREAM GOOD-QUALITY WRITING PAPER • CHEAP, TEXTURED, CREAM PAPER •
PVA (WHITE) GLUE • UTILITY KNIFE • LINEN TAPE, OR SEAM BINDING • VICE AND CLAMPS • 2 STRIPS OF WOOD • MULL, OR OPEN-WEAVE BANDAGE •
CUTTING MAT • STIFF CARDBOARD OR MILLBOARD (PASTEBOARD) • SCRAP OF THIN CARD (CARDBOARD) • SILK EMBROIDERY THREADS (FLOSSES) • GOLD PAPER •
PASTE (SEE BASIC TECHNIQUES) • BLACK BOOK CLOTH • CIRCLE CUTTER (CUTTING COMPASS) OR CRAFT KNIFE • BONE FOLDER

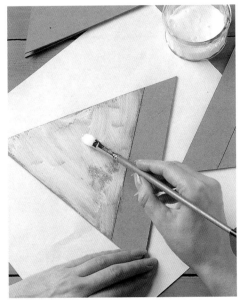

5 Cut four equilateral triangles from cardboard or millboard (pasteboard), 22 cm (8¾ in). Draw a 4 cm (1½ in) margin on one side of each. Glue together in pairs, leaving the margin edges unglued.

7 To make a fancy end tab, curl the end of a strip of card (cardboard) 12 mm x 4 cm (½ x 1½ in) and glue then wrap silk threads over the curl. Make two tabs, and glue one at each end of the spine, so the curl projects over the pages.

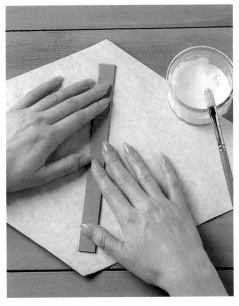

9 From book cloth, cut a diamond 2.5 cm (1 in) larger all round than the paper diamonds in Step 1. Cut a strip of board exactly the length of the spine. Glue the strip exactly in the mid-line on the paper side of the book cloth.

6 Apply glue to both sides of a purple "wasted edge" and slide it between a pair of boards at their unglued margins. Repeat to make the second cover.

8 Cut two pieces of gold paper to fit the covers exactly. Paste on to the covers and smooth out any bubbles.

10 Fold the book cloth around the book and press around the edges with your fingertips to transfer the outline to the book cloth. ▶

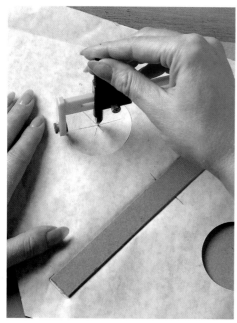

11 Use a circle cutter (cutting compass) or template and craft knife to remove a 5 cm (2 in) diameter circle from both sides of cloth.

13 Use a bone folder to smooth over the covers, eliminating any air pockets. Work outwards from the circle.

15 Glue along the overlapping edges of the book cloth, fold in and smooth over with a bone folder.

12 Trace the circle on to the gold covers. Apply glue to the gold back cover, carefully avoiding the circle. Smooth the book cloth in position. Repeat for the front cover.

14 Using a bone folder, tuck in the book cloth at the top and bottom of the spine.

16 Glue the end pages in place inside the front and back covers, and smooth in place.

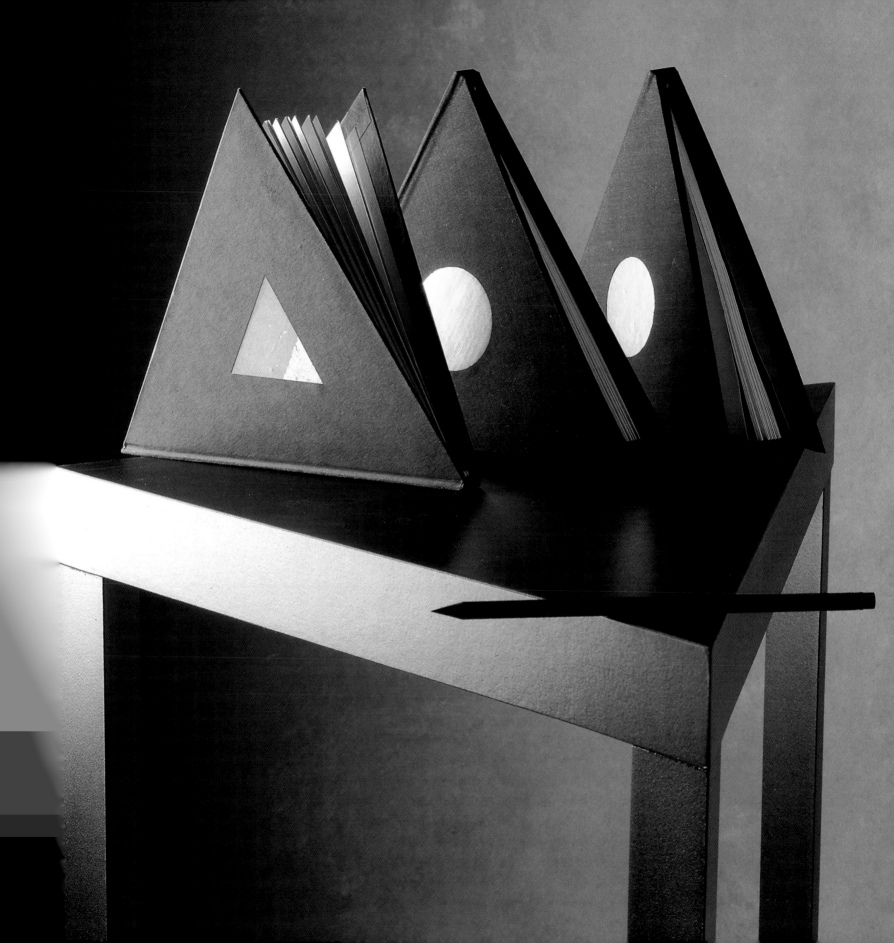

CLASSIC NOTEBOOK

THIS CLASSIC BOOK MAKES A PRACTICAL GIFT FOR THE BUDDING WRITER. ITS LINED PAGES ARE FROM AN EXERCISE BOOK AND ARE STITCHED USING THE ALL-IN-ONE METHOD. READYMADE BOOK CLOTH IS AVAILABLE FROM SPECIALIST SUPPLIERS, BUT YOU CAN MAKE YOUR OWN BY LINING FABRIC WITH A THIN SHEET OF PAPER. CUT THE PAPER LARGER THAN THE FABRIC, SPREAD ON PVA (WHITE) GLUE AND WHEN IT BECOMES TACKY PLACE THE FABRIC, RIGHT SIDE UP, ON IT. SMOOTH OUT ANY AIR BUBBLES AND ALLOW TO DRY.

1 Remove the staples from the 16 x 20 cm (6¼ x 8 in) exercise book(s) and carefully take out the folded pages. Group them into six sets, laying the pages one inside the other. Make a hole gauge (see Basic Techniques) and make holes in each set of pages using a bradawl (awl).

2 Make a "W" fold in two 16 x 20 cm (6¼ x 8 in) sheets of lined paper (see All-in-One Stitching, Basic Techniques). Cut two endpaper sheets to size and glue them to the outside edge of a "W".

3 Using the bradawl, make holes to correspond with the holes in the pages. With a long thread, stitch the sections together (see Steps 3–6, All-in-One Stitching, Basic Techniques).

4 Clamp the spine of the book between two strips of wood, and slip two strips of linen tape or seam binding under the stitching, across the spine. Glue a 17 x 3 cm (6¾ x 1¼ in) strip of mull along the spine (see step 8, All-in-One Stitching, Basic Techniques).

MATERIALS AND EQUIPMENT YOU WILL NEED

1-2 STANDARD EXERCISE BOOKS • SCRAP PAPER • PENCIL • METAL RULER • BRADAWL (AWL) • LINED PAPER • ENDPAPER • SCISSORS • PVA (WHITE) GLUE • NEEDLE • WAXED LINEN THREAD • VICE AND CLAMPS • 2 STRIPS OF WOOD • LINEN TAPE OR SEAM BINDING • MULL OR OPEN-WEAVE BANDAGE • CUTTING MAT • UTILITY KNIFE • CARDBOARD OR MOUNT BOARD • THIN CARD (CARDBOARD) • SILK EMBROIDERY THREADS (FLOSSES) • BOOK CLOTH • BONE FOLDER

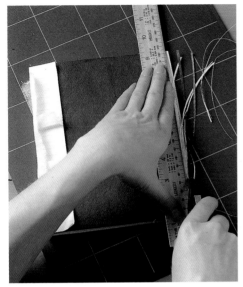

5 Lay the book on a cutting mat and, pressing firmly, trim the pages against a metal ruler using a utility knife.

6 Cut four 21.5 x 16.5 (8½ x 6½ in) sheets of cardboard or mount board, leaving a 5 cm (2 in) margin at the edge of each. Glue together in pairs, leaving the margin edges unglued.

7 Apply glue to both sides of one "wasted edge" (see All-in-One Stitching, Basic Techniques) and slide it between a pair of boards at their unglued margins. Repeat to make the second cover.

8 To make a fancy end tab, curl the end of a strip of card (cardboard) 6 mm x 3 cm (¼ x 1¼ in) and glue then wrap silk threads over the curl. Make two tabs, and glue one at each end of the spine, so the curls project over the pages.

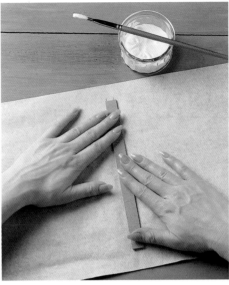

9 Cut a rectangle of book cloth and a strip of board the exact length of the spine. Glue the strip exactly in the mid-line on the paper side of the book cloth.

10 Position the book on top of the book cloth and cover it completely with glue. ▶

11 Fold the book cloth over the front cover and smooth with a bone folder, working from the spine outwards. Repeat with the back cover.

13 Using a bone folder or similar, tuck in the book cloth overlap at the top and bottom of the spine.

15 Insert an A4 (8½ x 11 in) sheet of paper under the endpaper at the back. Spread the endpaper with glue.

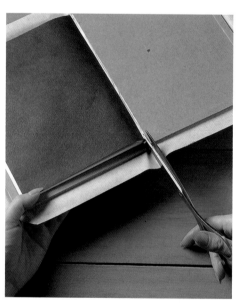

12 Trim off the corners of the book cloth, leaving an overlap the width of the cover board. Using a sharp pair of scissors, cut slits in the "wasted edge" to correspond with the edges of the spine, taking care not to cut the book cloth.

14 Stand the book on its spine and support it in that position. Open the front cover and glue down first the top and bottom overlaps, then the side overlaps. Repeat for the back cover.

16 Smooth the endpaper in place on the inside back cover, using a bone folder to eliminate any air pockets. Repeat steps 15 and 16 for the front cover.

June 1959] ALTERNATIVE MATHEMATICS

JAPANESE STORK ALBUM

JAPANESE BINDING IS DECEPTIVELY EASY TO DO AND, ALTHOUGH IT LOOKS DELICATE, IT IS SURPRISINGLY STRONG AND SECURE. FOR THIS ALBUM THE STITCHING "THREAD" IS A SOFT, PLAITED STRING AND, SINCE IT IS TOO THICK TO THREAD ON A NEEDLE, A LOOP OF WIRE IS TWISTED AROUND IT TO ACT AS A GUIDE. THE COVER IS MADE FROM A MOTTLED HANDMADE PAPER, DECORATED WITH A STORK MOTIF. YOU MAY PREFER TO DESIGN YOUR OWN MOTIF TO COMPLEMENT THE THEME OF THE CONTENTS.

1 From cardboard cut two rectangles 30 x 33 cm (12 x 13 in) and two strips 30 x 3.5 cm (12 x 1⅜ in). Lay each strip beside each rectangle, with a slight gap between. Paste a strip of mull or bandage along the join.

2 Cut paper for the cover, allowing a 2 cm (¾ in) overlap and paste on (see Basic Techniques). Turn the board over, trim the corners and paste the edges back.

3 Cut two sheets of contrasting paper to line the cover, ideally using a rotary cutting blade. From card (cardboard) cut 26 pages 29.7 x 36 cm (11¾ x 14¼ in) and 27 pages the same size from the glassine paper.

4 Using a bone folder, score a line on each sheet of card, 4 cm (1½ in) in from the spine edge.

5 Cut strips of card 4 cm (1½ in) wide, to fit the scored margins. Using a glue stick, glue a strip to each page.

6 Using a hole punch, punch four holes at equal intervals in each of these pages. Do the same with the glassine sheets. ▶

MATERIALS AND EQUIPMENT YOU WILL NEED

CARDBOARD • CUTTING MAT • CRAFT KNIFE • METAL RULER • MULL, OR OPEN-WEAVE BANDAGE • HANDMADE PAPER • PASTE (SEE BASIC TECHNIQUES) • HANDMADE PAPER IN CONTRASTING COLOUR • ROTARY CUTTING BLADE (OPTIONAL) • CREAM CARD (CARDBOARD) • GLASSINE PAPER • BONE FOLDER • GLUE STICK • HOLE PUNCH • SCISSORS • PLAITED STRING • BRADAWL (AWL) • PVA (WHITE) GLUE • THIN WIRE • SILVER FOIL • GRASSES AND STRAW • SCRAP PAPER • WEIGHTS

7 Cut two lengths of string 25 cm (10 in). Working from the front, make a hole with a bradawl (awl) in the front and back cover, halfway down and close to one narrow edge. Push each string through the holes from the front. Glue the frayed ends on to the inside.

9 Collate the pages, alternating card pages with glassine paper pages. Cut a strip of cover paper wide enough and long enough to fit over the spine. Fold the ends over as shown. (It may help to first apply a little glue to the spine with a glue stick.)

11 Use silver foil, grasses, straw and scraps of torn, handmade paper to decorate a plaque for the front of the album. Make a simple stork image or create your own design.

8 Glue the lining paper on to the inside of the covers, hiding the ends of the string. Pierce holes on the spine edge of each cover board to correspond with the holes in the pages.

10 Loop a piece of thin wire around a long length of string and twist the ends together to act as a needle. Bind the book in the Japanese style (see Basic Techniques), but here, because the string is bulky, tie the knot on the outside.

12 Glue the plaque in the centre of the front cover. Place a piece of scrap paper on the front of the book and weight the book until the glue is dry.

COOKBOOK

USE THIS UNUSUAL SCRAPBOOK FOR YOUR FAVOURITE RECIPES, DINNER MENUS OR INTERESTING FOOD INFORMATION. THE BOOK COVERS AND PAGES ARE CUT FROM HANDMADE INDIAN KHADI PAPER, WHICH HAS A LOVELY TEXTURE AND A NATURAL DECKLE EDGE. THE BOOK IS BOUND JAPANESE-STYLE USING A WAXED LINEN THREAD. THE PAGE DIVIDERS ARE DECORATED WITH EMBOSSED FOIL MOTIFS PERTAINING TO THE DIFFERENT CATEGORIES OF FOOD: SOUP, SAVOURY DISHES, FISH OR POULTRY, VEGETABLES AND DESSERT.

1 Arrange the handmade paper with page dividers separating different colours. The sheets of card (cardboard) will form the covers.

2 Using a ruler and craft knife, cut the punched edge off each of the page dividers and discard.

3 Using a bone folder, score a line 2 cm (¾ in) from the spine edge of each cover, page and page divider. Using a bradawl (awl) and a hole gauge, make holes along this line at regular intervals (see Basic Techniques).

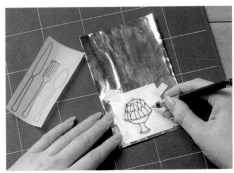

4 Make templates of a variety of foods, cutlery and kitchen implements. Copy these on to tracing paper and tape to aluminium foil. Using a ballpoint pen, emboss the details on to the foil.

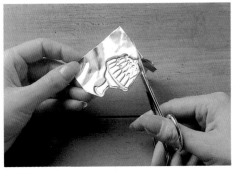

5 Using nail scissors, carefully snip out each embossed motif.

6 Cut a small rectangle of paper for each motif or group of motifs. Tear the edges against a ruler to give a deckle-edge effect. Glue each motif or group of motifs to its backing patch of paper. ▶

MATERIALS AND EQUIPMENT YOU WILL NEED

ASSORTED COLOURS OF KHADI OR ANY HANDMADE PAPER, A4 SIZE (8½ x 11 IN) • PAGE DIVIDERS •
2 SHEETS OF THIN CARD (CARDBOARD), A4 SIZE (8½ x 11 IN) • CUTTING MAT • RULER • CRAFT KNIFE • BONE FOLDER • BRADAWL (AWL) • TRACING PAPER •
MASKING TAPE • ALUMINIUM FOIL • BALLPOINT PEN • NAIL SCISSORS • PVA (WHITE) GLUE • LINEN THREAD • NEEDLE • BEESWAX • 2 LARGE PAPER CLAMPS

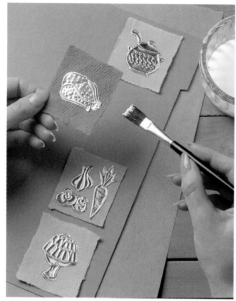

7 Glue all the patches with food motifs to the first page divider, then write the names of the recipes alongside them. Alternatively, glue each on to a separate page divider. Glue the patches with "cutlery" motifs to the front cover. Collate the covers and pages.

9 Clamp the book firmly on either side to hold it in position while you bind it. Stitch the book in the Japanese style (see Basic Techniques).

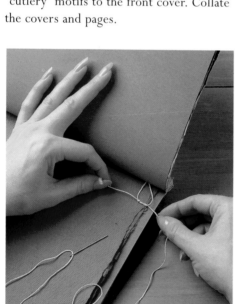

8 Pull the linen thread through beeswax before you begin stitching (see Basic Techniques). Tie a knot on the inside near the spine at the bottom of the book.

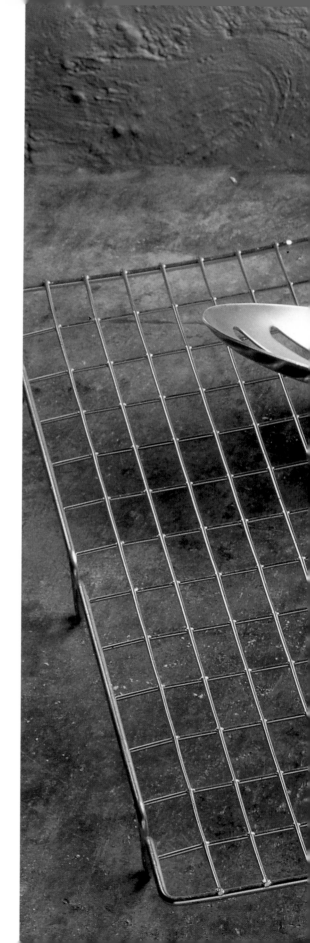

PAPERMAKING TEMPLATES

THE MEASUREMENTS GIVEN FOR EACH TEMPLATE ARE THOSE USED WITHIN THE INDIVIDUAL PROJECTS. WHERE NO MEASUREMENTS ARE GIVEN, THEY ARE REPRODUCED AT THE SAME SIZE, OR AN ENLARGEMENT SIZE IS SPECIFIED. FOR AN ENLARGEMENT, EITHER USE A GRID SYSTEM OR PHOTOCOPIER.

25 cm (10 in)

EMBROIDERED BIRD PP 86–87

PATTERNED PULP PP 43–45

EMBOSSED WRITING PAPER PP 39–40

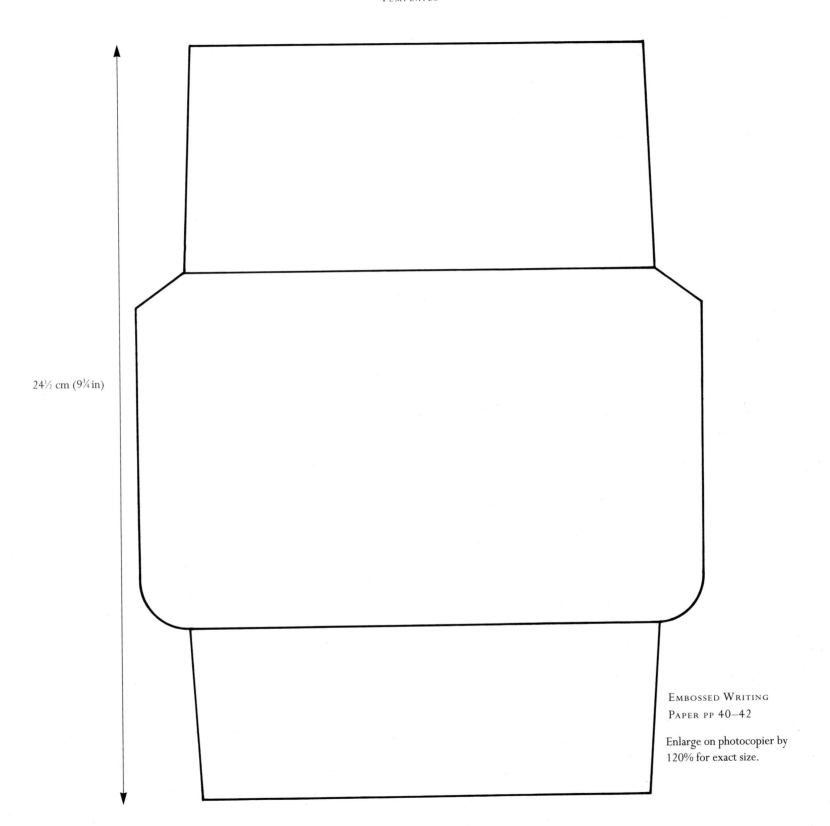

24½ cm (9¾ in)

EMBOSSED WRITING
PAPER PP 40–42

Enlarge on photocopier by
120% for exact size.

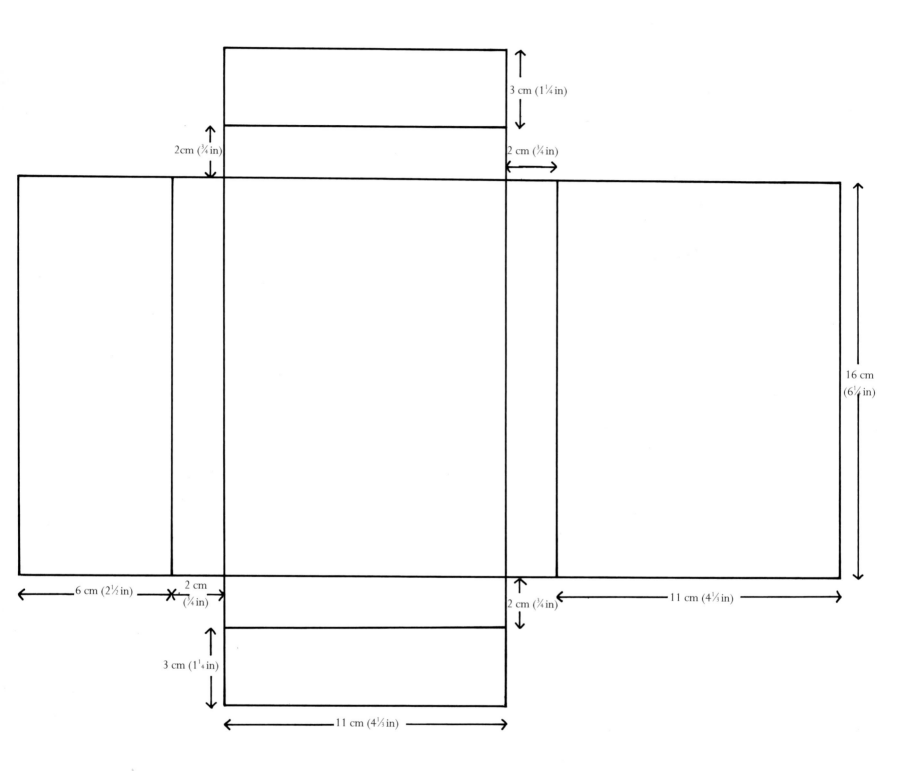

3 cm (1¼ in)

2cm (¾ in)

2 cm (¾ in)

16 cm
(6¼ in)

6 cm (2½ in)

2 cm
(¾ in)

2 cm (¾ in)

11 cm (4⅓ in)

3 cm (1¼ in)

11 cm (4⅓ in)

PAPER CUTTING TEMPLATES

THE PATTERNS FOR THE PAPER CUTTING PROJECTS ARE PRESENTED IN TWO DIFFERENT STYLES. FIRSTLY, THERE ARE SOME FOR WHICH THE WHOLE DESIGN IS GIVEN AND YOU EITHER HAVE TO TRACE THE WHOLE DESIGN, OR JUST A SECTION, USUALLY HALF OR A QUARTER, AND TRANSFER IT ON TO YOUR CHOSEN PAPER. SECONDLY, THERE ARE SOME FOR WHICH ONLY THE SECTION YOU HAVE TO TRACE IS GIVEN. FOLLOW THE STEPS FOR EACH PROJECT AND THEY WILL TELL YOU WHICH PART TO TRACE.

DECORATED LAMPSHADE PP 106–107

PAPER CAFÉ CURTAIN PP 112–113

MEXICAN PAPERCUT BUNTING PP 114–115

SHELF EDGING PP 116–117

PLACE MAT PP 118–119

18TH-CENTURY ITALIAN PAPERCUT PP 120–121

WHITE LACE SCHERENSCHNITTE PP 122–123

STAR CLOCK PP 124–126

1 2 3 4
5 6 7 8
9 10
11 12

BOOKMARKS PP 133–135

VALENTINES PP 127–129

DOVE LAMPSHADE PP 136–137

FRAKTUR-STYLE COLOURED PAPERCUT PP 141–143

DECORATED ELEPHANTS PP 146–148

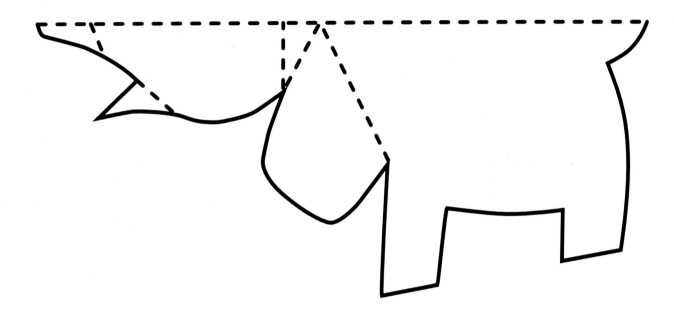

PAPER FLOWERS PP 149–151

CYCLIST COLLAGE PP 152–154

CAKE TIN PP 165–167

SNOWFLAKES PP 155–157

GREETINGS CARDS PP 158–161

PAPIER MACHE TEMPLATES

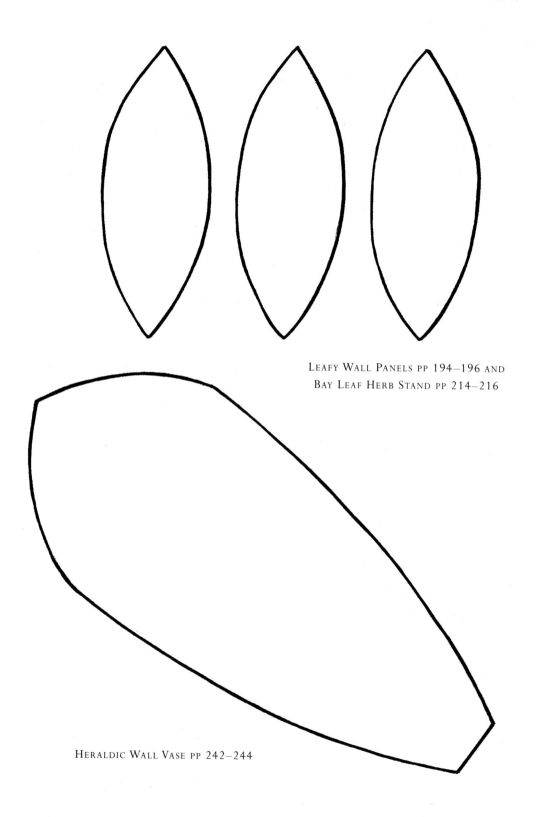

LEAFY WALL PANELS PP 194–196 AND
BAY LEAF HERB STAND PP 214–216

HERALDIC WALL VASE PP 242–244

GILDED FINIALS PP 202–204

PETAL PICTURE FRAME PP 245–247

EXOTIC BLIND PULLS PP 234–235

BAY LEAF HERB STAND PP 214–216

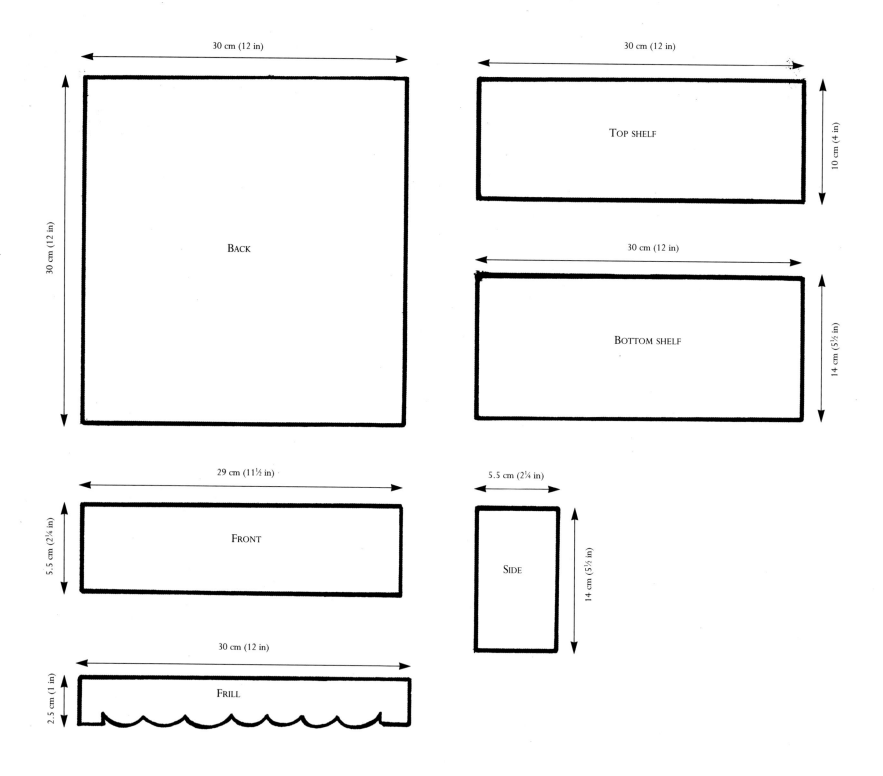

30 cm (12 in)

BACK

30 cm (12 in)

30 cm (12 in)

TOP SHELF

10 cm (4 in)

30 cm (12 in)

BOTTOM SHELF

14 cm (5½ in)

29 cm (11½ in)

FRONT

5.5 cm (2¼ in)

5.5 cm (2¼ in)

SIDE

14 cm (5½ in)

30 cm (12 in)

FRILL

2.5 cm (1 in)

CARDBOARD TEMPLATES

TRAY PP 305–307

GREETINGS CARDS AND GIFT TAGS PP 266–267

STORAGE BOXES PP 277–278

SHELF EDGING PP 270–271

CARDBOARD PLACE MATS PP 272–273

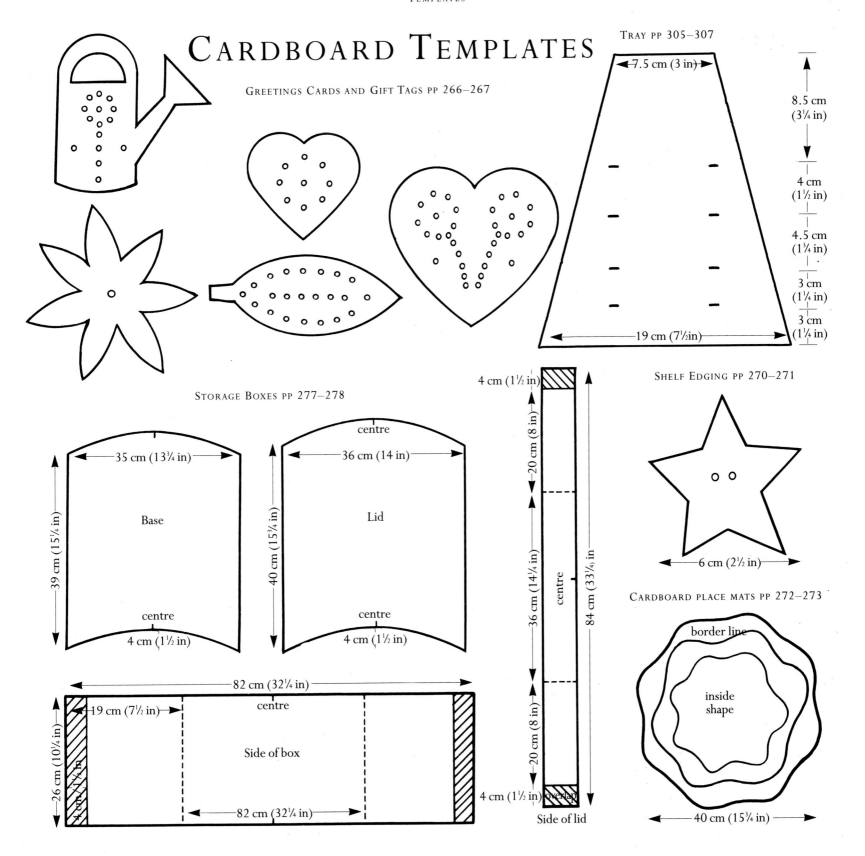

7.5 cm (3 in)

8.5 cm (3¼ in)

4 cm (1½ in)

4.5 cm (1¾ in)

3 cm (1¼ in)

3 cm (1¼ in)

19 cm (7½in)

35 cm (13¾ in)

Base

39 cm (15¼ in)

centre

4 cm (1½ in)

36 cm (14 in)

centre

Lid

40 cm (15¾ in)

centre

4 cm (1½ in)

82 cm (32¼ in)

19 cm (7½ in)

centre

Side of box

26 cm (10¼ in)

4 cm (1½ in)

82 cm (32¼ in)

4 cm (1½ in)

20 cm (8 in)

centre

36 cm (14¼ in)

84 cm (33¼ in)

20 cm (8 in)

4 cm (1½ in) overlap

Side of lid

6 cm (2½ in)

border line

inside shape

40 cm (15¾ in)

Doll's House pp 288–290

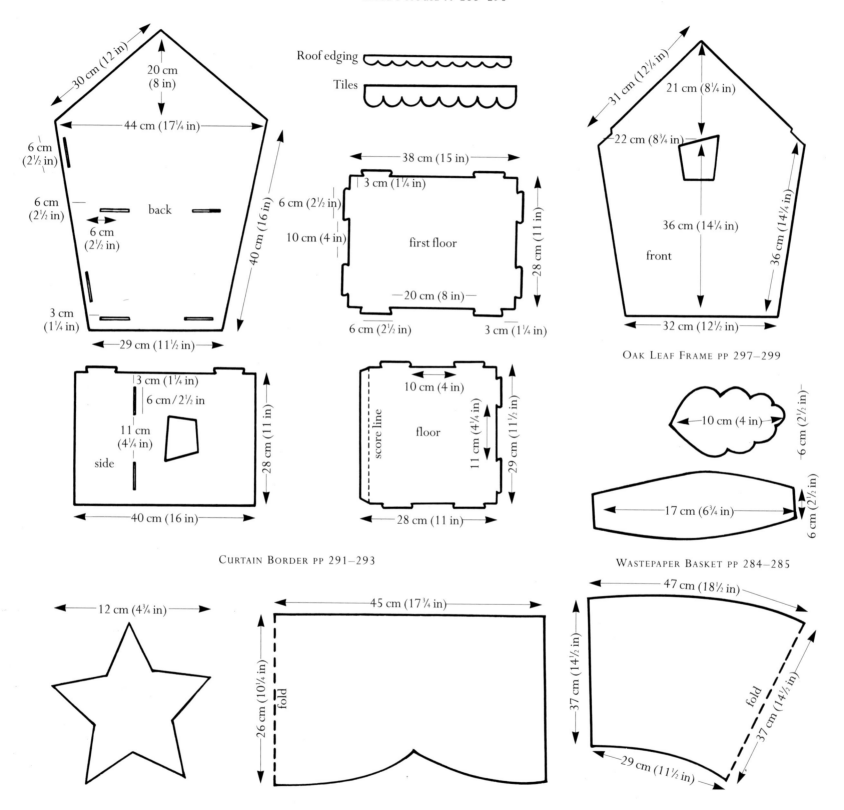

30 cm (12 in)

20 cm (8 in)

44 cm (17¼ in)

6 cm (2½ in)

6 cm (2½ in)

6 cm (2½ in)

back

3 cm (1¼ in)

29 cm (11½ in)

40 cm (16 in)

Roof edging

Tiles

38 cm (15 in)

3 cm (1¼ in)

6 cm (2½ in)

10 cm (4 in)

first floor

20 cm (8 in)

28 cm (11 in)

6 cm (2½ in)   3 cm (1¼ in)

31 cm (12¼ in)

21 cm (8¼ in)

22 cm (8¾ in)

36 cm (14¼ in)

front

36 cm (14¼ in)

32 cm (12½ in)

3 cm (1¼ in)

6 cm / 2½ in

11 cm (4¼ in)

side

28 cm (11 in)

40 cm (16 in)

10 cm (4 in)

score line

floor

11 cm (4¼ in)

29 cm (11½ in)

28 cm (11 in)

Oak Leaf Frame pp 297–299

6 cm (2½ in)

10 cm (4 in)

6 cm (2½ in)

17 cm (6¾ in)

Curtain Border pp 291–293

12 cm (4¾ in)

45 cm (17¾ in)

26 cm (10¼ in)

fold

Wastepaper Basket pp 284–285

47 cm (18½ in)

37 cm (14½ in)

fold

37 cm (14½ in)

29 cm (11½ in)

CARD TABLE PP 314–317

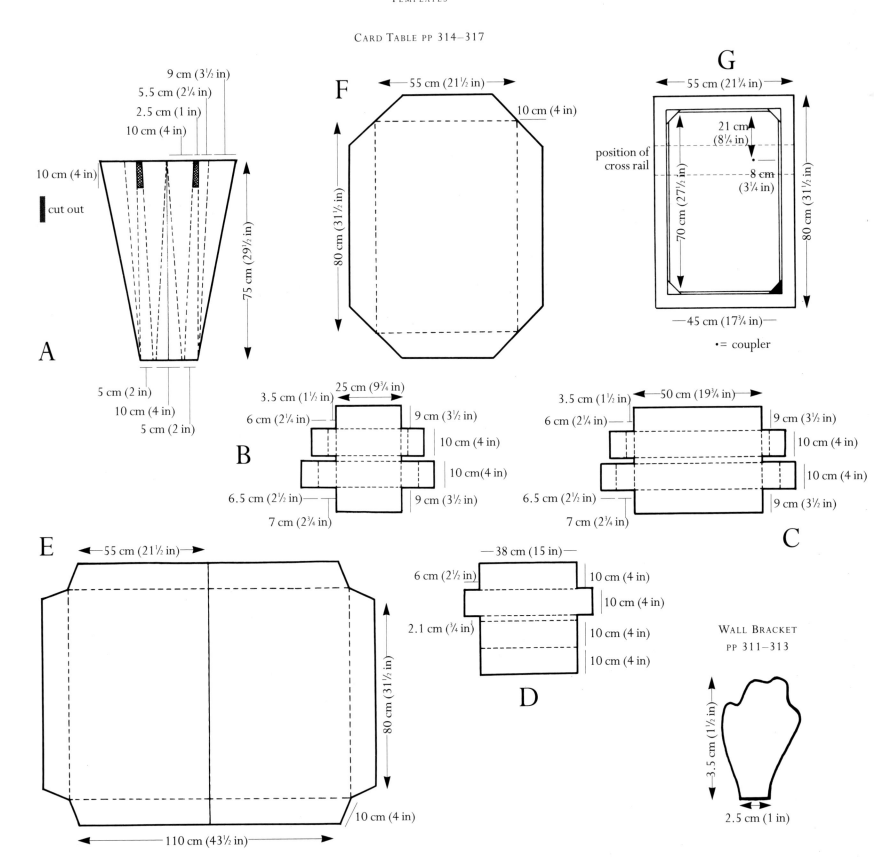

9 cm (3½ in)
5.5 cm (2¼ in)
2.5 cm (1 in)
10 cm (4 in)

10 cm (4 in)

cut out

A

75 cm (29½ in)

5 cm (2 in)
10 cm (4 in)
5 cm (2 in)

F

55 cm (21½ in)
10 cm (4 in)
80 cm (31½ in)

G

55 cm (21¾ in)
21 cm (8¼ in)
position of cross rail
8 cm (3¼ in)
70 cm (27½ in)
80 cm (31½ in)
45 cm (17¾ in)

• = coupler

B

3.5 cm (1½ in)
25 cm (9¾ in)
6 cm (2¼ in)
9 cm (3½ in)
10 cm (4 in)
10 cm (4 in)
6.5 cm (2½ in)
9 cm (3½ in)
7 cm (2¾ in)

C

3.5 cm (1½ in)
50 cm (19¾ in)
6 cm (2¼ in)
9 cm (3½ in)
10 cm (4 in)
10 cm (4 in)
6.5 cm (2½ in)
9 cm (3½ in)
7 cm (2¾ in)

E

55 cm (21½ in)
80 cm (31½ in)
10 cm (4 in)
110 cm (43½ in)

D

38 cm (15 in)
6 cm (2½ in)
10 cm (4 in)
10 cm (4 in)
2.1 cm (¾ in)
10 cm (4 in)
10 cm (4 in)

WALL BRACKET
PP 311–313

3.5 cm (1½ in)
2.5 cm (1 in)

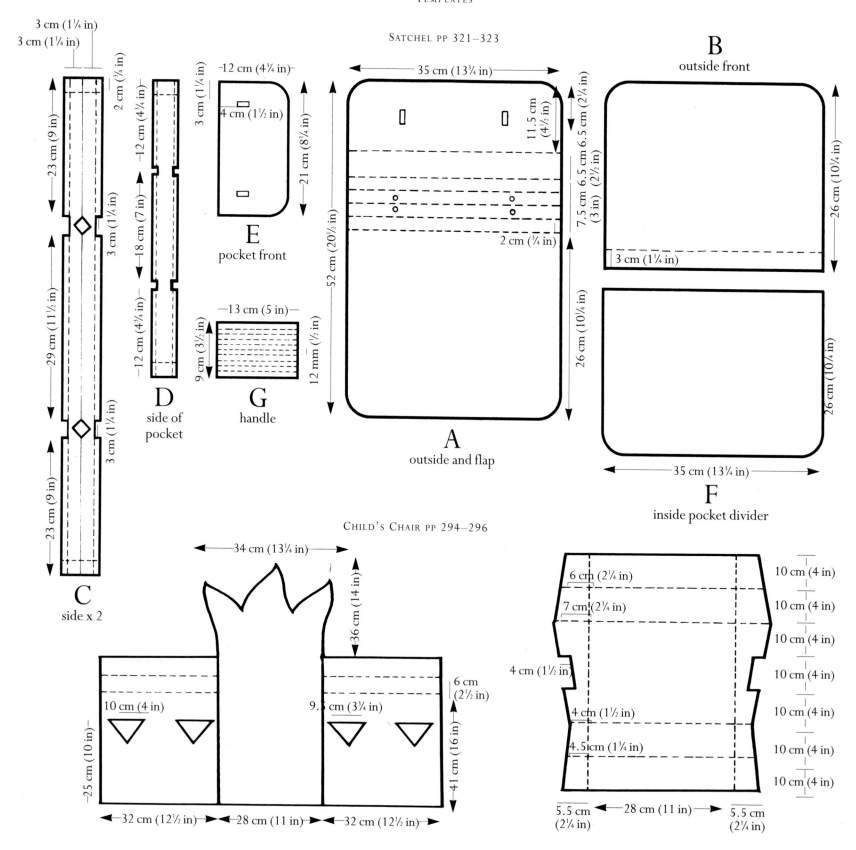

SATCHEL PP 321–323

3 cm (1¼ in)
3 cm (1¼ in)

23 cm (9 in)

2 cm (¾ in)

3 cm (1¼ in)

29 cm (11½ in)

3 cm (1¼ in)

23 cm (9 in)

C
side x 2

12 cm (4¾ in)

18 cm (7 in)

12 cm (4¾ in)

D
side of
pocket

12 cm (4¾ in)
3 cm (1¼ in)
4 cm (1½ in)

21 cm (8¼ in)

E
pocket front

13 cm (5 in)

9 cm (3½ in)

12 mm (½ in)

G
handle

35 cm (13¾ in)

11.5 cm (4½ in)

6.5 cm 6.5 cm (2¼ in)
7.5 cm (3 in) 6.5 cm (2½ in)

2 cm (¾ in)

52 cm (20½ in)

26 cm (10¼ in)

A
outside and flap

B
outside front

26 cm (10¼ in)

3 cm (1¼ in)

26 cm (10¼ in)

35 cm (13¾ in)

F
inside pocket divider

CHILD'S CHAIR PP 294–296

34 cm (13¼ in)

36 cm (14 in)

6 cm (2½ in)

10 cm (4 in)

9.5 cm (3¾ in)

25 cm (10 in)

41 cm (16 in)

32 cm (12½ in)

28 cm (11 in)

32 cm (12½ in)

6 cm (2¼ in)
7 cm (2¾ in)

4 cm (1½ in)

4 cm (1½ in)

4.5 cm (1¾ in)

10 cm (4 in)
10 cm (4 in)
10 cm (4 in)
10 cm (4 in)
10 cm (4 in)
10 cm (4 in)
10 cm (4 in)

5.5 cm (2¼ in)

28 cm (11 in)

5.5 cm (2¼ in)

SUNBURST CLOCK PP 300–301

CHANDELIER PP 302–304

WALL SCONCE PP 308–310

- - - scorelines for back
——— scorelines for front

diameter =
46 cm (18 in)

10 cm (4 in)

6 cm (2½ in)

3 cm (1¼ in)

3 cm (1¼ in)

12cm (5 in)

19 cm (7½ in)

8.5 cm (3¼ in)

9.5 cm (3¾ in)

3 cm
(1¼ in)

4 cm
(1½ in)

11 cm (4½ in)

13 cm (5 in)

11 cm (4½ in)

CHRISTMAS TREE DECORATIONS PP 324–325

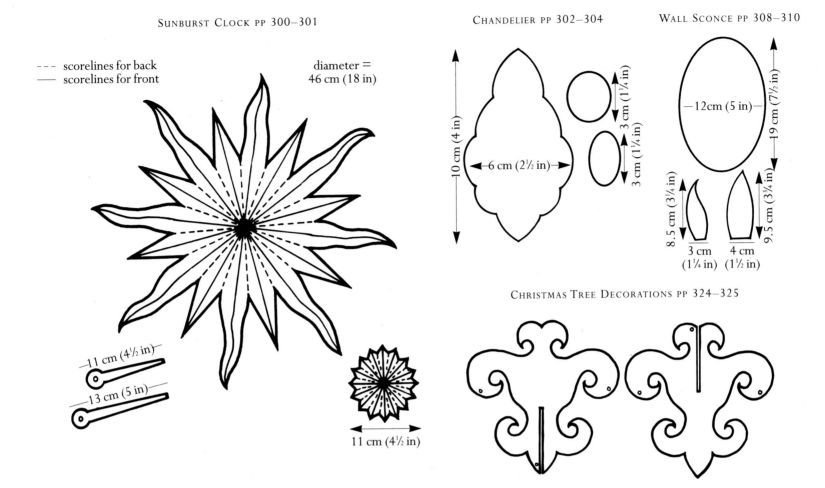

SUPPLIERS

Many of the projects in this book use paper or cardboard that you may have on hand or is readily available. If you want to buy paper, the range today is enormous. There are speciality stores, and most craft and hobby stores stock a good collection. Listed here are a few addresses of specialist shops:

United Kingdom

Falkiner Fine Papers
76 Southampton Row
London WC1B 4AR
Tel: 020 7831 1151

Khadi Papers
Unit 3
Chilgrove Farm
Chichester
West Sussex PO18 9HU
Tel: 01243 535314

Maureen Richardson
(hand-made papers)
Romilly
Brilley
Hay-on-Wye
Hereford HR3 6HE

Paperchase
213 Tottenham Court Road
London W1P 9AF
Tel: 020 7580 8496
14 St Marys Gate
Manchester M1 1PX
Tel: 0161 839 1500

Pulp and Paper Information
Centre
1 Rivenhall Road
Westlea
Swindon
Wiltshire SN5 7BD

Shepherds Bookbinders Ltd
76 Rochester Row
London SW1P 1JU
Tel: 020 7630 1184

United States

The Art Store
935 Erie Blvd E
Syracuse, NY 13210
Tel: (315) 474 1000

Colophon Book Arts Supply
3611 Ryan Road, S.E.
Lacey, WA 98503
www.the gridnet/colophon

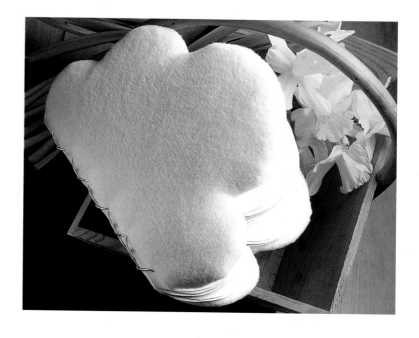

Creative Craft House
897 San Jose Circle, HC 62
P.O. Box 7810
Bulhead City, AZ 86430
Tel: (520) 754-3300

Dick Blink
P.O. Box 1267
Galesburg, IL 61402
Tel: (302) 343 6181

Fascinating Folds
P.O. Box 10070
Glendale, AZ 85318
Tel: (800) 968 2418
www.fascinating-folds.com

Gold's Artworks Inc.
2100 North Pine Street
Lumberton, NC 28318
Tel: (800) 356 2306

Jerry's Artarama
P.O Box 58638J
Raleigh, NC 27658
Tel: (800) 827 8478
www.jerryscatalogue.com

Kate's Paperie
561 Broadway
New York, NY 10012
Tel: (212) 941-9816
(800) 809-9880

Joe Kulbert Art & Graphic Supply
37A Myrtle Avenue
Dover, NJ 07801
Tel: (201) 328 3266

Nasco Arts and Crafts
4825 Stoddard Road
Modesto, CA 95397
Tel: (800) 558 9595
www.nascofa.com

National Artcraft Co.
23456 Mercantile Road
Beachwood, OH 44122
Tel: (216) 963 6011

Papersource Inc.
730 N Franklin Suite 111
Chicago, IL 60610
Tel: (312) 337 0798

Pearl Paint Co.
308 Canal Street
New York, NY 10013
Tel: (800) 221-6845

S & S Arts & Crafts, Dept 2007
P.O. Box 513
Colchester, CT 06415
Tel: (800) 243 9232

Twinrocker Handmade Paper
100 East 3rd Street
Brookston, IN 47923
Tel: (800) 757 8946
twinrock@twinrocker.com

Australia
A to Z Art Supplies
50 Brunswick Terrace
Wynn Vale, SA 5127
Tel: (08) 8289 1202

Art & Craft Warehouse
19 Main Street
Pialba, QLD 4655
Tel: (07) 4124 2581

Artland
272 Moggill Road
Indooroopilly, QLD 4068
Tel: (07) 3878 5536
Free call: 1800 81 5377

Artwise
186 Enmore Road
Enmore 2052
Sydney
Tel: (02) 9519 8237

Bondi Road Art Supplies
181 Bondi Road
Bondi, NSW 2026
Tel: (02) 9386 1779

Eckersleys
126 Commercial Road
Prahran, VIC 3181
Tel: (03) 9510 1418

Janet's Art Supplies & Books
145 Victoria Avenue
Chatswood, NSW 2067
Tel: (02) 9417 8572

Oxford Art Supplies Pty Ltd
223 Oxford Street
Darlinghurst, NSW 2010
Tel: (02) 9360 4066

The Paper Merchant
316 Rikeby Road
Subiaco 6008
Perth
Tel: (09) 381 6489

Quire Handmade Paper
PO Box 248
Belair 5052
Adelaide
Tel: (08) 8295 2966

INDEX

ACKNOWLEDGEMENTS

PAPERMAKING

The author and publishers would like to thank the following people who contributed projects to this section of the book:
Lindsay Bloxam, p49, 65; Wendy Carlton-Dewhirst, p29, 46, 53; Brenda Connor, p67, 86; Vivien Frank, p41, 89; Nicola Jackson, p56, 75; Anne Johnson, p27, 35, 79; Jenny Nutbeem, p32, 69, 81.

The publishers would also like to thank the artists who contributed work to the Gallery chapter of this section: Lindsay Bloxam, Wendy Carlton-Dewhirst, Elizabeth Couzins-Scott, Susan Cutts, Carol Farrow, Anne Johnson and David Watson.

PAPER CUTTING

The authors and publishers would like to thank the following people who contributed projects to this section of the book:
Penny Boylan p106, 108, 112; Madhu and Ray McChrystal p146, 149, 153, 165.

The would also like to thank Mexique for the loan of the Mexican papercuts.

The authors and publishers would also like to thank the following stores that kindly lent materials as props for photography:
The Holding Company
V.V. Rouleaux
The Shaker Shop
Yound & D Ltd
Paperchase

PAPIER MACHE

The author and publishers would like to thank the following artists for the projects and gallery pieces photographed in this section of the book:
Julie Arkell p176; Claire Attridge p175, 176, 177; Lisa Brown p234–235; Hannah Downes p175, 177; Emma Hardy p231–233, 239–241, 248–249; Deborah Schneebeli Morrell p188–190, 220–222, 245–247; Kerry Skinner p205–207, 217–219, 223–225, 236–238; Caroline Waite p197–199, 228–230, 242–244.

The following stores kindly lent materials as props for photography:
Joss Graham Oriental Textiles
V.V. Rouleaux
David & Charles Wainwright
The Old Station

CARDBOARD

The author and publishers would like to thank the following people who contributed projects to this section of the book:
Penny Boylan p266, 268, 286; Gloria Nicol p277, 272, 324; Andrew Gilmore p314, 321; Polly Pollock p326; Mary Maguire p319.

The following people kindly lent items for the Gallery section:
Tomoko Azumi
Carton Massif
Sarah Drew
Thomas Heatherwick
Polly Pollock
Lois Walpole
Nigel Westwood

BOOKWORKS

The author and publishers would like to thank the following artists for the projects and gallery pieces photographed in this section:
Susan Allix p339; Penny Boylan p69–71; Marcus Davies p387–389; Timothy C. Ely p338; Evangelia Biza p339; Heidrun Guest p384–386; Susan Johanknecht p336, 338; Peter Jones p338; Trevor Jones p336, 337, 339; Gavin Rookledge p337; Philip Smith p337–339.

Picture credits

The following agencies and museums kindly gave permission to reproduce pictures in this book:
p10, British Museum, London/ Bridgeman Art Library, London/ New York (top), Bibliotheque Nationale, Tunis/Lauros-Giraudon/ Bridgeman Art Library, London/ New York (bottom); p11, ET Archive (top); Oriental Museum, Durham University/Bridgeman Art Library, London/New York (bottom left); Jaqui Hurst Picture Library (bottom right); p95(bottom) and p96, the Abby Aldrich Rockefeller Folk Art Center; p170 Christie's Images/Bridgeman Art Library (top), Victoria and Albert Museum (bottom); p171 Victoria and Albert Museum/Bridgeman Art Library (top); p172 Bonhams, London/ Bridgeman Art Library, (top) Private Collection/Bridgeman Art Library (bottom); p173 David Lavender (top and bottom); p332, Victoria and Albert Museum; p333, The British Library (top and bottom); p334, The British Library (top), The British Library/Bridgeman Art Library (bottom); p335, The British Library (top), Christie's Images, UK/ Bridgeman Art Library (bottom).